Good Advice

Good Advice

Information & Policy Making in the White House

DANIEL E. PONDER

Texas A&M University Press
College Station

Texas A&M University Press expresses its appreciation for support
in publishing works on the presidency and leadership to

The Center for Presidential Studies
George Bush School of Government and Public Service
Texas A&M University

For a complete list of books in print in this series, see the back of the book.

Library of Congress Cataloging-in-Publication Data

Ponder, Daniel E., 1966–
    Good advice : information and policy making in the White House /
Daniel E. Ponder.—1st ed.
        p.   cm. — (Joseph V. Hughes, Jr., and Holly O. Hughes series in the
presidency and leadership studies ; no. 5)
    Includes bibliographical references and index.
    ISBN 0-89096-913-2 (cloth)
        1. Presidents—United States—Staff.   2. Political planning—United States.
3. United States—Politics and government—1977–1981.   I. Title.   II. Series.
JK552.P66 2000
352.23'0973—dc21

                                                            99-047705

To the memory of Patrick Joseph Fett (1959–96)
and
in celebration and anticipation of the life of Patrick Daniel Ponder (b. 1997)

Contents

Preface

This book is about the politics of presidential advice. Specifically, it traces how different modes of information (political and substantive) are integrated into workable policy for the president. As such, it takes its cue from many who have passed this way before. For example, advice interacts strongly with the various information perspectives in determining the bargaining terms a president pursues.[1] Matthew Dickinson notes that Richard Neustadt argues the best way to determine a president's optimal bargaining leverage is to acquire information in order to determine the trade-offs and consequences of various bargaining choices.[2] Neustadt himself holds that "a president is helped by what he gets into his mind. His first essential need is for information."[3]

In weaving an analysis of information and advice with staff dynamics, this book fits into the larger literature of the presidency by providing a detailed examination of the advisory process as it relates to the behavioral consequences of presidential incentives and the preferences derived from those incentives. It also examines the subsequent questions of organization and information gathering and dissemination. A collateral interest that further guides my analysis is whether or not there is a trade-off between the president's dependence on the competent policy advice of agents in the bureaucracy on one hand, and the White House staff, which is assumed to be responsive to the president, on the other. These two sets of advisers often differ in the kinds of advice they offer. In turn, these different advisory perspectives can lead to very different conceptualizations of the shape policy initiatives should take. Furthermore, they often differ in their analysis of outcomes relating to information gathering and processing, policy and political analysis, and the character of presidential relationships with other political actors. In short, these processes can yield outcomes that are responsive to presidential or bureaucratic goals, programmatic expertise, or combinations thereof. My purpose in this book is to trace these dynamics within Pres. Jimmy Carter's administration, and to draw lessons, where appropriate, for the larger enterprise of presidency research.

The idea for this book can be traced back to a seminar on the presidency and executive politics I took with Erwin C. Hargrove at Vanderbilt University in the spring of 1990. One of the readings was Terry Moe's seminal work on the politicized presidency.[4] I found Moe's emphasis on the decline of neutral competence and the rise of a politicized executive branch to be fascinating developments in the larger context of American politics and political institutions.

I subsequently determined that I could, through the study of a number of well-chosen cases, "turn Moe on his head" by showing that presidents do not necessarily centralize over time. I had a normative bias against centralization and hoped to prove that presidents need not centralize and, empirically, do not. However, as I got farther and farther into theories and hard evidence, I became more and more convinced that Moe was right after all. One thing I did notice was that, although Carter did centralize his policy-making apparatus in the White House, there was considerable variation in his Domestic Policy Staff's involvement. That finding led me to trace variations in the centralizing strategy and ultimately resulted in this book.

I benefited greatly from the valuable guidance the members of my dissertation committee provided me. For their hard work and endless patience, I thank Robert H. Birkby, George J. Graham, Hugh Davis Graham, and Benjamin Walter. Erwin Hargrove, the committee chair, deserves special mention. He was always finding subtle and, unfortunately, not-so-subtle flaws in my logic or analysis, provided unlimited encouragement, and shared freely his seemingly bottomless insight into American politics. He has continued to provide me with his unfailing support, including reading and rereading drafts of the book manuscript, with enthusiasm for the project and unfailing good humor. He has proven to be a most remarkable mentor and friend.

My list of debts is long, but I am happy to acknowledge them. Suzanne Werner was given the unenviable task of listening to me work out the problems and issues as I grappled with them. I did the same for her, which made it all the more special because neither of us had any real clue about what the other was talking about. She and her husband Tim fed me warm meals and let me sleep on their couch during my many data-collecting trips to Atlanta, and I thank them for their hospitality and, especially, their friendship.

Doug Lemke is a friend like no other. Intellectually curious, he was the perfect graduate school companion. We have remained friends and confidants through the subsequent humbling experience of job hunting and settling into academic life.

Many others affected my career in general and the many drafts of this book in particular. My friend Anna Mary Rizzi encouraged me at virtually every stage, and there is no question that I would not have pursued, much less completed, this project had it not been for her unfailing encouragement and support. I am in her debt. Jacek Kugler, Don Hancock, and Shrikant Dash all provided examples of what a scholar should be. David Moon has been the consummate department chairman during my time at the University of Colorado at Colorado Springs (UCCS), providing endless encouragement and enthusiasm for the project.

Many scholars from around the country provided encouragement and many useful suggestions as the manuscript moved glacially toward publication. In particular, I'd like to thank Paul Brace, Matt Dickinson, Paul Quirk, Frank Rourke, Andy Rudalevige, Steve Shull, Stephen Weatherford, and the late Marcia Lynn Whicker. Jim Pfiffner proved to be a patient series editor. I would also like to thank the two anonymous reviewers for Texas A&M University Press. I would like to particularly acknowledge "Reviewer #1," who provided exceptionally insightful and detailed commentary on various versions of the manuscript. For financial assistance and extra time to write, I am grateful to the Graduate School at Vanderbilt and to the College of Letters, Arts, and Sciences at UCCS. Our very capable administrative assistant in the Department of Political Science, Rochelle Henry, helped get the manuscript into its final form, and I thank her for her patience and good humor. I must, of course, absolve all these people and institutions from all errors of fact or interpretation. Any that might appear in this work are mine alone.

Some of the analysis presented here appeared previously in "Three Strategies of Presidential Policy Making: Politics and Policy in the Carter Administration" in Congress and the Presidency 23 (fall, 1996): 113–37; and "The Presidency as a Learning Organization" in Presidential Studies Quarterly 29 (March, 1999): 100–14.

My parents, Ed and Loretta, inspired me throughout my life to achieve whatever I wanted. Although I never quite made it to playing left field for the St. Louis Cardinals, their encouragement allowed my brothers and I to pursue whatever interests we had, never pushing but always demanding that we put forth our best effort in whatever we tried. For that freedom, as well as their support and love, I thank them. My brothers Tim, David, and Michael gave me comfort, peace of mind, and much needed distractions when I traveled back to Missouri. They truly exemplify the term "brothers."

Thanks go as well to my family—Heather, Zachary, Jacob, Gabriel, and Patrick—who supplied the diversions necessary for completing a book. They have my deepest affection and admiration, and they managed to maintain a positive attitude even when my mood turned sour as the pressures of finishing the manuscript mounted. I hope I can make it up to them.

Finally, I would like to acknowledge the people to whom this book is dedicated. Pat Fett was a scholar and a very close friend. He graciously invited me to write with him when the subject of congressional term limits was still in its infancy, and thus began an all-too-brief collaboration that quickly developed into one of the finest friendships I have ever known. Although his life was tragically short, his example of how to be a scholar and, more importantly, of how to live life, will stay with me for the rest of mine. His namesake, my son Patrick, who is just beginning his life, could not have had a better role model. It gives me great pleasure and pride to dedicate this book to them.

Good Advice

Part I
Theoretical
Underpinnings

CHAPTER I

Foundations of
Presidential Analysis

I t is no profound insight to note that presidents, like all of us, are often
faced with several alternatives when a choice must be made. But for occupants of the Oval Office, the consequences of those choices are usually quite public and often of a high-profile nature, carrying with them the
possibility of dramatic success or embarrassing backlash. As Roger Porter's
premise makes clear at the outset of his classic work on presidential decision making, the problem lies in the fact that "the President makes decisions on a multitude of issues about which he is not an expert."[1] Observ-
ing the information and advice that reaches presidents, and tracing what
they do with it, is necessary if one is to begin to understand the presidential policy-making process. The nature of the battles presidents wage trying to fulfill their role as the leader of public policy making is the subject
of a deep and rich literature. Much of that literature concerns the use of
information in the presidency, either implicitly or explicitly, and, by extension, the advisory processes bringing that information to the president. Indeed, it is hard to imagine a study about the presidency that is completely
silent on the general subject of presidential advice and information.

Some scholars give advisory and information issues center stage, as
does Alexander George in his pioneering work on the relationship between
advice taking and personality.[2] Others examine the means by which information is generated and the organizational structures for managing that
information.[3] However, few scholars focus *exclusively* on information or
advice, opting instead to integrate the two into a larger treatment of the
presidency and its attendant leadership problems.[4] Many treat advice as a
given, an issue that stands in the wings, outside the glare of the stage lights.

All of this is, of course, perfectly reasonable; the presidency is far more
than information processing. Still, whether the focus of study is on the individual occupying the White House at a given time, or on more general
issues of the presidency itself, the acquisition of information in the process
of policy making is usually present at some level. However, the systematic
study of presidential advising and what presidents do with that advice has

been unnecessarily lumped in with more general studies of decision making. Karen Hult argues that the subject of presidential advice has too often been equated with presidential decision making per se. She calls for studies that investigate the operations of advising the president by systematically focusing on advising and not just decision making.[5] This book represents an effort to accept Hult's challenge by delving deeply into the advisory dynamics of a single presidential administration.

My thesis is that although presidents have tended to centralize policy-making authority in the White House staff, the dynamics of staff participation and consequent policy success vary from issue to issue. This is consistent with a theoretical framework I call staff shift.[6] The dynamic nature of centralization changes not just from one presidency to another but within an administration, and from issue to issue. Resources such as staff time and attention are sensitive to factors such as presidential interest, issue priority, the intended scope of the policy initiative, and the changing cast of relevant actors in the American political system. These in turn lead to presidential decisions regarding staff allocation of time and attention. The nature, time allocated, and effort of staff activity shifts depending on the mix of White House–oriented factors and external considerations. Moreover, chances for policy success and failure do not necessarily follow from a centralizing strategy, but rather by a coordinated system of policy cooperation by presidential staff and bureaucratic agents, with the relative emphasis on one or the other being a function of the mix of political and policy imperatives.

Thus, while centralization of policy making describes recent White House decision processes, the *character* of centralization differs within an administration in both degree and kind depending on the confluence of these factors. For more than a decade, presidency scholars have noted the increased tendency of presidents and their staffs to exert close political control over nearly every aspect of the executive policy-making apparatus.[7] The primary purpose of this book is to enrich and qualify rational-choice approaches that trace the increasingly politicized nature of the presidency. It does so by delving significantly below the surface of a single administration to explore what the demands of policy centralization entail. It will take the rest of the book to elaborate these dynamics, and I discuss them more fully in relation to the larger issues of American politics and the presidency in the final chapter.

Studies of the presidency deal with issues such as the president's office and powers, his electoral strategies and relations with mass publics, the proliferation of interest groups, the nature of decision making, the implementation of advisory processes, and interinstitutional relations between the president and Congress, bureaucracy, and the courts. Many are concerned at one level or another with how presidents portray themselves or ready themselves for institutional combat. The manner in which presidents receive information through the advisory process and have it at their disposal for purposes of policy choice, and the methods by which they impart that information to others, is necessary (though hardly sufficient) for understanding either individual presidents or the office itself. All of this becomes even more apparent when scholars address the problems of presidential pursuit of public support, the consequences of variation in that support, and attempt to determine whether the president has been a success or failure in one, several, or all of these pursuits.[8]

By looking deeply into the Carter experience and exploring the variation in developments that have led presidents to centralize policy making in the White House, I seek to provide a descriptive analysis, grounded in a variant of the new institutionalist approach to political analysis.[9] This in turn allows for the development of a framework within which to understand how presidents and their staffs synthesize policy and political advice. Less importantly, and more tentatively, this analytical framework allows for some evaluative inferences, although the nature of those evaluations is subject to a reasonable level of uncertainty given the limited scope of the analysis. Nonetheless, the framework developed in the pages to come points to criteria that can be evaluated as to the policy consequences of their presence or absence for presidential governance.

Presidential success takes many forms and has many explanations. The combination of favorable resources, context, timing, skill, fortuitous events, and other considerations, place the president in an agreeable situation where the probability of success, be it policy, political, or both, is maximized. The absence of any one of these makes the unambiguous achievement of success more difficult, although not impossible. Just as persons who have been deprived of one of their senses experience heightened awareness in others, so must a president work harder at identifying realistic possibilities embedded in the relevant political or policy contexts. He must learn to sharpen his personal and public skills when one or more circumstances militate against the prospects for purposive presidential action.[10]

One of the subsidiary purposes of this book is to explore an underlying question concerning the use of advice and information in the presidency, one that cuts across many of the environmental circumstances listed above. That question, in brief, is: How do presidents and their staffs use, misuse, and even decide *not* to use the advice they get in the process of formulating policy? This is a tall order, and I grapple with only some of the issues raised by that question. To be sure, the role advice plays in presidential decisions is multifaceted and complex. *Political* circumstances (be they electorally motivated, partisan based, public-opinion oriented, prestige enhancing, or some other presidential interest) raise political questions that in turn necessitate political answers.[11] More rare, but still of great importance, problems of policy substance sometimes override political concerns, and the use of politically impartial analysis is preferred to political bargaining. Most often, however, political concerns become so intractable that the technical substance of policy is used as a bargaining tool to bridge the gap between the political and policy dimensions. Substance, in certain instances, can be sacrificed or altered in favor of enhancing the probability of political success. Thus, the optimum strategy is likely one that pursues a mixture of the best elements of both dimensions of politics and policy.[12]

These issues form the cornerstone for the analysis presented here. The chapters that follow take a long look at political and policy balance and the attendant compromises as they were played out in the domestic advisory process of the Carter administration, spearheaded by the Office of Policy Development (hereafter the Domestic Policy Staff [DPS]). At all times, a focus on the alliance between politics and policy, accentuated by the dynamics of staff shift, is given pride of place, especially as the necessities of each creep into the advisory process.

Regardless of the decision setting, politics and its practice are often about winning and losing in the public arena. Thus the question arises: How do policy makers parlay substantive advice, which often originates in bureaucracies, into the advancement of political goals? In other words, what are the dynamics of the political uses of policy information? These issues are systematically explored in this and the next chapter.

THE UTILITY OF RESEARCH ON PRESIDENTIAL ADVICE

With the possible exception of the U.S. Congress, the presidency has been the focus of more scholarly attention than any other single political institution. Studies of presidential advice and, by extension, how presidents receive information is no exception. Scholars of diverse methodological and conceptual stripes get at the issue in one way or another.[13] The fact that individual presidents have chosen to staff their offices and pursue various types of decision structures has made generalization about the institutional presidency difficult.[14]

Presidents seek information on many fronts, sometimes delegating decision authority to staff members or political appointees, and sometimes reserving it for themselves. Although the two domains of policy and politics probably overlap more than they stand as separate and distinct features of the American system, presidents and their staffs are faced daily with the tasks of sorting, discarding, modifying, rejecting, and accepting advice. They sometimes out of necessity must emphasize one over the other, but they rarely rely on one perspective to the exclusion of the other. Depending on the nature of the issue and the policy domain in which it falls (foreign or domestic, for example), staff members who enjoy close proximity to the president are not only given the task of providing political advice to the president, they are also responsible for integrating the policy and political realms. In his summary of comments made during a panel on which former presidential advisers discussed presidential advisory needs, Roger Porter observed: "Presidents inevitably are faced with the need to have advice both about the substantive effects of their policy choices and about the political implications of these alternatives. There (is) broad consensus that both strands of advice are important, (and) that bringing them forward in parallel is difficult." [15]

The analysis of decision structures for bringing these two strands of advice in parallel has become a source of lively debate among presidential scholars. However, there is a problem with focusing on decision structures. The problem concerns the difficulty of identifying the processes that are aided or impeded by various structures. Richard Tanner Johnson has identified three types of decision processes that have been linked, in one form or another, to the range of organizational patterns found in the modern presidency. These are *formalistic* (exemplified by Dwight Eisenhower and Richard Nixon), *competitive* (Franklin Roosevelt), and collegial (John Kennedy). Each has strong points, but they are also saddled with weaknesses and trade-offs. [16] Unfortunately, a major problem presents itself to analysts who apply Johnson's framework. Informal decision processes thrive in the presidency (as in virtually any organization), and thus hinder attempts to categorize presidents or policies into one or the other processes. In addition, multiple decision structures exist within any given administration. [17] The presidents mentioned above are the archetype of each pattern, but many other presidents defy easy categorization. As John Burke and Fred Greenstein argue, categories as they stand are too simplistic because they fail to account for the informal decision processes beneath the formal model. [18] Some of the patterns have been attributed to personal idiosyncrasies such as personality or management style. There is enormous potential variation in the factors affecting staffing arrangements and advisory processes, and this book examines intra-administration variation in style, substance, and process. [19]

NOTES ON THE PRESIDENCY AS AN INSTITUTION

Before going any farther I should explore two pretheoretical questions that have been debated in the literature and are relevant for my purposes in this book. The first asks simply whether the presidency is an institution that can be understood in terms of continuity and variation among designated variables over time. Along with others in the field, I contend that this is indeed the case. Such a determination is, on some level, necessary for maintaining the efficacy of focusing on just one administration, but at the same time keeping watch for what the experience of that one administration can tell us about the presidency in general.

However, it is fair to assert that studying the presidency as an institution is more difficult than studying other, more clearly demarcated, institutions, such as the U.S. Congress or legislatures in general. The sequential properties of the congressional process, for example, make the study of Congress as an institution easier to support. Most of what Congress does when making a law is governed by a previously specified sequence that is well known to members, and conditions their behavior. The specific rules, norms, and customs guiding member behavior in Congress thus can be thought of as institutions.[20] Congress and the institutions it creates internally form an arena within which individuals and their behavior can sometimes exploit the legislative process (by asserting gatekeeping authority to keep an unwanted bill from coming to the floor, for example). But individuals can only rarely change the nature of the institution itself. With the partial exception of the revolution that accompanied Newt Gingrich's rise to the House Speakership, the wholesale replacement of established institutional boundaries rarely obtained. Certainly, individual leaders can identify, define, and execute agendas, but must do so within a structure that remains relatively rigid and thus predictable. Institutional change occurs only gradually, and while strong leadership can be decisive, it is also vulnerable to the whims of undisciplined parties and, in the Senate especially, the prerogatives of the minority. The point is that Congress has a set of embedded rules and norms, both formal and informal, which make the study of congressional politics somewhat easier than the presidency when it comes to generating propositions about the institution.[21]

In his work on the evolution of social institutions, Jack Knight defines subtle differences in institutions and organizations. Institutions, according to Knight, are "sets of rules that structure interactions among actors," whereas organizations "are collective actors who might be subject to institutional constraint."[22] Knight's definitions need be only slightly altered to apply to the presidency. For my purposes, the presidency as an organization is relatively easy to identify. Actors coming together under various rubrics with readily identifiable responsibilities and tasks form the basis of the organizational presidency. Thus, the various components of the White House staff are considered as organizational entities, such as the Office of Legislative Liaison, the Office of White House Communications, the Domestic Policy Staff (DPS), and the like. They are differentiated by the definitions of their tasks, but those tasks and the dictates by which they are to be carried out may vary within and across administrations. Nonetheless, they are organizationally tied to the presidency. Similarly, the several offices created and housed in the Executive Office of the President (EOP)—such as the Office of Management and Budget (OMB), the National Security Council (NSC) staff, the Office of the U.S. Trade Representative, and the Council of Economic Advisers (CEA), to name but a few—are set apart by the responsibilities that govern their existence and the actions they take in the name of presidential policy making.[23] Indeed, the set of tasks that I refer to can be considered the institutions that parameterize the organizations which serve the presidency (as opposed to the executive branch or the whole of the national government). But institutions can be developed further and considered as not only the rules that formally govern organizational activity, but also as the aggregation of organizations within the White House and the EOP.[24]

On the other hand, when thinking of the presidency as an institution and not simply as a set of support organizations, one is struck by how few are the sets of rules that formally constrain presidents and their staff in choosing how to conduct business. For example, Article II of the Constitution is notoriously ambiguous on just what the proper scope of presidential authority is or ought to be. Although the policy-making process may follow a more or less regular pattern, the president is certainly not beholden to anything like the formal, sequential process that Congress follows, nor even a set of delineated, in-house, "by-the-book" procedures observed in most bureaucratic agencies. Rather, presidents implement their own procedures for engaging the political and policy process, and may or may not choose to use the various support organizations they have at their disposal in the same ways as their predecessors. There is wide variation in the extent to which presidents use their cabinets, for example. In the foreign policy realm there is a perceived trade-off between focusing policy efforts through the State Department versus relying on the NSC staff.[25] Even the functions performed by various support staffs that are ostensibly similar in focus and outlook can vary across administrations, although their general tasks remain more or less constant.[26] These trade-offs sometimes lead different presidents to structure policy making in ways conducive to personal style, institutional relationships, and other relevant factors. So, at least on the surface, treating the presidency as an institution in the same manner that we think of Congress or even the bureaucracy as an institution presents analytical problems.

Nonetheless, the presidency has developed in ways that allow scholars to think in general terms about the performance of the presidency as an institution in its own right, and not simply as an organizational apparatus that changes from president to president. Lyn Ragsdale and John J. Theis III used the features of autonomy, adaptability, complexity, and coherence to argue that the presidency emerged as an institution in the 1970s, with many of its organizational entities attaining stability and acquiring what they call a "distinctive identity."[27] Charles Walcott and Karen Hult, in their study of governance structures across presidential administrations, found that structures that were highly congruent to the situation or task at hand also tended to be highly stable. That is, they persisted across at least two administrations. Less congruent structures did not achieve such stability.[28] Finally, Matthew Dickinson's work on the growth of the presidential branch takes a decidedly legalistic approach to institutionalization. He describes institutionalized structures as "the positions and related incentives [which] are grounded in statute, executive order, or some other formal foundation." These works, taken together, offer further support of the proposition that the presidency, though less formalized and delineated in constitutional demands than Congress or even the courts, exhibits a reasonably high degree of organizational stability under successive presidents and can thus be studied as an institution.

Although the concept of institutionalization takes many forms, most scholars agree that an organization has become institutionalized when it can be characterized by the development of stable patterns of social interaction based on formalized rules, laws, customs, and rituals.[29] Since at least the Budget and Accounting Act of 1921, certain functions specific to the White House have become more or less permanent fixtures of the modern presidency. Expectations that the president will devise and submit a budget, manage an expanding executive branch, provide direction and coherence in domestic policy, and propose legislation for fine-tuning the economy have mandated an ever-increasing reliance on the entities of the OMB, the DPS, and the CEA. Yet it is important to note that a president can use these support staffs as much or as little as he wishes, but he would be ill-advised to get rid of them entirely. Even if a president did want to abolish one or all of them, the need to meet or exceed expectations heaped upon the office would make it politically and administratively dangerous for him to do so.

The second (and much shorter) pretheoretical question deals with whether or not advisory patterns and the policy-development process reveal theoretically interesting variations in institutional patterns. I contend that they do, examining the specifics of this debate later. For now, it is enough to say that the conflict between responsiveness and policy competence (if one exists) and the degree of centralization of authority in the White House and politicization of the executive branch or decentralization to the departments and agencies in developing policy has transcended individual *presidents*. It remains a subject to be evaluated by studies of the *presidency*, regardless of who occupies the Oval Office. By focusing scholarly attention on the institutional characteristics of the presidency, patterns of institutional performance present themselves and generate general testable propositions. If this approach has credibility, then examining the dynamics of a presidential support organization such as the DPS in one administration can be useful for understanding presidential actions more generally. For example, while the dynamics have changed over time, all presidents in the modern era face a highly fragmented and conflictual interest group system.[30] Party affiliation in the electorate has declined, and with it the level of congressional deference to the president.[31] The players in presidents' political and contextual environments may vary, but the substance of what they must face in terms of these environments remains remarkably consistent across time.

Defining Concepts

Stephen J. Wayne noted that presidency scholars have not, in general, "labored to articulate the definitions, assumptions, and relationships on which their research has been predicated."[32] Presidency scholarship has come a long way since Wayne's observation, and much of it displays the fruits of conceptual clarification and operationalization.[33] What follows is a brief explanation of the definitions of recurring concepts employed in subsequent chapters.

Advising is defined as "providing input into or support for presidential decision making."[34] An advisory role encompasses a number of functions. These range from exploring possible policy avenues to advocating the selection of a particular proposal alternative. As noted previously, advice is the means by which information is culled, synthesized, and integrated with numerous political and policy-related factors, ultimately providing the foundation upon which the president and/or his deputies decide from among several alternatives. I see advising as a type of investment made by the president. His choices are contingent on his and his staff's assessment of the degree of risk associated with the nature of the particular policy being considered and the strategy embedded within the information promulgated by the advice the president receives.[35]

Staff shift refers to the idea that while presidents tend to centralize policy making in the White House, there is variation in how this is done with regard to different policies. Presidential staffs have limited resources such as time, information, expertise, and so forth. Given these constraints, the policy-making strategy shifts in accordance with factors such as presidential interest, the nature and scope of the policy under consideration, and political concerns (such as congressional concern or interest group attention). Staff involvement is basically a constant in the policy process, but the nature of that involvement varies, reflecting the political and policy environment confronting them at any one time. Under various conditions, and with varying degrees of success, the staff will act as *director*, centralizing policy making tightly within the staff framework; *facilitator*, brokering agreements across policy jurisdictions; or *monitor*, delegating policy authority to external agents in the executive branch, but keeping a watchful eye on the progress and substance of policy development.[36]

Each of these strategies implies a different mix of policy and politically oriented information and advice. *Policy competence* is defined as policy substantive information, originating primarily in the departments and agencies of the bureaucracy. While I am sensitive to the existence of what Graham Wilson calls the "higher form" of neutral (what I refer to as policy) competence, which provides decision makers with policy expertise informed by political analysis, policy competence most often takes the form of long-term, policy-specific information, with limited (if any) reference to how policy proposals will affect political constituencies.[37] Information concerning political constituencies that does exist is predominantly a function of institutional memory manifest in the relevant bureaucracy. In the case of the Carter administration, this rationale extends to department heads given that they were chosen mostly on the basis of their *substantive expertise* and not on their proximity to the various constituency groups that politicization would imply.[38]

Responsiveness is defined as the extent to which advisers are sensitive to the president's political interests. For the purpose of this book, those members were located mostly (but not exclusively) in the DPS. I note exceptions when needed. More specifically, responsiveness refers to an emphasis on short-term political goals, the likely reaction of various publics (e.g., Congress and interest groups), and the strategies for dealing with these various actors. Richard Neustadt contends that much of the president's bargaining position was determined by prestige—both within Washington and beyond the Beltway.[39] Whether or not this is the case, the president's responsive agents are charged with guarding his professional prestige, which in turn serves to protect his public prestige.[40] Responsiveness thus entails protecting the president's political interests while taking into account the substantive impact of policy by subordinating it to the concern for political imperatives. It is better, in light of the above, for the president to fight and lose on an issue of importance to him and have the content of that issue remain faithful to political imperatives than to win on an issue that is sound in terms of policy substance but does irrevocable damage to his professional or public prestige.

Closely related to responsiveness, of course, is the concept of *politics*. Politics, as it is referred to in this book, includes traditional conceptions employed in other writing on this topic. These factors include partisan demands, constituency pressures, concern with public opinion, and the like. Stuart Eizenstat and his staff in the DPS were responsible for protecting President Carter's interests; agencies and departments are, of course, less responsible. Politics does imply constituency and institutional (e.g., congressional) pressures, but overall it entails the desire to remain faithful to presidential goals. As with probably all presidents, Carter had sets of goals that can be broadly classified as policy and political, although the two are not mutually exclusive. For him, the art of presidential politics was doing the political in the right way. Put another way, his goals were to combine "right" policy with sensitivity to political realities, although policy was not to be subjected exclusively or with sole reference to what would succeed in the political world. Consistent with Carter's worldview, the purpose of the DPS was to integrate the substance of policy with political interests and purposes. This goal-oriented behavior, thus conceived, is consistent with politics. Indeed, the main difference between the Carter administration from those of his predecessors and successors is that he employed generalists rather than specialists in his staff arrangements. This is a marked change from the hierarchical, differentiated, and functionally specialized staffs of other administrations.[41]

Given the generalist thrust of the Carter staff, and depending at least partially on the circumstances surrounding an issue as laid out in chapter 2, the DPS developed, facilitated, or monitored policy formulation decisions. Since the staff was not exclusively concerned with the politics of an issue, the organizing principle of the DPS was to integrate the president's policy and political interests.[42] While politics can take a number of forms, it is more than a game of positioning. Walcott and Hult argue in their analysis of White House organizational governance that politics also includes "coping with the attendant uncertainty and conflict" that characterizes so much of the internal workings of organizations and nation-states.[43] My use of the concept of politics here is thus quite similar to theirs. Politics is part and parcel of organizational routine and the concomitant staff dynamics within the White House. Descriptions of staff struggles, disagreements, and jurisdictional disputes litter the analysis presented in the empirical chapters. Politics also includes the question of turf, with the White House maintaining strong ties to policy formulation decisions which, after all, must conform at least minimally to the political interests of the president. My concept of politics does differ slightly from Walcott and Hult's, however, in that the acquisition, control, and dissemination of information is emphasized by the advisory framework detailed in chapter 2.

When examining specific policies, the analysis takes a presidential perspective as to what are deemed successes and failures. *Policy success* is determined by the degree of cooperation and coordination among the various players. The criteria of presidential satisfaction, defined as getting what is feasible from the process as well as accurately assessing the political implications of an issue, is the measure of that degree of cooperation. Successful cases are, as I argue in the chapters that follow, characterized by such cooperation and coherence. This idea of success leans heavily on the idea that presidents can win or lose at roll-call time in Congress—but only if they have fought and won in terms of principle while maintaining or controlling the content of that principle. Stephen Skowronek defines good political leadership in the same terms: "Successful political leaders do not necessarily do more than other leaders; successful leaders control the political definition of their actions."[44] Thus, while presidents may not get a particular policy through Congress, if they can "control the political definition" of what they were trying to accomplish and make their case to the public, they are, according to my framework, more successful than a president who gets a bill passed but in the process loses all control over what he was trying to accomplish, letting it be defined for him by his political opponents.

A breakdown or unevenness of cooperation in the advisory process, on the other hand, characterizes *failures*. These can easily lead to a failure to deliver to the president the type of policy for which he expressed a preference. Such advice can bastardize the president's stated preferences, cause policy failures in the political arena, or both. But losing in the political arena does not necessarily mean failure. There are times when a president's position can be enhanced by fighting on matters of principle rather than bowing to powerful interests that severely distort the intent of his proposals.

Much of the preceding discussion and the subsequent analysis refers to various *processes*, each with their own distinct dynamics. As I note below, the processes that concern me here are the domestic policy formulation processes. These are defined as the formal and informal interactions of White House staff members (usually, but not exclusively, members of the DPS), and the attendant governmental institutions (e.g., bureaucratic departments and/or agencies) and publics (e.g., policy-specific interest groups). Studying process itself can be problematic. Conceptions of process have tended to be reified in the social science literature.[45] Process needs to be explained on its own terms, and integrated into the overall discussion rather than simply taking on the characteristics of the actors executing a set of tasks. I try to avoid this reification problem throughout this book by treating process as a specified set of actions taken and routines followed in response to events or circumstances. Thus, people (e.g., staff members) and process are and should be kept analytically distinct. People within an organization follow routines, and those specified routines can be identified as process. Anthropologist Andrew Vayda and his colleagues note that "discerning recurrent sequences of intelligibly connected actions and events" is one possible way to conceptualize process.[46]

Following their lead, I thus conceptualize process in White House–bureaucratic relations as a set of connected actions that follow a more or less specified routine. No one process, or identifiable set of interactions, dominates all advising. Rather, process and roles shift as presidential incentives and staff resources expand or contract.[47] A smooth process is one in which each actor is aware of his "proper" place in the process. He does not seek political gain in a covert manner (e.g., by "hiding" information), and the responsive agent acts as an "honest broker" by bringing all relevant issues to the president's attention, giving considered expression to the importance of each. This conceptualization is similar to a notion of "organizational routines," drawn from the literature on organizational learning. Martha Feldman, for example, defines organizational routines as "complex sets of inter-locking behaviors held in place through common agreement on the relevant roles and expectations."[48] For the purposes of this book, then, the idea of the proper role played by the various actors is derived from what the president or his staff deemed to be appropriate within the broader advisory strategy pursued. Those roles should be made clearer within each case study chapter.

Although the term is admittedly ambiguous and slippery, I conceptualize the *smoothness* of a particular process as the absence of relevant policy actors who hinder the process. It is an environment in which no one is attempting to impede the progress of the policy proposals.[49] *Collegiality* is present in the process when actors work together, minimizing the adverse effects of bureaucratic policy turf wars. These definitions of ideals will be sharpened and clarified as the case analyses progress. One objection can be made that it is the contentious issues that are most likely to make it to the president's desk. It should be noted, however, that a smooth process is not totally free of dissension. Dissension, conflict, and their resolution can often bring about the "best" information and advice. Matthew Dickinson and others have pointed out that Franklin Roosevelt thrived on such dissension.[50] My conception of cooperation and coordination in the policy process is based on the idea that a smooth process is one in which the dissension is coordinated by the president's staff. It is when a staff's coordinating capacities fall short and dissension spins out of control that the likelihood of policy failure increases.[51]

The presidential advisory process detailed in the empirical chapters is characterized in two roughly distinct but partially overlapping phases, the first being the construction of broad *principles* that convey broad programmatic goals. The second is the development of the *proposal*, which attempts to weld policy substance and technical detail with the political goals embedded in the principles guiding proposal formulation. The proposal, then, is the document that goes forth to both the public and to other institutions, usually Congress, where the fight for passage begins. The importance of how broad-based, often ambiguous or symbolic principles move into the real world of formulating proposals should not be underestimated. As one Carter administration staff member put it: "Just attending to all the technical details of putting together a real proposal takes a lot of time. There's tremendous detail in the work. It's one thing to lay out a statement of principles or a general kind of proposal, but it's quite another thing to staff out all the technical work that is required to actually put a real detailed proposal together."[52]

Both aspects of principles (largely political in nature) and proposals (more technical in detail) will be examined as integral parts of the processes under consideration, for it is in the effort to move from principles to proposal that policy and politics are likely to interact most strongly.

The perception of the political possibilities surrounding an issue is the degree to which the actors succeed or fail to assess the parameters of political feasibility. One level, this is the very essence of responsive advice, and certainly of a higher form of policy competence, integrating political estimations with policy substance. Thus, when referring to a policy process, *coordination and cooperation* are formally defined as a multilateral advisory relationship with unilateral mediation of policy direction. More simply, at least two (and usually more) organizational entities provide information in the form of advice, and one entity (in this case, the DPS) plays a mediating role by bringing to the president a synthesis of all arguments and, where necessary or explicitly requested, advocates one or another of these perspectives.[53] Coordination and cooperation thus are identified as the capacity of policy actors to work with and through the acknowledged pivot in the policy process, namely the DPS.

Suboptimizing behavior, or *suboptimization*, refers to the tendency for bureaucratic agencies or organizations to engage policy strategies that are beneficial for the advancement of the parochial self-interest of that organization but might only serve to hinder the overarching goals of the government or bureaucracy as a whole. This is a problem more commonly referred to as the agency problem in information economics.

OVERVIEW OF THE BOOK

The book is divided into three sections. The first, comprising chapters 2 and 3, provides a theoretical and methodological foundation for the empirical chapters. Chapter 2 develops a new institutionalist approach to studying presidential advice and use of information, including the idea of seeing presidential advice as a type of investment, and the theory of staff shift that informs the descriptive, analytical, and evaluative dimensions of the book. Chapter 3 offers an overview of presidency research and the data and methods upon which the empirical analysis proceeds.

The second section applies the theoretical insights developed in previous chapters to an empirical analysis of six policy-making cases. Two cases are analyzed in each of three chapters, detailing strategies of presidential staff in the policy-making process. The chapters examine variation in the tendency for presidents to centralize policy making in the White House. Chapter 4 is focused on the use of staff as policy directors, taking a dominant role in forging the direction and substance of policy. This is the most controlled of the various centralizing strategies. Carter fully centralized the development of a youth employment initiative and the creation of a new Department of Education. Although the presidential staff directed policy in the White House, there was still a function to be completed by the bureaucracy—namely, providing substantive advice that was then filtered and integrated into the substance decreed by the president's staff. Both organizational entities (the White House staff and bureaucrats) played important parts in the "staff as director" strategy. However, it is the ability of the staff to sound out the politics of the issue and weld this information with the analysis of policy substance that emerges as the most crucial element in this particular process.

Chapter 5 considers the "staff as facilitator" strategy. It undertakes an analysis of how policy and political substance are mixed. This particular strategy was employed in constructing Carter's second energy proposal (after the first process failed miserably), and welfare reform. This strategy is essentially a partnership between presidential staff and executive branch officials, be they career civil servants or political appointees. The policies that are likely to be staff facilitated are likely large-scale and cut across multiple jurisdictions. Proposals are too large and volatile to be delegated to one particular agent and too technical to be run from the White House. Thus, presidents seek a mix between responsiveness and policy competence. However, in policies with multiple jurisdictions, there is likely to be a great deal of intrabranch dissension. The success of the policy process is then at least partly contingent on the ability of the White House staff to broker or "facilitate" a compromise between the warring jurisdictions. The degree to which White House involvement is insinuated into the policy process also emerges as crucial to policy success. In the case of welfare reform, the DPS was not brought into the process until late, by which time proposals were already muddled and substantial damage to President Carter's professional prestige had been done. In contrast, the second energy program (Energy II) enjoyed strong DPS input from the beginning, and many of the problems plaguing welfare reform were avoided. These dynamics are examined in detail.

Chapter 6 looks at the strategy of using the staff as a monitor. White House engagement in the process is different in degree and kind from the other two strategies. A delegated strategy entails staff monitoring policy processes that are played out mostly outside the walls of the White House. As such, a premium is placed on the higher form of policy competence that resides in the executive branch's agencies, departments, and bureaus. Policy competence is not eschewed in the other strategies, of course, but it appears to be critical to both the political and policy success of presidential initiatives. Policy parameters are set by the administration but the development of policy is largely left up to civil servants and political appointees in bureaucratic agencies. The president's staff monitors the substance of policy development with an eye toward political feasibility and substantive viability. Carter's experiences with civil service reform and national health insurance fit squarely within this strategy. The fact that a president entrusts development of a policy priority to agents in the bureaucracy raises issues of presidential control. If a president has a bureaucratic agent sensitive to both his political and policy needs, then the concerns regarding substantive and political aspects of policy are lessened. However, if policy making is entrusted to an agent with a self-interested approach that differs from the president's, the president risks being hamstrung by a policy that is not in his best interests—or at least not in line with his preferences.[54] It is thus incumbent upon the staff to monitor the degree to which policy making comports with the president's desires. Staff participation in actual policy making is muted in the monitoring strategy but rises or falls with the degree to which the substance of policy is developed with regard to the president's preferences. Monitoring policy made by civil servants is an important function for insuring policy fidelity to presidential preferences and assuring the coherence of the president's program.

The concluding section reiterates the lessons drawn from the study. In it, I sort out the empirical implications that emerge throughout the book, noting that thinking of centralization is not so much a matter of compartmentalization but of a continuum reflecting differing levels of presidential and staff involvement. I go beyond that, though, to an assessment of presidential research in general, and what a new institutionalist approach can add to the many other theoretical tools being used in presidency scholarship today. Using a new institutionalist approach can help bridge a gap between scholars who focus too much on variation and individual idiosyncrasies and those who wish to move almost completely to a purely institutional approach to the presidency. The new institutionalist approach I offer relies heavily on the idea that to truly understand the presidency, one must understand not just presidents but the different conditions under which their incentives ebb and flow and how their preferences follow. This book cannot provide a full accounting of how this occurs, but it does, I think, provide a rationale for understanding the need to do so. By taking a step in that direction, we move toward an understanding of presidential policy making that can account for variation and constancy. Work in the presidency field has been moving in that direction, and this book seeks to move with it by offering an approach that assists in that undertaking.

CHAPTER 2

Presidents, the Presidency, and Information

A Framework

There are at least two conflicting views of presidential management of policy formulation and the information requirements for policy making that accompany those management strategies. Both are centrally concerned with the use of varying perspectives proffered in the advisory process. The first holds that the president's interests are best served by relying on expert advice from career civil servants in the bureaucracy, thus enjoying gains-from-trade by utilizing their policy competence. The second (and dominant) perspective contends that presidents have pursued responsiveness to presidential preferences by relying on a dual strategy of centralization and politicization. That is, presidents use the White House staff and rely on presidential appointees placed deep in the bureaucratic apparatus to develop policy initiatives, relying on experts in the civil service for policy implementation and technical advice. In doing so, presidents maximize presidential influence over policy formulation.[1]

One other perspective has emerged as a sort of middle ground between the centralization/politicization and departmental/careerist approaches. It is one that counsels presidents to pursue a mixed strategy that incorporates responsiveness and policy competence in one integrated policy-making process.[2] The empirical chapters provide an exploration of the nature of these three perspectives, examine the plausibility of a middle ground that incorporates the "best" elements of policy competence and responsiveness gained in the course of advising the president, and present empirical case studies of the dynamics of these processes as they took shape in Pres. Jimmy Carter's administration. I analyze only one administration in order to fully consider a broad array of advisory participants, trace White House involvement in the policy process from beginning to end, examine variation among cases, and discern the consequences of relying on advice bent toward one or the other type of information, placing policy-making responsibility in various decision locations (in-house versus the departments and agencies). The analysis, I argue, points to the necessity for a revised theoretical framework incorporating suggestions for research that will engender testable propositions about presidential use of advice.

Scholars studying the American presidency have long debated the relative merit of relying on policy planning and analysis done by neutrally competent experts in bureaucratic departments as opposed to structuring policy making in the White House by their own responsive agents. It has been commonplace to refer to information developed and posited by bureaucrats to be of neutral competence. There are, of course, many problems with calling policy substance neutral competence. Almost nothing can be truly neutral in the sense of being value free. I use the term policy competence to represent something a bit closer to the realities of policy making. The death of the politics-administration dichotomy engendered an extensive literature that explicitly argues that policy makers fight for programmatic goals.[3] Given that presidents and their staffs need both strategies of policy making but may rely on one or the other depending on the nature of shifting environmental circumstances, research is necessary to answer the empirical questions this issue raises. What are the conditions under which presidents are likely to choose one strategy over another? Do different institutional modes of thought enter into presidential policy making? Do presidents seek an appropriate balance between these modes of thought? If so, what organizational processes are most conducive to achieving that mix? These are some of the questions on which I try to shed light in the case analyses and draw inferences as to the interplay between these information strategies. In turn, these strategies illuminate procedural, substantive, and political imperatives illustrated by the Carter experience that are likely shared by all presidents. I turn now to the task of more fully clarifying my use of responsiveness and policy competence.

THE PRESIDENCY, POLITICS, AND POLICY: POLICY COMPETENCE AND RESPONSIVENESS

As implied in the preceding discussion, the literature on presidential organization and management focuses on the manner in which presidents structure their administrations for executive policy making. Much of this received knowledge has gathered around the relationship between relying on department heads and political appointees to render advice and make policy decisions as opposed to career civil servants in the bureaucracy. Both are involved at some level in policy making, and both offer advice to the president. The nature of presidential advice can be broadly conceived as covering policy substance, political analysis, or some combination of the two. This section details these modes of advice in some depth.

Two leading analysts of the presidency and policy making fall on different sides of the analytical fence. James Fesler argues for a strong presidential reliance on bureaucratic actors in the executive branch, whereas Terry Moe traces the tendency of presidents to centralize policy making in the White House.[4] According to Fesler, presidents would benefit from following the advice of bureaucrats who are intimately familiar with the details of policy substance and who can thus be counted on to maximize the potential for policy effectiveness. Moe argues that presidents seek to govern in a hostile political world, and while the pursuit of policy competence is notable, they are driven by the realities of the political environment to seek policy responsiveness. Presidents, the argument goes, are best served by a group of close political staff and advisers who are responsive to the president's political position and goals. When centralization is not feasible, presidents are driven to rely on their appointment powers to politicize the bureaucracy and maintain a sort of decentralized responsiveness.[5] Moe argues that the presidency is essentially a solitary position, and as such the president needs a team of consultants and advisers who act, first and foremost, in his interest and have primary responsibility for policy formulation. Information can be policy oriented, but it must be run through a political filter in order to maximize responsiveness to presidential preferences.[6]

Policy Competence

The concept of neutral (hereafter policy) competence emerges directly from the tradition of public administration identified most closely with Woodrow Wilson and Max Weber.[7] As such, it has deep roots in the politics-administration dichotomy where bureaucrats implement policy within the parameters of general guidelines set by legislatures and/or politicians. According to this theory, career bureaucrats manage these policies within the broader framework set by political leaders and do so in a routinized, specialized, and efficient fashion.[8] Indeed, orthodox public administration theory deems the appropriate relationship between political appointees and career bureaucrats as one based on the policy competence of the latter.[9]

Herbert Kaufman defines policy competence as the "ability to do the work of government expertly, and do it according to explicit, objective standards rather than to personal or party or other obligations and loyalties." He further contends that those in positions of policy implementation are expected to "formulate policy on non-political premises."[10] Although the politics-administration dichotomy addresses implementation questions, its theoretical premises can be adapted to the degree of policy competence used in the policy-formulation stage of policy development.

As a tool for policy development, policy competence is focused on policy advice that is less political and more reflective of long-term goals than is often the case with advice from those in positions responsive to the president.

Graham Wilson notes the existence of at least three types of policy competence. The first is simply technical or scientific proficiency. To use his example, the Department of Agriculture should be able to predict the volume of wheat produced at any price when no one else can. The second type is the practical policy knowledge manifest in a department. This knowledge is essentially institutional memory, so not only is the department charged with providing policy competence of the first form, but assessing the prospects for implementation by other governmental entities, industry, or other relevant governmental actors. The third type of policy competence is what Wilson calls a "higher form," combining political assessments with scientific and practical judgment—in essence, a hybrid of the first and second types. Not only is information substantive, it also includes assessments of the political impact of the proposals, the likelihood of passage in the Congress, and other similar considerations.[11] Given its relevance to presidential decisions, one component of my research is to explore the degree to which this higher form was achieved (if ever), and whether there is evidence that such policy competence even exists in a presidential administration.

Much of the discussion over policy competence is couched either in generic terms or, more specifically, on the relationship between politicians and civil servants.[12] In an attempt to link the advantages of policy competence directly to the presidency, James Fesler argues against centralizing decision making in the White House and for relying on bureaucratic expertise. He argues that it is difficult for political appointees, characterized by brief tenure and often minimal governmental experience, to view policy making from an explicitly long-term perspective. Appointees often distrust careerists, and this limits the possibility for careerists to effectively present their accumulated experience and historical knowledge. Fesler sees this barrier as unnecessarily restricting the possibility for effective action because it restrains the free use of expertise, and could be potentially damaging to long-term policy effectiveness.[13]

Consider, for example, the case of the Bureau of the Budget (BOB). The creation of BOB was intended to "mark the initial American effort to provide neutral competence staff support to achieve greater coherence in the executive branch."[14] From 1939 until about 1960, BOB had great influence in presidential policy making and agenda setting. It was staffed mainly by career civil servants who were also exceptionally competent individuals. The bureau's main function was central clearance, screening requests from agencies and departments to determine whether or not they fell in accordance with the president's stated objectives.[15] For Fesler, this supports the notion that policy competence can be responsive to the president (a point to which critics of the policy-competence paradigm often object) while taking advantage of the expertise of careerists using criteria for policy analysis developed independent of the administration.[16]

Responsive Competence

Others attack the information question from a different angle. Employing a principal-agent framework, these scholars are concerned more with political than organizational imperatives. Although policy competence is valued, it is subordinate to the need for responsiveness. Presidents are driven to centralize policy making in the White House and concentrate on pursuing responsiveness because government institutions cannot be expected to be sympathetic to the president's agenda. Bureaucracies remain while presidents come and go. Parties have declined as mechanisms for presidential control of the administrative state.[17] Agencies charged with a task counter to their standing mission (which is often the case when a new president arrives in Washington) are perceived to be intransigent at worst or lacking responsiveness at best unless they are infested with presidential loyalists. Thus, in order to get what they want, presidents have to pursue a centralized/politicized strategy of policy making in order to sidestep the obstacles erected by the perceived entrenchment of departments and agencies.

Thomas Weko has provided the most thorough empirical examination of the agency framework as it is applied to presidential policy pursuits.[18] His powerfully argued study of the growth of the White House Personnel Office shows both the strengths and weaknesses of that approach. Weko's analysis confirms rational-choice-based explanations that the aggrandizement of the presidency via politicization has some roots in the decline of national parties, and that the development of the White House Personnel Office and, more generally, the White House Office "is far more a product of the institutional system than the leaders who occupy it."[19] He also shows that the growth of the system cannot be accounted for entirely by rational-choice theory. The decline of old constraints (i.e., political parties) were replaced by new ones (i.e., the increased importance of the mass media and the "disintegration of 'policy networks'" in response to the dispersion of interests, and the concomitant splintering of authority in Congress).[20] It thus was well within the parameters of presidential self-interest to control policy making in the White House where possible, and to increase the means of control over departments rather than let them pursue their own interests more or less divorced from presidential supervision.

The implications of Weko's analysis underscore the importance of institutions in framing choices as well as the importance of individual influences. The analysis presented in this book stands on the shoulders of his findings and notes that while presidents *do* tend to centralize decision-making authority for the sake of responsiveness, there is much intra-administration variation in how they go about it. Most presidents have de-centralized decision making at one time or another, entrusting decisions to bureaucrats outside the immediate scope of presidential authority.

However, in centralizing policy making and advice, simply having a "guiding hand" in directing policy making toward presidential preferences is not the same as enjoying monopoly rights over authoritative decisions in a particular policy area. Information and advice must come from some-where, and presidential loyalists are subject to cognitive limitations and time restrictions such that they often process information that is far more substantive in orientation than political.[21]

Presidents have delegated authority in important policy areas to agents outside the White House even when those agents are the products of a po-liticized process. Recent examples include the information processes in the Truman administration, where Clark Clifford pulled ideas from sub-stantive information forwarded by departments to the White House. This modus operandi also characterizes much of the policy making in the Eisen-hower administration, the creation of the Peace Corps under Kennedy, and the constant influence exerted by the BOB and other departments un-der all presidents. Beginning with the Nixon administration, a shift took place in which the domestic policy organization in the White House as-sumed policy-making responsibility by co-opting ideas from work done in the departments.[22]

Other empirical work supports the contention that presidential pol-icy choices are not always (or even mostly) formulated within the White House. In the context of an innovative and painstaking research project, Andrew Rudalevige provides convincing evidence that the source of many presidential proposals, even those classified as priorities, are in the depart-ments or mixed between the White House and the departments.[23] Politi-cization can explain some of these, to be sure, but politicization has gen-erally been couched in terms of policy implementation and not necessarily policy development per se. At a minimum, Rudalevige's data suggest the need to rethink the parameters of centralization. However, as I argue be-low, this apparent discrepancy between theory and observation is explain-able with an analytic approach I call staff shift. This approach represents an effort to reconcile these different perspectives.

Politicization (useful more as a tool for assuring that the *implemen-tation* of policy conforms to the president's goals and preferences than

contributing to policy formulation per se) can be a generally effective way
for the president to control the content of policies for which he will ultimately be held responsible. Still, politicization can fail. One of the reasons
for presidents to take care in choosing loyalists to spearhead their program
in the executive branch's departments and agencies is to minimize the possibility that department heads will "go native" and become beholden to the
organizational culture of their respective staffs. Indeed, despite politicizing efforts, relations between the White House and the departments have
been strained and characterized as "conflictual."[24] The shortcomings of
the politicization strategy doubtless contribute to the tendency of presidents to eschew any form of truly cabinet-type government. Because politicization cannot always provide the president with the sort of political
protection he needs, centralization of policy making and funneling advice
in the White House is pursued in tandem with politicization, and an attempt to understand their integration makes up the core of this book.

    For analytical purposes, I focus on the shifting nature of DPS dynam-
ics in the Carter administration. The DPS is an appropriate White House
organization to study because it was at the forefront of the effort to synthesize information, give advice, get feedback, revise advisory perspectives,
and so on. I argue that staff allocation of scare resources such as time, effort, and interest shifts when process variables such as presidential interest,
scope of policy, bureaucratic input, and public attention change.[25] Having
a broad array of information available for presidential consumption is crucial for advisory processes where the staff seeks to protect presidential
preferences in a politically uncertain environment. Therefore, I conceptualize information as going hand-in-hand with advising because most of the
information that finds its way to the president's desk can be broadly cate-
gorized as political, policy substance, or some mixture of the two. Advising, then, can be thought of as a means to reduce uncertainty by providing the president with, among other things, estimates of the political and
substantive impact of his policy initiatives.[26] In addition, advisers can track
what the president already has in the policy pipeline and offer analysis on
how well new policy initiatives can be expected to be received given the
necessity to coordinate policy proposals and integrate them with the agendas of other institutions.

    Within this general framework, advising is the method by which pres-
idents arm themselves to get what they want and need from the process of
collecting information. Some scholars argue that research on the presidency focuses too much on presidential-bureaucratic relations and not
enough on the presidents' relationships with their advisers.[27] Thus, the information perspective integrated into an advising framework is necessary
for a thorough analysis (with the attendant concerns on political versus

policy competence). However, the empirical portion of this book is guided explicitly by Hult's suggestion to highlight the advising portion of the presidency-staff-bureaucracy triangle, how this advisory process synthesized and presented information alternatives to the president, what the president did upon receiving that information, the variation in the centralization strategy, and the consequences for President Carter's policy goals.[28]

Advice as Investment

It is useful for clarifying what I mean by the importance of advice to conceptualize presidential acceptance or rejection of advice as a kind of investment strategy. I assume that presidents want advice that will enhance the prospects for policy and political success, and will invest greater or lesser amounts of energy in pursuit of such, depending on their policy goals and the level of uncertainty existing in the political environment. When the president's central, policy-relevant constituencies are pleased with his actions, and the policies advocated and developed by him and members of his administration adequately address the nation's problems, the president is in an enviable position. Boldness of policy can set a president apart in the political system and contribute to distinguishing his record. As Stephen Skowronek reminds us, a president will seek "to exercise the constitutional powers of his office in his own right and for his own purposes."[29] But presidents, especially those who are progressively ambitious and in their first term, are not likely to systematically pursue high-risk political strategies.[30] The advisory sources to which the president ultimately listens and the subjective judgment of information content thus are akin to an investment strategy. Presidents who are told by their close advisers that a proposal will alienate large segments of their constituency (or that failure to pursue a particular policy direction is likely to incur the wrath of high-profile interests) will be less willing to follow the course originally set. Often, for every piece of advice accepted, especially dealing with controversial issues characterized by several viewpoints (such as those analyzed in the empirical chapters of this book), significant opportunity costs are incurred by rejecting competing pieces of advice. Relying on staff members to protect political interests cuts personal transaction costs, but the president is ultimately responsible for bearing the political burden of failure. This is true no matter who is responsible for giving the advice, be it "good" or "bad," however those terms are defined from president to president, or from policy to policy.

This is not to argue that presidents will necessarily execute the policy component of their office by simply bowing to the dictates of public-opinion polls. To adhere to such a view is to seriously distort the notion of the president as leader. Democratic theory holds that representation of interests need not always assume the form of constituency preferences.[31] For presidents, this difficulty is exacerbated by the enormous heterogeneity of viewpoints espoused by those they represent. The problem is eased only slightly by the fact that presidents cannot hope to achieve harmony with all of the American people. Furthermore, presidents have increasingly been at odds with their core supporters, especially their political party, in an attempt to forge and maintain a broad governing coalition.[32] Indeed, presidents can and do undertake risky investments as far as advisory information is concerned. However, as my evidence will support, advisory considerations take stock of what political interests and public constituencies can be persuaded to support if the president's position is controversial. Moreover, advisers pursue questions of how that persuasion can best be handled from strategic positioning, which constituencies *cannot* be persuaded, how best to minimize the risk of the investment, and the like.

Of course, presidents and their advisory staffs have an idea of how some of their larger proposals will play with the public. The presidential campaign, for example, provides a natural forum for testing the waters of public opinion. Once in office, however, the public is only part of the president's worries. Congress, interest groups, and even cabinet members in the administration have something to say (sometimes a *lot* to say) on the proposal under consideration. Further, Congress and groups can mount their own public campaigns should the impetus to oppose the president prove strong enough. Cabinet members have this recourse available to them as well, but they are not as likely to use it given the fact that they work at the pleasure of the president and can be fired if their opposition becomes too vocal or is otherwise damaging to the administration.

The president's decision to invest in one or a combination of advisory perspectives thus is contingent on a number of factors that together define a presidential risk factor. A president may pursue a high-risk strategy if the potential payoffs are high, but even those must be informed by analysis that helps the president maximize his return on investment and minimize the risks involved. In an environment of imperfect information, and lacking an enforcement mechanism to prevent interested political forces from reneging on a deal forged by a combination of presidential appeals and large expenditures of staff resources, the risk factor can never be cut to zero. But minimizing the risk factor, or at least identifying the relevant contexts, political and otherwise, within which policy activity will be pursued is the essence of conceptualizing advice as investment and risk assessment.

One important consideration that can both help and hinder a president is that there is an abundance of information in the American political system. Groups, lobbyists, subnational governments, interested citizens, think-tanks (both partisan and nonpartisan), political parties, politicians, civil servants, the media, congressional committees, task forces, and academic institutions and centers, to name just a few, are all potential sources of all types of information. These diverse resources reduce information asymmetries and uncertainty, but at the same time raise the costs of collecting, synthesizing, and disseminating that information, as well as incurring the opportunity costs of choosing among several perspectives, and of necessity discarding others. The president invests in certain strategic routes based on the best information he can find consistent with his policy goals, and his acceptance or rejection of this advice is based on the transaction and opportunity costs associated with his choice. This does *not* imply that policy failures are necessarily the result of a president investing in bad advice. The point is simply that the mode of choosing among enormous amounts of information is analogous to investment decisions, and good investments sometimes go bad. This perspective of advice as investment strategy is implicit, and is often made explicit, in the course of analyzing the cases in chapters 4, 5, and 6.

Presidential Incentives and Preferences

Thinking about advice as a kind of investment suggests the need to specify presidential preferences and incentives since staff attention, presidential personal activity, and the mixture of policy and politics will likely be influenced by the president's preferences which are, as I explain below, closely related to his incentives. Investment strategies are likely the outgrowth of preferences for certain outcomes over others, and incentives about how and when to best achieve those outcomes. For the purposes of this book, I use the term incentives to refer to various structural features of the political system that obtain at the time and form the culture around a particular policy proposal. Such features include partisan strength in Congress, perceptions of bureaucratic intransigence, intra-administration dissension, interest mobilization, problem identification, and the like. These make up various incentives and disincentives that militate either in favor of or against presidential action. Preferences, then, are largely, although certainly not exclusively, derivative of incentives.

I conceptualize preferences as being of two kinds. First, there are *pure preferences*. That is, a president has a set of issues that he feels strongly about and would implement in a perfect world unfettered by political pressures. The second are *realistic preferences*, or those that are adapted to meet the realities embedded in the political context. For example, a president

might wish to put forth a large-scale domestic program but public opinion presents strong resistance to such a program; competing institutions
signal ambivalence or, worse, strong opposition; and budgetary constraints
minimize realistic possibilities of implementing the policy even if it were
to pass. The president's pure preferences would lean heavily toward pushing the program, but the realistic preferences would give him pause for
thought given the no-win nature of this particular issue.

A president's preferences can be formed internally in accordance with
his own sense of what is right and wrong, good or bad. Like voters, presidential preferences can be adaptive, rather than fixed, and modified with
the acquisition of additional information or changing circumstances.[33] For
the purposes of my analysis, preferences are at least partly influenced from
sources or circumstances external to the White House. They are also
formed with some reference to and understanding of structural and/or institutional features of the political system. Thus, while a president might
otherwise prefer to pursue a particularly unpopular or institutionally non-
viable policy, his preferences for action, which are partially influenced by
the set of disincentives surrounding the issue, discourage him from doing
so. Unless otherwise stated, I will refer to preferences as partially derivative of the incentive structure, although they are by no means fully determined by those incentives.[34]

Presidential goals are similar, but they differ in that I refer to them as
being part of a larger, big-picture conception of what the president wants
to leave imprinted on the American political landscape. Later in the book
we encounter the example of the creation of the Department of Education.
On its face, Carter's pure preference was for a large, all-encompassing department. His goal was to have a department that systematically dealt with
all aspects of education policy. But the incentives manifested by the political environment, made up of a bureaucratic, congressional, and interest
opposition, were not at all conducive to obtaining such a department. Carter's pure preference thus was scaled down to a more realistic preference
consistent with the political realities impinging on policy formulation. His
preference for analytical purposes was for a smaller department than he
had originally envisioned but one that held more promise of passage and
implementation than did his larger plan. This simple description, which
will be fully detailed in chapter 4, illustrates that an element responsive
to presidential preferences, when consistent with incentives, is not only
desirable for the president, but constitutes a kind of political-survival imperative. That responsive element is triggered by deep White House involvement in the policy formulation process, and is considered crucial in
institutionalist accounts of presidential choice. The framework I develop

in the following sections brings these concerns to the forefront in an analytical way.

Developing the Framework:
Presidential Action and the New Institutionalism

In order to make sense of the ways in which presidents use (and, perhaps,
are used by) the institutional system that envelopes them, analysts of the
presidency need a theoretical grounding from which to sort out the seemingly endless array of facts and anecdote that characterize presidential
studies. The analytical perspective I employ in this book is adapted from
an approach that is being applied more and more by scholars of the presidency, namely, the new institutionalism. There are at least two approaches
to the new institutionalism: sociological and economic.[35] The sociological
approach emphasizes the informal rules, norms, and roles that guide institutional activity, recognizing the importance individuals have on institutions and society. It also stresses that institutions can in turn affect society and restrict individual autonomy. The economic approach underscores
the importance of formal rules that structure action, and gives credence to
the preferences and goals of political actors.

Combining the two into one framework is especially appropriate for a
study of the U.S. presidency.[36] The advantage of doing so is that it places
individual presidential action within structural boundaries defined by myriad characteristics of the institution. These include formal rules, procedures, histories, spatial boundaries, temporal orderings, environmental
contexts, and other relevant factors that temper (but do not quash) the actions of individuals within organizations. Institutions thus are actors in
their own right. Their individual contexts and cumulative experiences order political life and, to an extent, do so consistently over time without direct relevance to the individuals occupying them.[37]

By adopting an approach that recognizes formal and informal institutional constraints, both formal (e.g., constitutional and statutory obligations) and informal (e.g., the expansive public expectations for policy and
political success that have grown up around the presidency), as well as the
goals, preferences, and prospects for individual autonomy (however muted
those may be) that the individual has in structuring his policy-making environment, presidency studies can benefit from focusing on what presidents in and of themselves bring to the table in terms of individual traits.
These in turn impact the contours of the institution itself within a set of
parameters that are more or less rigid and fixed. The presidency is autonomous and is not a "prisoner" of the system within which it operates, but

rather acts in an adaptive mode to its environment, no matter who sits behind the president's desk. With the help of a single perspective, we thus
can come to a more thorough understanding of how the individual impacts
the institution. Perhaps even more important, we begin to see how the institution shapes and conditions the president's actions, decisions, and imposes limits on leadership.[38] My work here utilizes a variety of approaches
to institutional analysis, and concedes the necessity to understand the lag
between institutional patterns and rationality. This is, of course, a tricky
problem because the lag may reflect political preferences derived from system incentives.[39]

Before moving to the next section, one other point needs clarification.
While I use a new institutionalist framework to examine the dynamics
of policy centralization in the White House, this book does not test the
rational-choice paradigm as it relates to the institutional presidency. The
propositions I derive from the cases I present must be tested on other cases
for affirmation. The new institutionalist paradigm can only be tested by
the degree of analytical leverage it offers, and no single case study or even
set of cases presented can either nullify or validate the approach. While I
hope some of the findings presented in the following pages will help illuminate the usefulness of new institutionalist approaches to the study of the
presidency, a systematic inquiry into the propositions put forth in the literature is beyond the scope of this study. At a minimum, a full assessment
of this approach would necessitate examining several administrations, assessing the variation within and between presidencies.[40] Although the research presented in this book examines six policies and three strategies of
advice and information usage, as well as the impact of a host of contextual
and structural factors on the policy decision, it does not constitute a test of
a theoretical framework in any meaningful sense. Rather, I use the framework heuristically, helping to add meaning to description, extracting substance from an analysis that can ultimately provide insight into how centralization was carried out in one presidency, and more generally aid in the
process of advancing theoretical propositions ripe for systematic analysis
across a range of presidencies. I go a bit farther by providing evaluations
derived from the theoretical framework, but again this does not test a theory. While the scholarly debate has long been engaged, few comprehensive analyses dealing with the empirical relationship between the different
types of information coming to the president via the advisory process and
the choices made by presidents based on their interpretation of that advice
exist in the literature. This book fits squarely within that category. Having
explained my use of a version of the motivational approach to new institutionalist analysis, I turn now to developing a theoretical framework that
builds on insights extended from this approach.

Applying the Framework: Three Strategies of Presidential Management of Information

Political scientists who study the presidency, organizations, or policy making, need categories that describe variations in presidential control of policy making. When politics and policy collide, presidents and their staffs must make decisions about where to get advice, what kind of advice is needed, and how to integrate policy substance with political necessity. Insights gleaned from institutionalist scholarship suggest the nature of presidential constraints as they affect policy formulation. Furthermore, presidents have limited time horizons, so their personal resources such as time, energy, and attention are at a premium.[41] They are disadvantaged in the sense that there is relatively little they can do unilaterally. They must constantly vie for agenda space with competing institutions such as Congress, the bureaucracy, and state governments.[42] White House staffing units are charged with aiding in the policy-development process, but they too are saddled with limited time and resources. Information costs, coupled with time constraints, imply that although policy making is centralized in the White House, it is not of one kind. In other words, not all policies (nor even all presidential priorities) are fully directed by staff. Time and attention are limited, so in an effort to cut information costs during the development of policy priorities, the location of policy can shift in accordance with the president's preferences, the nature of policy, public and political opposition, or any combination of these.

Samuel Kernell has noted the change in American politics from "institutionalized pluralism" to "individualized pluralism." This change makes for an increasingly atomistic system within which presidents pursue positive, purposive action.[43] An increasingly atomistic system exacerbates the degree of uncertainty and increases both transaction and information costs for the president and his staff. It is therefore consistent with the goal of policy centralization for presidents to delegate policy-making authority to the executive branch, but still have those policies monitored by internal staff. That is, the nature and scope of staff participation will shift. The responsibility of the staff changes from directing policy development to one of monitoring the progress of policy formulation, with responsibility manifested in actors external to the White House. Having disseminated the responsibility for policy formulation while maintaining a sort of policy headquarters in the White House cuts (but cannot fully dissipate) the costs that the American political system imposes on presidents and their staffs in the pursuit of critical information so as to decrease the level of bargaining uncertainty.[44] This is consistent with centralizing tendencies because the White House Staff (specifically, the DPS for purposes of this study) plays an active part regardless of policy-making location. But the nature and scope of that activity, especially the nature of staff attention to policy formulation, shifts to meet the necessities of both internal presidential imperatives (such as policy priority and interest) and external factors (such as the nature of political opposition, the scope and reach of the policy under development, and so forth). More specifically, as I argue in the empirical chapters, the functions of staff shift vary in accordance with factors such as issue salience to the president, policy scope, and public attention.

Presidential Incentives and Staff Shift

In placing presidential use of information within the general framework just laid out, supplemented with the analytical lens of advice as investment and the discussion of presidential incentives and preferences described earlier in this chapter, three possible presidential strategies suggest themselves. These strategies, in turn, suggest different responsibilities of the advisory unit charged with overseeing policy choice in the White House. The first strategy is to locate policy-making responsibility primarily in the White House.[45] In accordance with this strategy, the DPS functions as *policy director*, maintaining a preponderance of control over policy making in the White House while giving priority to pursuing responsiveness. If the nature of the policy under consideration is wide, touching on several jurisdictions, the responsibility of the DPS shifts to that of *policy facilitator*. This strategy is most likely to be pursued when the president delegates authority for policy making to his staff and bureaucratic agents in roughly equal measure. As facilitator, the DPS coordinates the work of both the bureaucratic agents and internal White House staff.[46] Finally, the president may choose to decentralize policy formulation by giving responsibility to the relevant bureaucratic agency or department. In this instance the DPS would act as *policy monitor*, letting bureaucracies develop policy while monitoring its content to assure it comports with the president's wishes. Both responsiveness and policy competence are found in varying degrees in each category. The question then becomes: What are the consequences of varying relationships between policy competence and responsiveness? I now elaborate on each of these strategies.

Staff as Policy Director

Centralization is characterized by tight policy control from the White House. Issues that fall within the purview of this strategy are likely to be politically charged, so their formulation is directed by the DPS to ensure a high degree of responsiveness. Responsiveness thus takes precedence over the search for policy substance, although policy competence is likely to play some part in the formulation process. Policy is never made in a vacuum, and presidents are almost certainly not averse to organizational competence. The critical point is that the responsive agents in the White House (e.g., DPS) synthesize information and coordinate the workings of the agencies or departments. Policy making is directed outward from presidential staff to the bureaucracy. Bureaucrats become important for implementing White House directives rather than wielding a degree of independent authority. Advice coming into the White House from the departments is used as the baseline from which to work but is politicized to the extent that it does not interfere with the president's articulated preferences.

Staff as Policy Facilitator

Under different circumstances, the DPS serves as policy facilitator. The strategy employed can be termed a *mixed* strategy because there is a potential for tension in the realm of policy competence. One major reason that staff attention shifts from that of director to facilitator is that the nature of the issue under consideration falls across two or more departmental or agency jurisdictions. The fact that the proposed policy involves more than one department or agency is an incentive for the White House to maintain some semblance of control. However, it does not employ full centralization because it is unrealistic to expect to control policy development when issues are extraordinarily broad and complex. In this case, control problems exist because the issues are highly politicized and cut across departmental jurisdictions.

Staff as Policy Monitor

As noted above, policy can be delegated to departments or agencies for development. In this strategy, policy formulation is transferred primarily to civil servants and/or political appointees. The role of the DPS is to monitor policy development. Policy may or may not fall within the jurisdiction of politicized agents, but policy-competent civil servants often provide the information used for policy decisions.[47] To the extent that politicization is not part of the equation, there is a responsive element, but it is subordinate to the pursuit of policy competence. In a sense, then, this strategy could be considered as one of "decentralized centralization." In other words, policy formulation is decentralized, but only under the supervision of White House policy staff. This has the advantage of cutting White House transaction costs by placing the burden of policy development on those in bureaucratic departments and/or agencies, while at the same time

maintaining creative control over its content. Policy expertise takes precedence over but does not fully suppress responsiveness as the White House
monitors formulation to maximize consistency with presidential goals.

In sum, the theoretical framework developed here suggests that there
may be no one best way to disseminate, collect, analyze, and use advice.
President Carter, as I will show in the following chapters, pursued all three
strategies with both positive and negative results. Thus, something besides
simply centralizing policy making in the White House must be the crucial
factor (or factors) in having achieved a successful process.[48] I argue that
the variation in the centralization tendency of presidents is a crucial component in eliciting policy and political success. Indeed, each process yields
examples of unsuccessful and successful cases of policy making. Other crucial factors include coordination between the president's responsive agents
in the White House and the bureaucrats in the departments, and the character of that partnership. The advisory patterns in the Carter administration were both effective and ineffective in their pursuit of both good process and good policy. The conditions and circumstances surrounding each
result are the analytical focus of each chapter, always focusing the micro-
scope on the question of how policy advice was used for political purposes.

POLITICAL CONTEXT AND THE INTERPLAY
OF ADVICE AND INFORMATION

Although policy competence can never be value free, policy perspectives
on governmental action do exist and are substantively, rather than politically, motivated. According to rational-choice perspectives, presidents
have incentives that render them unable to resist emphasizing political advice at the expense (but not the eradication) of that which is substantive.
Policy competence thus is potentially intransigent and not conducive to
change in policy direction or in producing innovative thinking. It is also
incapable of formulating imaginative approaches to problem solving.[49]

In order to overcome these pathologies, centralization, or the pursuit
of "responsive competence," pulls policy making into the White House
and advises presidents as to the political imperatives of the policy under
consideration. The same forces naturally lead presidents to politicize the
executive branch with presidential loyalists. The result is the maximization
of responsive elements that consider a president's political obligations to
be of paramount importance. This is consistent with the assumption that
if the president is going to be held accountable for policy decisions, then
that policy should conform to standards or guidelines that are politically
palatable to the president. Even more than politicized loyalists, policy
making becomes the province of the president's staff. The staff may seek

advice, but policy making is pulled inward. It is made in the White House and mandated to the bureaucracy for implementation. Those who encourage such a system argue for a presidential version of policy competence. They contend that the American system, characterized by diffuse authority, multiple access points, dispersed interests, and (with a few exceptions) divided government, creates incentives to concentrate policy making and coordination within the White House Office (WHO) and, to a lesser extent, the EOP.[50]

An argument in favor of relying on policy competence would encourage presidents to recognize the advantages of substance, rely on cabinet officers (be they politicized or not) more than White House staff, and trust the expertise and professionalism of the career civil service. The problem that others see with these prescriptions is that they are not commensurate with a realistic vision of a president's resources, political incentives, and institutional constraints. The institutional configuration of American politics is not altogether amenable to a president and the policies he wishes to develop and implement. Presidents thus need to centralize policy development in the White House because efforts to do so will result in increased influence over policy making. There may be costs associated with a reliance on centralization, such as a loss of substantive knowledge and historical memory in a given policy area, to be sure. However, while these problems are readily acknowledged, forces pushing presidents in the general direction of centralization as a strategy appropriate for amplifying political preferences are too strong to be resisted.

Presidential decisions to centralize policy development in the White House or with presidential loyalists in the bureaucracy are determined by presidential incentives to activate priority policy proposals. With regard to these incentives, Moe writes: "What (the president) wants is an institutional system responsive to his needs as a political leader. He values organizational competence, to be sure, but what he seeks is 'responsive competence,' not neutral competence."[51] This choice of information may either grow in a deterministic way or as the result of deliberate action. Nelson Polsby argues that centralization is a conscious decision. Richard Nixon, for example, used a set of new, less-experienced cabinet officers in his second term, reflecting a conscious effort to centralize policy making in the White House and keep the locus of control firmly within his grasp. The assumption was that those with less political experience and few ties to interest groups would not block renewed efforts at centralization.[52]

However, these theoretical assertions do not always jibe with empirical observation. Jimmy Carter, for example, used three different and distinct strategies for pursuing advice and information in the course of policy formulation, all of which were consistent with the tenets of policy

centralization. In addition to pursuing a mixed strategy, with the DPS facilitating between the White House staff and the executive branch, Carter
sought both policy and responsive competence in roughly equal measure,
often eschewing politicization altogether and relying instead on bureaucratic professional expertise for advice. Thus, the decision as to which
strategy to employ is sensitive to a host of contextual variables and is not
simply a by-product of the political context within which the president
must govern, although as argued previously, that political context is important for shaping presidential preferences. Moe captures the essence of
that context but overstates his case when he claims that there has been little
variation in how presidents have managed their policy-making function.
Graham Wilson, for example, notes that "Moe's claim that American aca-
demics who study public administration have been biased in favor of the
bureaucracy is decidedly odd for a subfield that has been preoccupied with
issues such as 'capture,' 'iron triangles,' and . . . 'issue networks.'"[53]

My work moves toward integrating these perspectives by demonstrat-
ing intra-administration variation in how policy making was centralized in
the Carter presidency. Carter's DPS acted in three distinct ways, depending on the policy being developed. The implication of my analysis is that
the pursuit of these three staffing strategies (i.e., staff as facilitator; staff as
director; and staff as monitor) and both types of information (i.e., political and policy) can be viewed as complements rather than substitutes for
one another. Indeed, access to information and control of its dissemination are veritable holy grails for actors in the American political system,
given the constitutional system of separation of powers, checks and balances, and the consequent asymmetry of institutional incentives that such
a system engenders.[54] Seeking advice from a host of sources, and having
staff execute its policy-related tasks concomitant with the necessity engendered by the specifics of policy enhance the prospects of presidential success in the political and policy arenas. Indeed, success in the policy arena
has significant implications for increasing the president's prestige in the
political arena, implying that the two arenas may really be one.[55]

Of course, White House–executive branch relationships are fluid.
This fluidity stems from the similar, if not always exactly identical, perspectives growing from their shared, intrabranch perch overlooking politics and policy. Thus, to think of the categories of policy competence and
political information as mutually exclusive would be to miss the point. The
point is *not* that the two have nothing to do with one another and exist in
a zero-sum environment. Rather, there are no real institutional barriers
around either the White House or the rest of Washington; information
and advisory patterns are themselves fluid. While White House staff members and executive branch officials may sometimes see things differently,

they can and often do work together, many times to the satisfaction of both. Indeed, I make no assumption that policy competence implies that policy makers ignore political values or interests. Rather, I assume policy competence is neutral in the sense that it is removed from the presidential office, has a long-term perspective, and yields substantive policy information with little reference to impacts defined as political in electoral or interest group terms. This can come from either White House–centered operations or the executive branch more generally. This is an admittedly narrow perspective, but it is reasonable to note that the political information that informs and rounds out analysis of policy substance comes at a number of points in the process. Policy can, for example, be made to accommodate political interests and tailored to fit the contours of the political landscape. Policy also can be fashioned without regard for political imperatives. Once the principles and programmatic goals are agreed upon, efforts can then be made to add political nuance post hoc or, in the purest sense, make the case for policy on its own terms, thus attempting to persuade political interests as to the efficacy of the policy in question. Viewing the political pursuit of policy advice as a *continuum* ranging from heavy White House involvement to a mixture between White House and executive branch players and finally to the other extreme of bureaucratic carte blanche subject to relatively light White House monitoring thus is more useful and accurate than viewing centralization as a dichotomy or even a taxonomy. I elaborate the dynamics of such a continuum later in this chapter.

In short, the analytical question that arises when examining the various trade-offs between the two types of advice centers on the convergence of presidential preferences and the appropriate means for converting those preferences into purposeful policy action. Reliance on experts in the bureaucracy may raise problems of a president's control of his own administration, but an overly centralized decision structure may produce policy proposals that lack substantive depth or, somewhat paradoxically, political plausibility given the rejection of institutional memory that is implicit in the pursuit of responsiveness. There is a need, then, no matter what advisory strategy is pursued, to combine political and policy analysis. As I have argued, it is quite often the responsibility of the advisory unit within the White House (in this study, the DPS) to mediate between the two. The nature of staff activity thus shifts relative to presidential preferences.

The Shifting Responsibilities of the DPS

Beginning with Herbert Hoover, most presidents have benefited from some sort of institutional apparatus charged with overseeing the domestic policy-making process.[56] The position of domestic policy adviser can be traced at least as far back as Clark Clifford under Harry Truman. With the possible exception of Dwight Eisenhower, every president since has designated at least one person to serve as an assistant for domestic policy. Lyndon Johnson set up a formalized office of domestic policy, which has become a mainstay of the institutionalized presidency. The office has undergone a number of name changes, ranging from the Domestic Council in the Nixon and Ford administrations, to the Domestic Policy Staff in the Carter years. It was changed to the Office of Policy Development during the Reagan and Bush presidencies, and back to the Domestic Policy Staff under Clinton. Regardless of the extent each president has chosen to utilize this staff, the point remains that the domestic policy apparatus is part of the "deep structure" of the presidency.[57] Given this continuity, focusing on the responsibilities, political viewpoint, and inner workings of the DPS under the Carter administration is appropriate. Additionally, it is instructive to focus on the DPS and domestic policy in general because the responsiveness element is manifest in their interaction.[58] Presidency scholars might benefit from pursuing an understanding of the dynamic interplay between the president and the bureaucracy, as mediated by the DPS.

Although presidents have varied in the ways in which they have set up and used their domestic policy-making units, they have been reasonably consistent in defining the primary function of the staff as giving advice, protecting the president's political interests, and coordinating policy formulation. If this is the case, and I contend it is, then delving deeply into the internal workings of one administration can tell us much about the dynamics of White House policy making. This is buttressed by the proposition that many of the external forces in the political environment the White House has to contend with (including a fragmented Congress, geographically and ideologically dispersed interests, increasing media scrutiny, a seemingly independent bureaucracy, locally oriented parties, and heightened public expectations) remain relatively constant from one administration to the next. In this respect, while the experiences of any one administration are difficult to generalize, an in-depth study of the DPS can be useful for theory advancement and modification. Studying the Carter administration is as good as any other for gaining a sense of the variation in policy centralization and advice. I will have more to say on this topic, as well as present further justification for studying Carter and domestic policy making more generally in chapter 3.

The DPS in the Carter administration was not originally designed to formulate policy. Initially, as Shirley Anne Warshaw notes, "the domestic policy office was responsible only for review of departmental policy proposals and not for the initial development of the proposals by the departments."[59] Carter had more than doubled the size of the staff from that which existed in the Ford administration. He abolished the Domestic Council, but retained the staff, and put Stuart Eizenstat in charge of the DPS. Eizenstat was one of Carter's most influential White House advisers, and they enjoyed a close working relationship.[60] Margaret Wyszomirski observes that during the Carter years, the DPS participated in a wide range of issues and was involved in nearly as many stages of the policy-making process as Nixon's Domestic Council. However, the role it played was substantially different. Carter's DPS acted in an advisory and coordinating capacity rather than as a directing force. The official description of the office stressed analysis and advice functions, as well as multiphased policy-coordinating responsibilities ranging from the formulation stage to strategic planning for legislative enactment.[61]

Further understanding can thus be gained not only by exploring the capacity of advice to provide policy competence and responsiveness, but also the extent to which the DPS was an agent of policy facilitation, performing the dual functions of synthesizing analysis and offering advice. The focus on staff dynamics is further justified on the basis that, with the explosion of White House staff that has occurred since 1939, coupled with the various ways in which the staff has been used over time, the president's responsive agents in the White House undertake many of the day-to-day responsibilities for crafting his domestic agenda along with the character and content of that agenda. This staffing explosion has been long recognized as an important component to be understood if one is to understand almost any aspect of the institutional presidency.[62] I argue below that while the responsibilities of the DPS varied systematically across the range of centralized, mixed, and decentralized strategies, it was active in policy formulation—especially in the centralized strategy, less so in the mixed, and even less so in the decentralized realm. In short, the level of activity and energy expended by the staff can be conceptualized as a continuum rather than as amenable to more or less strict categorization. As the president's and staff's priorities, incentives, policy scope, and political environment shifts, so does the degree of time, attention, and resources exerted by the staff. But staff resources are not the only important variable in analyzing advice and information. Other organizational entities interact with the White House staff, further shaping the nuance of the relationship between politics and policy. An introduction to these resources is the subject to which I now turn.

Other Organizations and Functions Conducive to Policy Making
A host of factors interact with one another in the process of presidential policy making. Looking at these factors through a new institutionalist lens helps sort out and make sense of these clusters of variables. In designing

qualitative research, problems of evidence and inference present formidable problems to be overcome, especially concerning the level of uncertainty that should be reported by the researcher as to the veracity of any conclusions drawn. One of the ways to assuage this concern is to multiply the observable implications of the theory. I use the several groups, political party considerations, political promises, congressional liaison, task forces, and such to analyze the dynamics of centralization. I will expand on this in chapter 3, but it is necessary at this point to show that focusing on these other entities in the advisory process helps to get around some of the inferential problems encountered in qualitative research.[63] Several organizational resources, be they institutionalized parts of the presidency or not, are used by presidents for collecting information through the advisory process. The information perspectives they yield may be about politics or policy, depending on the president's preferences. Task forces are one example of such resources; cabinet councils are another. Systematically examining their dynamics is instructive. By inquiring into the problem at hand, it makes possible a comprehensive analysis of their impact on presidential advice and the consequent decisions made on the basis of information offered.[64] Two of the functions performed by these task forces and, on occasion, the White House staff itself, are outreach and interest group liaison. This process is vital to any advice, regardless of whether it is policy or political in nature. Interest groups, for example, provide substantive analysis useful for collecting, synthesizing, and utilizing policy specific information, although the group itself often has a political agenda.[65]

Another important function is assessing the impact of various policy proposals on myriad interest groups and constituencies.[66] The groups can provide a service for presidents by offering useful syntheses of policy and political information, both of which are of importance to the White House because both perspectives are presented at one time. Consultation with interest groups can provide another perspective, perhaps different from the bureaucracy, that a president centralizing policy formulation can use to fend off otherwise convincing arguments by civil servants or career bureaucrats. The more open the initial advisory process, the more likely it is that those charged with policy making will be able to make a determination about the tenor and content of policy. They will also determine what is acceptable to the president's stated purpose and be better able to approximate (though certainly not duplicate) conditions of perfect information.

The use of task forces in performing outreach functions are thus two important ways in which presidents can get the type of information they need, especially in the initial stages of policy development. Information gathered at these stages is important because it helps to formulate policy early and avoid expending political capital in unnecessary fights. In addition, outreach is also important for maintaining close contact with members of Congress and political parties and, in return, receiving political feedback that might be missed in the process of cultivating interest group relations. Indeed, external political institutions such as Congress and, to a much lesser extent, parties have an active role in policy formulation and the identification of political imperatives that in turn can have tremendous impact on the type of strategy the president pursues. Each of the empirical chapters that follow will thus take special notice of task forces, outreach, and congressional liaison functions. Where they are absent, the possible impact of their absence is assessed.

CONCLUSION

The task of this concluding section is to reiterate the framework and assumptions on which the analysis and interpretations in the balance of the book rest. This chapter has sought to build an analytical focus that helps explain intra-administration variation in presidential advice, and the assimilation and use of the information imparted to the White House from myriad sources.

I have argued that presidents seek advice from myriad sources so as to maximize their chances for policy and political success. The different kinds of advice brought to the president via the advisory process are integral for policy making and decisions. A president's decision to invest in various advisory approaches is an attempt to reduce uncertainty in an atomistic American political environment. In order to cut the transaction, information, and opportunity costs imposed via an effort to reduce uncertainty as to political consequences of various policy choices, presidents centralize policy making in the White House staff. This is not to say that they listen only to advice coming from staff members. Instead, the staff serves as a co-ordinating body for several avenues of political and policy advice, originating from many different sources such as bureaucracies, competing political institutions, task forces, relevant interests, and the like. I thus pay special attention to the interplay of two different, but not necessarily conflicting, types of information. The first is *policy* (often termed neutral) *competence*, which emphasizes policy substance, more or less without primary concern for political considerations. The second is *responsive competence*, which is designed to protect and adhere as much as possible to the president's political interests and his stated policy goals and preferences. The intersection of each with the other constitutes a major part of the analysis presented in the empirical chapters.

Where this book differs from other analyses on presidential advice and

advisers is its focus on the dynamics of the centralization process. Scholars
have long established empirical and theoretical explanations for why presidents pull policy-making functions into the White House. What my
analysis adds to the literature is a focus on why presidents might not only
look beyond the walls of 1600 Pennsylvania Avenue, but also come to rely
on the capacity of external participants to formulate policy. The president
and his staff clearly have incentives to maintain some sort of active presence in the formulation process, regardless of where policy is made. Thus,
the participation levels of staff members shift depending on factors such as
the scope and breadth of the policy under consideration, the nature of the
political contagion surrounding the issue, the level of presidential interest,
the profile of interested parties, and similar considerations.

Given the nature of constraints illuminated by institutionalist approaches, staff advisory participation and effort varies systematically across
policies. I account for this by sketching an explanatory theoretical framework of staff shift. The shift comes in the level of participation exerted by
presidential staff members. These strategies are empirically identifiable in
the Carter administration. I have assigned three labels depending on the
degree of policy formulation exhibited by the staff: (1) staff as director,
when policy is fully centralized in the White House with only advisory
functions played by external actors; (2) staff as facilitator, when presidential staff act in tandem with bureaucracies and affected groups, coordinating activities of these participants and assuming an active part in policy
deliberation; and (3) staff as monitor, when resource constraints make it
feasible for presidents to delegate policy-formulation responsibility to bureaucrats or political appointees in the executive branch while maintaining
a strategy of actively overseeing the progress of policy development. Although staff shift is similar to economic theories of resource allocation, it
says little if anything about *how* presidents determine their programs. Paul
Quirk reminds us that ideas, for example, can be of utmost importance in
determining policy substance, even more so than the push and pull of interest group competition and political compromise.[67]

Other approaches that view policy centralization as a more or less natural response to the constraints of the American political system imply that
presidents will employ their staff as akin to what I have called "policy de-
velopers" with little active input from bureaucracies beyond technical advice. The staff-shift framework developed here makes a weaker claim, but
one that is consistent with the view of the American political system as a
set of constraints on presidential action. The claim is simply that presidents can spread their policy-making net far and wide and rely on an abundance of information sources, using staff resources in such a way that they
maximize chances for policy responsiveness while at the same time cutting

information costs in relation to presidential incentives, preferences, contexts, policy characteristics, and the like.

In sum, my argument is that we can account for variation in policy by examining the nature of advice brought to the president, how that advice is used, and the degree of staff involvement. Although my analysis focuses on the experiences of only one administration, I posit that much can be learned given the institutional requirements of the presidency, such as a domestic advisory process. Variation in policy advice, political imperative, and information usage are thus made consistent with the empirical tendency of presidents to centralize, and all responsibilities assumed by the staff in bringing advice and counsel to the president are integral parts of the centralization strategy.

CHAPTER 3

Analytic Method

The enterprise of presidential research by political scientists has long been criticized for being atheoretical, containing little cumulative knowledge beyond anecdotal evidence and plagued by unconnected sets of propositions. In particular, political scientists who attempt to derive broad generalizations based on very few cases (sometimes only one) are criticized for engaging in work more properly and competently handled by historians.[1] This problem has been addressed in recent years by scholars who have examined either a relatively large number of presidential administrations or a large number of policy proposals across one or more presidencies. Considerable progress thus has been made on the theoretical front. The most fruitful areas of research so far have focused on presidential-congressional relations, dealing specifically with the effect of public support for the president and the impact of presidential legislative skills on programmatic success in Congress, and presidential actions in pursuit of pubic support.[2]

Still, the charges leveled at the presidency subfield by scholars who lament the dearth of cumulative knowledge and theoretical advancement in presidential studies are hard to ignore.[3] They have been trumpeted so loud and long that their claims have more than a little veracity to sustain them. Nonetheless, it is fallacious to assume that historical, case-based analyses have little to contribute to our understanding of the presidency.[4] As noted earlier, the progress of institutionalization in the presidency and the use (or misuse) of organizational resources increase the prospects for understanding the dynamics of the presidency in more general terms, even though the analysis may be based on lessons derived from the study of just one or a few presidents.

In the study of the presidency, important questions arise that cannot be addressed by quantitative techniques, just as questions arise that cannot be answered with a qualitative approach. A corollary holds just as well: If we only utilize data that can be gathered across administrations, then scholars are prohibited by logistics such as time and resources from asking other critical questions. Recently, scholars have begun to confront this problem head-on. Most notably, Gary King and his colleagues have shown that the underlying logic of causal inference is the same regardless of whether one uses quantitative or qualitative methodology.[5] It is important that case-based qualitative analysis focus on some aspect of the institution or a president in relation to institutional realities. If some generalization or contribution to theory building is desired, this concern becomes even more imperative. It is virtually impossible to generalize if the unit of analysis is the *president* rather than some aspect of the *presidency*.[6] Presidents come and go, but various components of the institution remain, and presidents are well-advised to learn as much as they can from the experience of their predecessors.

Analysis of a single administration can provide theoretically informed, descriptive inferences as to the rich dynamics of the presidency, and in so doing raise important questions and shed light on how the tasks of the presidency (and being president) are discharged. Thus, while generalization based on one president may rest on shaky ground, such need not be the case when using case analysis as a heuristic device, adding to and refining the current state of theory in the presidency subfield. This is especially appropriate when the number of cases can be multiplied. Instead of looking at one president, for example, one can describe multiple policies in multiple contexts in order to determine whether patterns appear, and how such patterns affect, change, or reinforce theoretical development. It is in precisely this endeavor (i.e. descriptive inference informed by theory) that a theoretical perspective such as the new institutionalism described in the last chapter has special utility. Such a perspective can supply meaning to description, allowing an interpretation that is sensitive to both institutional realities and individual influences in how presidents acquire, analyze, and use policy and political advice.

This position is also consistent with the argument put forth by King, Robert Keohane, and Sidney Verba when they state that "abstract, unobserved concepts such as utility, culture, intentions, motivations, identification, intelligence, or the national interest . . . can play a useful role in theory *formulation*; but they can be a hindrance to empirical *evaluation* of theories and hypotheses."[7] It follows, then, that variables such as these can and should be incorporated into analysis when they have observable characteristics. For example, some of Carter's actions as president were a direct outgrowth of his worldview.[8] I cannot hope to measure directly his worldview in any meaningful or empirically verifiable way. However, as I show in the case studies, the perception of his worldview influenced how the White House staff went about its work. Many of the documents I use in the analysis bear this out, and allow for at least the indirect evaluation of the impact of the president's worldview on policy formulation. I am not concerned with whether or not the staff accurately estimated Carter's perspective on various issues. The point is that the president's individual characteristics tempered the manner in which staff members carried out their tasks. Thus, it buttresses the new institutionalist theoretical argument I set out in chapter 2 that at least passing reference to individuals can and should be made when individual characteristics exhibit empirically observable characteristics that affect institutional and organizational performance.

All of this is not to argue that it is easy to get beyond the vicissitudes of the individual in an analytically meaningful way. Far from it. The methodological problem emerges from the very nature of the presidency itself. While some patterns of presidential activity are identifiable across administrations (e.g., the continued use of some sort of domestic policy apparatus), it is also true that some of what constitutes presidential performance is attributable to idiosyncratic elements of the individuals occupying the Oval Office at any given time. Any attempt to list these variables would have to include factors such as personality, differing historical circumstances, changing institutional configurations, differences in personal and organizational style, and the like. It is extremely difficult, however, to get a handle on many of these variables, especially personality.[9] Case-based analyses provide presidential scholars with a host of contextual variables with which they must come to terms when trying to build on to an existing theoretical base. In this sense, a case-oriented research design can provide a forum for theory building and evaluation, but cases must be studied comparatively. Otherwise, there is no variation within or between cases, which enable us to differentiate the systematic from the idiosyncratic, the general from the specific. Further, as mentioned previously, comparative case studies are invaluable as heuristic tools in that they can generate theoretically based hypotheses emergent in the analysis of the case and ripe for broader empirical investigation. Finally, and perhaps most importantly, such studies are enormously useful for surveying theoretical claims and providing a basis for either casting doubt on or supporting the veracity of a particular theory.[10] However, it must be noted that no single case or piece of datum, evidence, or observation can, in itself, falsify any explanation. It can, at best, raise questions about the veracity of theoretical explanation, but it cannot fully reject that explanation unless something more complete and persuasive is offered.[11]

This book seeks to help the enterprise of theory construction by using extended comparative case analysis of policy making in the Carter administration using the modest theoretical framework and institutionalized setting described in chapter 2. Using comparative case analysis as my foundation, I describe, explain, and, where possible, evaluate presidential action with regard to the tension between responsiveness and policy competence in the course of getting and using advice.[12] More importantly, following Paul Quirk's lead, my unit of analysis is six different policy formulation decisions rather than the president himself. In each case I explore the similarities and differences that characterize the use of information in pursuit of the success of those policies.[13]

DATA AND METHOD

The bulk of the data used for this study come from archival materials in the Jimmy Carter Presidential Library in Atlanta. Presidential archives offer a wealth of resources of which political scientists have made too little use.[14] Since the analysis focuses mainly on the Domestic Policy Staff and advisory relationships, I combed through thousands of pages in the papers of Stuart Eizenstat, DPS chief throughout the Carter presidency. Data culled from these papers is supplemented by information from other collections such as Chief of Staff Hamilton Jordan, along with other relevant papers.

There are many limitations to using cases as tools for theory generation. Jeffrey Cohen notes that single case studies do not aid the theoretical enterprise because they lack a comparative framework. They thus are unable to distinguish the unique from the general.[15] The analysis presented in this book is consistent with Cohen's viewpoint because it seeks comparative advantage through the analysis of multiple policies and the concomitant proliferation of factors available for investigation. Although concentrated within only one administration, the cases are presented from a new institutionalist framework that describes the nature of the interaction between person and institution. What emerges, then, is a portrait of advising and information that might be instructive for analyses of other administrations given the relative constancy of a domestic policy advisory process. The selection of cases and the method for analyzing the documents will be detailed below. First, however, it is important to explore the theoretical reasoning for selecting the Carter administration and the DPS as the contextual basis of this study.

WHY CARTER? THE PRESIDENT AND DOMESTIC POLICY

An analysis of policy making in the Carter administration provides a useful starting point for testing propositions put forth in the literature examining presidential use of information and advice. Candidate Jimmy Carter brought with him to the White House a public goods philosophy of governing. In his analysis of Carter's political leadership style, Erwin Hargrove defines Carter's particular type of public goods philosophy:

> Carter did not believe in fashioning policies according to calculations of political advantage or strategy, but he understood perfectly well that at the end of the day compromise might be necessary. His conception of leadership required a focus on "public goods" when policy was initiated but permitted compromise in due course. . . . Carter saw his own approach to leadership as antithetical to the tactics of compromise and bargaining practiced by legislators. . . . (He) preferred a comprehensive policy proposal that attacked all facets of a problem. . . . The public might rally behind a comprehensive proposal that appealed to public goods. *The power of the policy to sustain itself is strengthened by comprehensiveness, which implies a long-term view rather than a quick fix. . . .* Carter thought of himself as a political leader. . . . For (him) political leadership was not so much doing what's right instead of what's political as it was *doing the political in the right way.*[16]

As a Democrat guided by such an expansionist governmental philosophy, it is not unreasonable to expect Carter to use staff to take charge and direct the conduct of policy making, centralizing the bulk of domestic policy formulation in the White House. One reason for this is that Democrats in general tend to strive for large-scale domestic agenda items. Moreover, this tendency can be exacerbated by a public goods philosophy, where mobilizing constituencies for political gain may not hold the same import as doing the "right thing." As a consequence, policy making would be drawn into the White House, driven in part by a strong political motive to avoid having policy priorities dismantled in the bureaucracy. If the president is going to expend large portions of political resources advocating large initiatives and be held accountable for their content, then logic holds that the president and his staff should control the substance of those initiatives. If this was to be expected, then Carter's administration is an excellent one with which to check the veracity of this claim. However, as I argue in the chapters to follow, this was not always the case. To be sure, policy centralization was the modus operandi, but its practice varied according to various factors, and will be detailed in the empirical chapters.

Carter, like most presidents, went to Washington with an eye toward cabinet government and a reliance on expertise as guiding principles for policy making. His public goods philosophy led him to choose *experts* to head the government departments. Only two cabinet members could be said to have close ties to the interest groups most closely associated with their particular departments: Robert Bergland at Agriculture, and Cecil Andrus of Interior. Presumably this foreshadowed a no-nonsense approach to governance, based on the criterion of expertise, and a willingness to formulate sound, substantive policy addressing the major problems facing the nation. In an early assessment of Carter's cabinet, Nelson Polsby observed: "It is not their high level of education . . . that observers have fastened upon in noticing the odd resemblance between this Democratic cabinet and the Republican cabinets that immediately preceded it. Rather it is the curious neutrality of the Carter cabinet toward the vast stew of interest groups, both within and outside the government, that make up the traditional Democratic coalition."[17]

Carter quickly abandoned any notions of cabinet government, regardless of the fact that his cabinet officers boasted few political ties to their policy constituencies.[18] Cabinet government was, he discovered, too unwieldy to manage. Furthermore, while his cabinet officials tended to be of one type (i.e., experts detached from political pressure), they would not necessarily maintain the degree of responsiveness that he would have liked.[19] All of this supports the notion that Carter would most likely centralize policy decisions in the White House using staff to direct policy content. However, although this was partially the case, it was only one pattern among several. Carter pursued all three strategies in policy making, varying the degree of attention and concern allocated by his DPS. This is especially noteworthy given that all of the policies studied in this book were policy priorities, and, as I demonstrate below, all successful cases had one thing in common regardless of the role played by the staff, or the nature of the process (policy substance or highly politicized). That element was responsiveness, although it is somewhat different from the type of responsiveness predicted by a theoretical framework relying on a dichotomy between policy competence and responsive competence.

In short, Carter's administration makes for an interesting and informative study because of the theoretical paradox it presents. On one hand, his approach to governing leads to the theoretical expectation that policy making, especially on domestic priorities, would be directed predominantly by his DPS. On the other hand, he valued expertise, which leads the expectation that he would place a high value on policy developed by civil servants in the bureaucracy, relying on policy competence. The fact that domestic priorities were not deterministically driven into the White House, even after Carter abandoned the ideal of cabinet government, lends credence to the notion that our understanding of the process behind the tendency of presidents to centralize policy making is in need of revision. Indeed, it is not my purpose to set out a comprehensive theory of presidential use of advice, but rather to describe how the DPS and various bureaucracies interacted in marshaling their resources for political action. In doing so, I investigate the conventional wisdom on both sides of the coin and propose a direction toward a more comprehensive theory of presidential decision making.[20]

Choosing Cases

Recall from chapters 1 and 2 that the study employs a categorization scheme combining two dimensions, advisory strategy and policy success or failure. The analysis presented in chapters 4–6 considers the character of the processes using the theoretical framework as a guide to finding identifiable patterns and explaining variation in presidential advisory strategies. In doing so, it is my intent to shed light on variations in the formulation process and show that each strategy is not a priori better or worse than any other one. The comparative analysis of within- and across-category cases is employed in order to get at these problems; it allows for a close inspection of policy making and is sensitive to patterns that may not otherwise be identifiable in more cursory examinations of presidential action over a number of administrations. Analyzing six policies in a comparative framework brings with it the further advantage of expanding the number of relevant impact variables that are so important for illuminating theoretical relationships. By looking at six cases and three strategies, I examine interest groups, Congress, task forces, public opinion, and the like, thus greatly multiplying the observable implications of the underlying theory.[21] My work thus fits into the literature on the presidency that sees policy and policy making as fertile ground for examining crucial questions of presidential leadership, institutional relationships, and intrabranch decision making.[22]

The method for choosing cases is most accurately labeled "intentional." That is, the choice of cases was not the product of a consciously representative sample, and purposely so.[23] In order to get at the types of questions laid out above, I needed to identify policy decision situations that fit into each of the identified categories. Second, in order to explore the necessity of centralizing policy making, I selected cases that were presidential priorities. Holding several factors constant (i.e., the administration, the priority of an issue to the president, noncrisis situations), I chose cases based on both the primary independent variable (information strategy) and the dependent variable (policy success or failure). It is difficult to fully disentangle constant factors that impinge on presidential decision making, and my analysis makes no claim to do so. Probably no series of variables

Table 1. Policies, Location, and Success or Failure

Staff as:	*Success*	*Failure*
Director	Youth Employment Initiative	Creation of the Department of Education
Facilitator	Second Energy Program	Welfare Reform
Monitor	Civil Service Reform	National Health Insurance

can be uniformly transferred into analyses across administrations. However, variables such as presidential interest, staff resources, staff expertise, scope of the policy under consideration, and the impact of congressional, task force, and interest group concerns are important factors to examine within any administration. Nevertheless, the arrows of causality do not always point in the same direction, nor are they likely to have a constant impact and exert the same force across procedural and policy outcomes. Analysis such as that presented in this book can help sort out these interrelationships, but more systematic inquiry across a host of administrations is needed in order to generalize as to their importance.[24]

Finally, I analyze noncrisis domestic policy making. A focus on crisis decision making is useful for the purpose of gaining insight into the bureaucratic nature of White House processes, the flexibility and plausibility of the advice offered, and the outcome associated with various decision-making patterns. However, it does not offer insight into policy and politics as usual. An attempt to identify patterns within and across administrations, as well as to understand the dynamics of presidential action, must take into account how policy is made on a day-to-day basis. This requires examining noncrisis situations because severe time constraints, fluid participation by actors, and other exogenous considerations are present in different ways in times of crisis. Noncrisis domestic priorities provide a solid base to examine policy making in the White House and begin searching for sources of continuity and variation in presidential policy making.[25]

With these in mind, I set out to identify cases in each of the three categories. Table 1 illustrates the categorization of the cases within the relevant strategy. Close reading of several primary and secondary sources related to Carter's domestic agenda led to table 1, which illustrates the cases along with their concomitant strategy. The cases tell the story of policy formulation and use of advisers and advice, integrating secondary sources with White House documents.

The policies that I determined fit the categories are as follows: youth employment and the creation of the department of education in the centralized strategy, with staff actively directing the direction of policy proposals; the second energy proposal and welfare reform in the mixed category, with staff serving as facilitators between the White House and the bureaucracy; and civil service reform and national health insurance in the delegated strategy, where staff monitored policy proposals formulated mostly outside the White House. Furthermore, I selected one policy in each category because it was successful and the other because it failed. Finally, all cases were considered presidential priorities both by Carter himself and as identified by empirical work.[26]

A Note on Limitations of the Empirical Analysis

The empirical analysis presented in this book focuses on six policy formulation decisions. Although this does have the advantage of multiplying the observable implications of the theoretical framework, it is, after all, derivative of one administration. My main purpose is to describe the interplay between the institution and the individual in the procedures and routines of an advisory process. Generalization to all administrations is impossible. Nevertheless, given that the analytic focus is advising in the presidential office (i.e., domestic policy making and staff dynamics)—a factor that has been more or less constant since at least the Nixon administration and with roots extending even farther back—the study provides insight into the internal workings of advisory systems and thus helps to illuminate theoretically interesting relationships. In doing so, it provides fodder for future research, but it does not offer any firm conclusions about presidential advising over time.

Second is the problem of assigning policies to the categories of success and failure. Absent any objective criteria from which to judge, the determination of policy success and/or failure is necessarily subjective. This is out of necessity, however. By taking a presidential perspective, one has to reconstruct presidential preferences from the documentary evidence collected in support of the analysis presented. In order to minimize the effect of this limitation, I have taken care whenever possible to rely on the documents for the determination of success or failure. If the president and/or his staff considered the policy under consideration a success, then I consider it a success. I limit my use of public speeches or memoirs because there are obvious problems with relying on post hoc justifications for action most often found in these primary sources, based as they are on the necessity of putting on the best face for the public. This problem, critical as it is, should be minimized via the use of documents. Most of the data collected for this study come from confidential memos intended for internal consumption and not for public scrutiny.[27] I thus assume that the language and assessments found in these confidential memoranda more accurately represent the views of the relevant players than do those found in memoirs and speeches. Whenever possible I have used internal correspondence as my basis for judgment.

Third, a case can be made that the Carter administration is not the most appropriate one to examine as a preliminary test of my theoretical proposition concerning staff shift. Perhaps a better administration to study whether or not staff shift occurred might be Nixon's, or even Reagan's. Clear domestic policy priorities and distrust of bureaucracies coexisted in both of those administrations. It thus is possible that staff direction of policy making was more constant in those administrations than in Carter's.

There is merit to the point. Indeed, it is highly plausible that the higher the level of presidential distrust of bureaucracies, the greater the tendency to strictly centralize policy making in the White House staff.[28] Scholars have long observed that Carter structured policy making in such a way that it flew in the face of the various forces that pulled policy making into the White House. Bert Rockman, for example, notes that Carter, though a highly activist president, clearly was not a "White House centrist" until at least the summer of 1979.[29] As I argued previously, Carter initially thought he would decentralize almost all policy making, simply using the DPS as a *monitor*, or at most *facilitator*, charged with coordinating the work of departments and agencies.[30] Apparently, he did not anticipate that it would sometimes be necessary to authorize the staff to take responsibility for directing policy formulation. Nixon and Reagan thus are excellent examples of where to look if we want to make the case that decentralizing some policy responsibility in the form of facilitation or monitoring exists in all administrations. But theory is not particularly helpful in categorizing Carter. His efforts on behalf of a public goods approach to governing, as well as his stated desire for cabinet government coupled with his persistent (and ultimately frustrating) eschewing of political purposes, points us in both directions. One could also feasibly make the argument that since domestic priorities were not clear in the administration's scheme of things, Carter would ultimately centralize, or have his staff direct the path of policy decisions on those issues he identified as clear priorities. I will show this was not the case.

A fourth limitation of the study is the focus on domestic policy priorities. The treatment of these priorities does not fully consider the day-to-day processes of policy making. Many of the items on which the president and his staff work are neither domestic, nor priorities. Economic and foreign policy demands weigh heavily on the White House, and it may be that an exploration of their dynamics is more pressing. Domestic policy is, according to many of the theorists cited in chapter 1, almost always centralized in the White House, even though decentralizing pressures may be hard to resist given the complexity of issues and the myriad actors, both within and outside the government, with a stake in policy outcomes. It thus should not be surprising that the framework of staff shift demonstrates that presidents shift the burden of policy formulation contingent on various factors. What staff shift does do, and can do best by focusing on domestic priorities, is highlight the consequences of presidential or staff overload, how it is dealt with, and with what consequences. This allows for an evaluation of the relevant factors such as the nature of the policy itself and limited presidential capital on the prospects of success or failure.

Fifth, a study such as this, relying as it does on documentary evidence, is susceptible to the inherent limitations of the written record. Much informal communication takes place, telephone calls are logged but often not fully noted, and oral histories are often tainted by the passage of time. These problems should be assuaged somewhat by the fact that Carter, more than many presidents, littered official and unofficial memoranda with comments, suggestions, and questions. This makes it possible for one to get a flavor of exactly how the president responded at any one time, what he was thinking, who he wanted matters referred to, and the like. In addition, many formal documents, especially those that relate to the establishment of principles and the strategy of proposals, go through several drafts. The researcher thus has the chance to see the original drafts, response memoranda from various affected interests (both within and outside the government), and how the political interests brought to bear on an issue change the nature, scope, and character of the issues under consideration. I refer to these whenever possible. Nonetheless, most of my data come from documents and thus are susceptible to possible distortions of interpretation that might not occur with a more complete record.

Finally, in a point related to the fourth limitation, other political beings such as interest groups, parties, constituencies, and competing institutions have much to do with initiating and propelling policy proposals forward. The study looks inward at the White House and the shifting participation levels in response to varying transaction costs imposed by the relevant political and policy environments. I attempt to integrate this inward focus with an analysis of various participants from outside the executive branch. However, in so doing, I neglect to fully examine the basis of participation of these competing institutions.[31] A full understanding of the contributions of these various external actors would require focusing on *their* internal dynamics, a focus well outside the boundaries of this study. I do not fully investigate their interests, preferences, and consequent participation strategies, nor do I examine the transaction costs associated with such participation. The focus remains locked on the presidency and the use of staff and staff shift to illuminate a president's relationship with the policy environment.

Conclusion

The major task of this book is to describe and, where appropriate, provide a causal explanation of policy advisory dynamics within a presidential administration. Using six policies in the Carter administration, I illuminate aspects of a broader question, namely how do presidents who are policy conscious and must of necessity act in a highly charged political environment go about achieving their goals? While I examine only one president, the study has implications for theory building in a comparative framework, generating hypotheses for further testing on a larger cross section of presidents.

The analysis presented in the following chapters examines variation both within (success versus failure) and across (differential advisory sources) categories. Using the comparative case approach, I examine the interplay of policy and political context, presidential preferences, the nature of the policy under consideration, and especially information, on the type of advisory strategy that is employed, focusing specifically on how staff dynamics shift in tandem with these other factors, and with what consequences. Examining six cases empirically increases the number of observable implications of the staff-shift theory and the range of variation of the variables identified by the framework. From there, I examine what contributes to success and failure of both policy and process, and present arguments as to whether the outcome was determined by strategy or by some other factor or set of factors, such as limited presidential capital resources.

Part II

Jimmy Carter's White House

CHAPTER 4

Staff as Policy Director

The Department of Education and Youth Employment

T his chapter examines the DPS in the staff-shift framework when policy making is highly centralized and tightly controlled from within the White House. In this strategy, advisers are charged with fully directing policy formulation, using outside sources only tangentially and directing the course and content of the proposal. The tendency for presidents to concentrate policy making in the White House has been well documented. The Brownlow Committee report, issued in 1937, called for presidents to be equipped with some sort of in-house help, and thus is commonly viewed as the genesis of the modern presidential staff (although hardly at the level or with the power it has gained in current American politics). Almost a half-century ago, Richard Neustadt analyzed the use of the EOP, specifically the BOB, as a central clearinghouse for legislative initiatives going to Congress from the departments. While this is not fully comparable to using staff as policy directors, the core of the increasing tendency to centralize policy making in the White House or EOP can be traced back at least this far.[1]

As the nation moved from the New Deal to the relative calm of the Eisenhower years, and into the turbulent 1960s, presidents became increasingly suspicious of whether or not the bureaucracy was amenable to presidential objectives. More and more, the EOP and the White House staff (WHS) were used to try and control bureaucratic intransigence. Indeed, the broader organizational apparatus of the "institutional presidency," specifically the EOP, grew up around the perceived presidential necessity to acquire responsiveness. This imperative was even more pressing given that the White House was hampered by weak means for monitoring what the bureaucracy was doing and how bureaucratic action affected a president's policy agenda. Even before Watergate was in full throttle, Erwin Hargrove observed bluntly:

> The growth of the Presidential bureaucracy as a separate institution from civil service and other departments has not really

enabled the President to direct those sprawling bureaucracies in an effective way. *This . . . is the paradox of the drawing of initiatives and the centers of power into the Presidential orbit.* Such action signifies recognition of the great difficulty the President and his aides have in learning about the bureaucratic actions in the implementation of Presidential policies, or in securing responsiveness from the departments and agencies to Presidential directives. The linking mechanisms necessary for program direction and learning about their actual results, which should exist between the White House and the great departments of state, are rudimentary. *The result is to compound the draining of power to the center.*[2]

By the time Jimmy Carter assumed the reins of government, policy centralization had become the modus operandi of presidential operatives. Carter's background virtually assured he would rely on cabinet government and bureaucratic expertise. Within a short period of time, though, policy centralization had seized on the Carter White House, and for good reason. Politicization, which had been a mechanism for both guiding and implementing policy making, had let the president down. More and more, President Carter gave the instruments of power to the WHS, especially the DPS.

The goal and purpose of centralization is not really to control the bureaucracy, for this is largely an impossible task. However, as Hargrove suggests, it is a supplement to the politicization of the bureaucracy, and helps to remedy the situation where the institutional presidency is ill-equipped to adequately understand and control the activity of the bureaus and departments of the executive branch. Centralization thus is necessary for the protection and articulation of the president's policy preferences, given that his incentives are largely derivative of the political and policy system. Centralization need not be characterized by the full, heavy-handed control of the WHS. The staff-shift framework suggests, though, that policies that are of primary importance to the president are candidates for such direction from the DPS. Issues that are politically imperative for the president, highly controversial, and carry substantial opportunity for presidential gain consistent with the investment perspective are most likely to be heavily directed by staff. That is not to say that only those policies that are controversial or of high priority will be fully centralized. Rather, they are the most likely candidates for the staff to direct. Advice coming from outside the White House is likely to be technical, helping fill gaps in the staff's knowledge base, and not as part of a broader collaborative effort. In this way, it is much like the description offered by Hargrove. Policies, especially high priorities, are pulled into the presidential orbit and handled almost exclusively by White House operatives, leaving policy advice from outside to support and validate the direction in which the president wants to go.

This chapter details President Carter's experience with the staff as strategy director in two policy areas: the creation of a Department of Education and the youth employment initiative. Scholars who have examined the trend toward centralization cite a number of factors that are sympathetic to the development of centralized policy making, especially the institutional configuration of American politics.[3] According to this perspective, the institutional configuration is composed of "separate institutions sharing power."[4] Each is seeking the maintenance of its power base, struggling against usurpation by the other institutions and targeted by groups seeking to apply pressure for personal gain. But such is the governmental status quo in a pluralistic democratic system characterized by multiple access points, frequent elections, and checks and balances.

Although the presidency remains the focal point of the governmental apparatus in the American system, some analysts maintain that its power has declined relative to other institutions.[5] While it is true that presidents propose budgets, for example, it is equally true that Congress asserts its independence and has been unwilling to give presidents all or even most of what they wants in terms of policy. While this chapter does not examine the Reagan administration, his presidency serves as a brief example of the usefulness of this strategy. After the initial budgetary successes of 1981, Congress was frequently willing to give the president an aggregate spending amount close to what he requested. However, it shifted the allocation of dollar amounts to items more in tune with congressional tastes. Reagan's defense budget requests, for example, were pared down in favor of other social programs. Reagan did succeed in increasing overall defense spending, but not to the extent that he preferred. He was equally successful in eliminating or scaling back a number of social programs and agencies. He did this by centralizing decision making in the White House and governing by unilateral administrative means (e.g., executive orders). It is this state of affairs—bolstered by the fact that Reagan sought to achieve his goals after his first two years in office by means of centralized decision- and policy-making strategies—to which scholars often point in support of their propositions concerning the utility of employing this strategy.

The central argument of this chapter is that a fully centralized, staff-directed strategy for policy formulation and offering political advice does not always produce superior results. The new institutionalist perspective employed in this book suggests that it is this strategy where DPS policy-making efforts are greatest in terms of resources expended. Resource costs are likely to be greatest since the staff is directly involved in every aspect of the process, using outside sources only for auxiliary purposes.

The strategy carries with it both positive and negative implications. On the positive side, using the staff as policy director can help to ensure that the content of policy conforms closely to what the president desires. It affords greater control for the WHS and avoids many of the pathologies of hierarchical organizations, such as intransigence and suboptimization. However, it has the potential to miss much of what is good about bureaucratic advice, or policy competence. Fully centralizing policy making can insulate the president from advice and information that might be helpful and can cause him to misinterpret the risk factor in pursuing one or another course of action. This in turn can result in over- or underestimating the risk factor as it pertains to the political climate. Such a system would undermine the advisory investment strategy of presidents and further contribute to increasing the political risk factor.

This particular pathology can be overcome if the president utilizes a "multiple advocacy" approach in which he seeks many different advisory viewpoints. But such an approach would need to be even more carefully monitored by staff operating in a fully centralized system, because the president can quickly become overwhelmed with too much information. Moreover, the whole framework of using staff as policy director can be undone by the infiltration of affected interests directly into the policy formulation process. In addition, it is doubtful that a multiple advocacy approach would be of much utility for the president in making domestic policy as opposed to foreign policy, where most applications of the multiple advocacy approach are observed. The high-profile, priority issues in domestic policy—although no more complicated or important than foreign policy—often cross many jurisdictions, affect many different interests, and are susceptible to the myriad problems of coalition building. They thus must all be systematically addressed to ensure legislative passage, making such an advisory framework unmanageable. Foreign policy shares many of these roadblocks, to be sure, but presidents are generally given the latitude they need in setting foreign policy agendas to their taste. With regard to domestic policy, if presidents wish to fully centralize policy making in the White House, multiple advocacy may play a muted role, but it must also be carefully structured so as to maintain fidelity to the goals of centralization and top-down political and substantive control by the DPS.[6]

Carter's experience with the strategy of using the staff as policy director is instructive because it brings into focus how a staff-directed policy formulation process can be useful for presidents wishing to maximize responsiveness (such as the youth employment initiative). It also shows how it can close presidents off from the kind of advice they need from others within the EOP, WHS, and even political appointees in the executive branch. These actors can further assure that policy proposals maximize responsive competence.

In addition to the empirical trends of centralization, one can say something about the normative implications of directing policy formulation from within the White House, which may also be positive or negative. The positive case has been set out above. The negative case would include arguments about choking off legitimate channels of communication and information, as well as the more general danger of creating an impression of tyrannical or imperial tendencies in the office of the presidency. The most obvious example would be the Nixon administration, which governed by means of executive fiat in order to implement many of its policies, both foreign (e.g., the surreptitious bombing of Cambodia) and domestic (e.g., the impoundment of more than 14 percent of the funds targeted for water projects).[7]

It does not necessarily follow from the logic of either one of these perspectives that presidents are ill served or well served by fully centralizing policy formation in the DPS. Nevertheless, I argue that presidents maximize their chances for policy and political success in a maximally centralized policy advisory process if three criteria are met. First, the type of policy desired must be such that it can be easily controlled from the White House. That is to say, the proposal should not cut widely across agency or departmental jurisdictions. Second, the DPS must, to the best of its ability given resource, time, and information constraints, reliably assess the politics of both time and the policy itself. In other words, it must determine if the public is in favor of the proposed policy or, at the very least, that it is not composed of a majority hostile to the president's position. Finally, bureaucrats responsible for carrying out the president's plans and/or a sufficient number of legislators willing to carry the president's fight to the Congress must be marshaled in favor of the proposal. In addition, the controlling agent in the White House, often (but not always) the DPS, must maintain a dominant role while remaining sensitive to the legitimate and informed input by agents in the bureaucracy. Sensitivity to input from advisory sources outside the White House is not inconsistent with the centralization strategy, but it is consistent with the notion of staff shift as long as the staff retains a principal role in developing policy. Most important from a presidential perspective, it increases the probability that the president's preferred position will be both politically and substantively sound.

In the sections that follow I focus on the DOE and youth employment cases but I do not provide a full account of either policy initiative. Rather,

I concentrate on describing the parts of the stories that illuminate the process and the degree of coordination and control (or the lack thereof) and the combination of political and policy advice embedded in the creation of each proposal.

UNSUCCESSFUL STAFF DIRECTORSHIP: THE DEPARTMENT OF EDUCATION

The first case, the creation of a Department of Education, is considered an unsuccessful case of staff shift, maximizing policy centralization by using the DPS as a policy director. The primary reason for this classification is that, though Carter's preference (in spite of his incentives) was for a broad-based, all-encompassing department, he failed to get it. Instead he had to take what amounted to little more than the Office of Education surgically removed from the Department of Health, Education, and Welfare (HEW). Much of this failure can be traced to the advisory process, as I demonstrate below.

Background

Education was a priority for Jimmy Carter going back to the early days of his political career, continuing through his tenure as Georgia governor, and on into his campaign for the presidency.[8] Coupled with his interest in education and its reform was a strong commitment to reorganization, which may have stemmed from his frustration with a decentralized education bureaucracy that lacked coordination.[9] In refining his views on education, Carter was at least partly influenced by a report to the National Education Association (NEA) on the need for a new federal department. The report advocated coordinating intergovernmental and interagency programs that touched on education programs. The report further argued that a new department would best serve education needs if it were used to upgrade services and consolidate all of the institutions within the education system.[10] This schema envisioned the presidency as a driving force behind reorganization, arguing that success could be achieved only if Carter energetically committed the resources of his office to the education debate. The report concluded that the education system would be best served by asserting strong leadership from the top.[11]

Pressure for a New Department

Carter's direct commitment to the creation of an education department stemmed from the 1976 presidential campaign. In a series of stump speeches, Carter pledged to the NEA and, by extension, the American public, that he would make the creation of a comprehensive new education department an administration priority. He insisted he would not simply upgrade the status of education within HEW. The core of his plan was to consolidate the various grant programs, job training, early childhood education, literacy training, and the like, which were at that time scattered throughout the government. By making education reform and reorganization a priority, Carter committed himself to addressing the NEA's concerns, and thus locked himself in early. By the end of the primary season a large portion of Candidate Carter's committed delegates were NEA coalition members. Indeed, 1976 marked the first time in its history that the NEA actively worked on behalf of a presidential candidate. In addition, it had formed a coalition with the United Auto Workers (UAW) and other trade unions, which together wielded considerable political power. When the Democratic Convention convened in New York City in the middle of July, the NEA could offer the candidate a "disciplined bloc of 172 votes." [12] Number one on their agenda was, of course, creation of a new department, and Carter's acceptance of NEA political support more than implied a presidential commitment to establishing it.

The Political Climate

As is often the case in American public policy making, the political climate created a series of obstacles that would have to be disposed of via the advisory function. The first political obstacle appeared when it became clear that the proposal championed by the NEA polarized education groups. Those who favored the new department saw it as an opportunity for comprehensive education reform, especially for coordinating education policy by vesting much policy responsibility in the federal government. Conversely, the mostly conservative opposition worried that a new department would increase the role of government in domains traditionally the province of state and local governments. Those in support argued that a new department would increase the status and visibility of education, provide access to the president, coordinate dispersed education programs, provide a mechanism for the president to develop a coherent set of education policies, and serve as a vehicle for federally induced change in the decentralized system. [13] Those opposed based their opposition on the premise that a department would signal an increased federal role, thereby usurping traditional state and local sovereignty over education, politicize education programs, and disrupt the balance between private and parochial schools. [14]

Beryl Radin and Willis Hawley describe the dynamics of the situation as follows: "The momentum from the constituency for the creation of a cabinet level department was aided by a tendency within Democratic administrations to look to the federal government as the locus of new social policy." [15] However, "tension between the perceived power of the president to effect reorganization and the unwillingness of the Congress to give such power has been a characteristic set of conflicts in all contemporary reorganization efforts. This dynamic was an important element in the development of a separate department."[16]

While the president's pure preference was to pursue education without regard to political concerns, his realistic preferences were tempered by incentives structured by external forces, some of which had little to do with education. For example, an immediate problem was that Frank Moore, director of the Office of Legislative Liaison (OLL), and his staff were under heavy fire for what many perceived as incompetence in handling congressional relations. In addition, collegiality between high-level members of the administration began to break down as serious dissension manifested itself.[17] Finally, Carter himself appeared unwilling to enter into the necessary political compromises, as evidenced by the experiences of Energy I and welfare reform.[18] Given these political obstacles to policy change, neither reorganization in general nor the creation of a new department in particular would be easy matters to effect. Carter's pure preferences would later yield to a more realistic vision of what could be accomplished—a vision tempered by the incentives embedded in the political climate.

Developing Principles: Task Forces in the Initial Phase

President Carter's advisory process consisted of at least two phases: the development of principles and the transformation of those principles into concrete proposals. Principles are often of a broader, more abstract nature, laying out the intended goals of the nascent proposal. It is in this first articulation of presidential policy that pure preferences are most likely to present themselves. Responsibility for identifying significant groups and their political agendas is often given to task forces appointed by the president and responsible only to him. Armed with this broad responsibility, task forces play an important part in presidential advising, encompassing an opportunity for the president to gain outside perspectives while avoiding the turf battles sometimes characteristic of bureaucratic politics. Pure preferences can be floated to these groups, with less satisfying, more controversial components of those preferences being tempered, removed, reworked, or even elevated within the program, depending on presidential goals.

President Carter commissioned a task force to coordinate disparate attitudes and group expectations as they pertained to various priority issues. The task force, dubbed the President's Reorganization Project (PRP), was to conduct a study of several issues and make recommendations based on their findings. The PRP, supervised by Harrison Wellford, was housed in the OMB and consisted of individuals both from within and outside the government. Carter was a great believer in such support-oriented organizations. According to Radin and Hawley, by March, 1977, "the reorganization staff would begin work on several priority items on which the President had promised immediate action."[19]

The creation of a department of education was first included in these priorities. The PRP was responsible for probing all facets of reorganization and reported directly to the president. Before the various task forces connected with the PRP began their work, they were given broad guidelines and targeted goals. The task force responsible for the issues surrounding education worked within the Human Resources Study Team and was headed by Patricia Gwaltney, a career civil servant and former Senate staff member. The DOE project took precedence over other staff work. The original members who began their work in the summer of 1977 were drawn almost entirely from the career civil service, specifically OMB and various parts of HEW. Political scientist Willis Hawley was appointed director of the education study. In contrast to the Hawley-led White House group, HEW secretary Joseph Califano appointed his own groups to study reorganization. Unlike the Hawley group, Califano's group touched only lightly on the education question. It recommended consolidating student loan programs into a proposed Bureau of Student Financial Assistance. Most importantly, and in direct contrast to both presidential incentives and preferences (both pure and realistic), the group did not propose anything other than a minor shift in HEW's Office of Education (OE), located within HEW.[20]

The important task of assessing the political implications of reorganization was given to a related but distinct high-powered political task force consisting of Vice Pres. Walter Mondale, budget director Bert Lance, DPS chief Stuart Eizenstat, and, somewhat paradoxically, Califano himself. Together with the team working in the PRP, the two task forces examined the politics of various organizational options.

The general goals for the new department were listed in the following DPS memo:

> We believe that the current Federal organization of Federal education programs—with education sandwiched between the major health and welfare activities in HEW and with so many education programs in other departments—severely limits the Federal Government's ability to build on past successes and to provide visible and effective leadership to meet new opportunities.

The primary mission of this department will be to assist States and localities which are principally responsible for education in America.

The establishment of a Cabinet Department of Education will:

—Increase the visibility and status of education and related programs.

—Improve the management and coordination of education programs at the Federal level by bringing programs now scattered throughout the government under one official.

—Increase the accountability of education and related programs to the Congress, President and the public both as a result of increased visibility and more focused responsibility and leadership.[21]

In order to meet these goals it was necessary to identify the most appropriate institutional structure to handle the new education function. This identification, it was felt, was crucial to the prospects for programmatic success. The PRP toyed with five structural proposals, finally winnowing the available choices to three.[22] These three included, first, simply elevating the status of education within HEW; second, creating a separate department with broad authority; and, third, creating a separate department with very narrow authority. Attempting to garner as broad an advisory base as possible, Carter asked Vice President Mondale and Secretary Califano to also explore the available options. Mondale argued for a fully functional cabinet-level department. Califano, who was adamantly opposed to creating a new department, suggested that the issue be made the subject of a joint study between OMB and HEW, with the cooperation of affected interest groups. The White House chief of staff, Hamilton Jordan, joined Mondale in his advocacy of a separate department. Jordan, mindful of the president's political interests, pushed Carter to be faithful to his campaign promise and propose creating a department.[23] However, Jordan advised the president that the political incentives were such that it mattered little whether the department was broad or narrow in scope.

The atmosphere within which the study was conducted was highly competitive and conflictual. The NEA pushed for Carter to keep his word. Califano, who wanted to maintain responsibility for education in HEW, lobbied for the administration to keep an open mind and explore other options.

Understanding the use of the task force and the actions of Califano and his staff are illustrative of the tension between policy and political advice.[24] Such an understanding adds to the more general theoretical issues presented in the centralization strategy and the politics-administration dichotomy. Members of the OMB task force, directed by Eizenstat and the DPS and presumably responsive to the president's preferences, recommended the creation of a narrow department on political grounds. This would satisfy important constituencies, fulfill political promises, and address Carter's concerns regarding diffusion and lack of coordination in the education bureaucracy. The analysis was heavily couched in political terms and in the orthodoxy of classical reorganization, which emphasizes economy and efficiency. Califano and his staff also pitched for economy and efficiency, but added an argument for policy coherence, holding that these goals could best be achieved if education were consolidated and upgraded within HEW.

The staff-shift framework suggests that the DPS would be most heavily involved in coordinating advice, keeping control to itself given the high-priority status education held with Carter's core constituencies. The staff was further burdened in that affected bureaucracies, most notably HEW, were not simply called upon to offer advice, which is consistent with centralization theory. Instead, the department, especially Secretary Califano, actively opposed taking positive action on a plan that was at once consistent with the president's political incentives and his pure and realistic preferences. From a new institutionalist perspective, reference to the institutional imperatives of the education issue and Carter's personal commitment to education can accommodate both. They are not solely attributable to the dictates of politics, but also to the president's sense of where he wanted to go with education. Califano, who had his own base of political support on Capitol Hill, would prove to be a formidable opponent. Califano would do so by playing on the dual and sometimes conflicting nature of advice that was coming into the White House, advice not simply meant to provide information and insight so as to reduce the president's risk factor, but to oppose and resist the president's stated goals. In this sense, politicization failed. It failed not in the implementation sense, but in the sense that the president had to count political appointees as agents of resistance. This situation, where the DPS risked losing policy control in the centralizing strategy, led to various discrepancies between the political and policy orientations of advisory sources. It is to these discrepancies between political and policy advice, both within task forces and in direct White House–bureaucracy confrontation, that I turn to next.

Developing Proposals: Facing Intrabranch Dissension
Presidents are often faced with dissension from within their ranks. Politicization, which is often employed as an implementation tool, can also be used as a helpful device for controlling policy formulation. But when

bureaucratic pathologies, such as agency or department capture, or administrative turf wars, enter the equation, presidents must spend precious time and effort dealing with these inconveniences. Other times, the dissension is more serious, as when an administrative appointee actively opposes the president's policy goals and, by extension, the direction in which he wants to take the country. Such dissension is especially serious in its effect on the advisory process. As I and others have suggested, an effective process is one in which many different viewpoints from many different sources are synthesized, assessed, and brought forth to the president's desk. When an appointee actively and consistently opposes the president, the lack of information, the strategic advice, and the political basis of the maverick appointee can poison the process by exacerbating the relative asymmetries in the principal-agent framework. Such a situation works in immediate opposition to the president's investment interests. With strategic advice and information working at cross-purposes with the president, the president and his staff must incur the costs of formulating counterstrategies.[25] These costs include forgoing policy analysis, based as it is upon information exchange. When that information is hidden or slanted by an appointee with an independent political base, the political costs of keeping control of policy formulation and minimizing political damage are considerable. Although the president and his appointees are likely to disagree often, once the president reaches a decision it is imperative that he have at least tacit support of those in his administration most directly involved with the policy.

Dissension can occur at any or all points in the policy formulation process, affecting advisory relationships and creating issues of presidential credibility. At the point of developing policy proposals, though, the question becomes one of ends and means. When agreement has been reached on principles, the ends have been set. It is reasonable to assume that administration operatives are on board with broad questions of policy direction. But when the discussions turn to means, or the concrete proposals that comprise the substance of the proposed policy, dissension is more likely to occur. The president can be the beneficiary of such dissension if disagreements are aired in private. But when disagreement is made in public, or at least in full view of the president's competing institutions, he risks political damage at best, and the loss of control of his administrative apparatus at worst. This is exactly the problem President Carter ran into regarding education policy, especially in regard to his HEW secretary. It is that set of problems that I now describe.

The history of education policy during the period April to December, 1977, clearly indicates that the relationships among relevant policy actors, especially within the executive branch, were complex and fraught with tension. The PRP competed with the DPS for the president's ear, and both claimed to act on his behalf and with his authority. HEW was active as well, constantly arguing for maintaining HEW as it stood by simply upgrading education within it rather than forming a second department. Organizations that were potentially affected by reorganization (e.g., HEW, the Department of Agriculture, the Department of the Interior, and the National Science Foundation) resisted change on the grounds that it was unnecessary or potentially harmful to their interests.[26] Such deep and seemingly irreconcilable differences presented formidable obstacles to policy coordination and group cooperation.

Cooperation among administrative operatives was rare. At a minimum, organizations need a basis for possible agreement or, at the very least, muted dissension within their ranks in order to function smoothly. The education process had none of that. Even worse, there was no common basis for negotiation. This type of dissension is not new to presidents, but occupants of the Oval Office differ in their approaches to handling it. How presidents handle dissension, or minimize its adverse affects, is crucial to policy success and administrative cohesion. President Kennedy seems to have dealt with this type of dissension in an effective manner. He invited all affected parties within the administration to disagree with proposed policy and to do so loudly if they were so disposed. However, once he made the final decision, everyone was expected to fall into line.[27] Carter, who often exercised the same tactic for encouraging discussion, did not do so in this case, though he might have benefited from employing it.

The evidence suggests that Carter felt he benefited from dissension among cabinet members, or between the cabinet and the White House staff, gaining as many differing viewpoints as possible.[28] This served to increase the level of advisory information from which he could cull alternatives, ultimately making a decision that was highly informed. But this case seems to be different in that the effects of dissension were often damaging or even destructive to the administration. He was unable to deal with elements within his administration that were straying from his preferred course, and were polarized as to the efficacy of the proposal. These elements strayed not only from his pure preferences, but even from his realistic preferences. For example, the Bureau of Indian Affairs battled for continued control over certain Indian education programs; the Agriculture Department fought to keep food programs; and Head Start at first wanted to be included in a new department but later reversed itself. In addition, substantial opposition was voiced from outside the administration, and that opposition illustrates the tenor of discussions among the president's external and most trusted advisers. For example, Adm. Hyman Rickover, Carter's mentor from his days as a navy submarine captain, wrote a letter to Beth Abramowitz of the DPS setting out three fundamental objections to the creation of a new department: (1) a department would give educators too much control over education policy and budget; (2) it would lead to decreased accountability for student performance on the part of educators; and (3) it would make parental involvement in the process and oversight impossible.[29] Similar arguments were made by members of Carter's own administration. Not surprisingly, the most vocal objections came from HEW secretary Joseph Califano. In his memoirs, Califano summed up his position in the following manner: "With respect to the separate department of education, the eye of Carter's camera was on the politics of renomination and reelection, and over time he seemed only to sharpen its focus. . . . My concern . . . stemmed from a fear that [it] threatened to breach the healthy limits on federal involvement in education."[30]

He continues, "I stressed that the President needed fewer constituency departments, not more people reporting to him, if we were to have a *bureaucracy responsive to presidential leadership*."[31] He also stressed the necessity of keeping the H, E, and W modules together within one department because maintenance of that combination "was essential to the success of such efforts" as child immunization.[32]

One of the catalysts exacerbating dissension within the administration was the question of whether a department, if created, should be narrow or broad in scope. In a premeeting memo he prepared for Carter, Califano criticized the idea of a narrow department:

> While the federal government should serve as trustee of the chance for all children to enjoy educational opportunity, a Department of Education is very likely to be dominated by an assertive, nationally organized interest group—the NEA. While individual teachers are dedicated, institutional interest groups necessarily focus on economic self interest. In this context, creation of a narrowly based Department of Education will dump the NEA's agenda directly on the President's desk. This controversial agenda which, among other things, seeks nearly a four-fold increase in federal elementary and secondary spending, much greater use of federal funds for general aid, and federal guarantees of collective bargaining for teachers, is not likely to become, and should not be federal policy.[33]

This memorandum marks Califano as an astute political tactician. In essence, he argued *for* a department even though he was politically, substantively, and philosophically *opposed* to it. He did this by focusing ostensibly positive attention on an extremely broad-based department because he knew that the prevailing political climate militated against such a massive undertaking. In the same memo just cited, he broke his argument down into a case *against* a department (i.e., the narrow option) and the case *for* enhancing education within HEW. While affirming the president's preference for a broad department (i.e., the untenable option) he presented no sustained argument in favor of a large department given his opposition to any department at all. This analysis strongly suggests that he was presenting what appeared on the surface as substantive policy advice, but that substance was instead a political agenda in disguise. Califano's case against a department was broken down into several parts, including his "concerns" in regard to the president's "multiple roles as policy-maker, organizer, and manager of the executive branch, maker of the executive budget, and leader of an administration in being."[34]

Even when Califano did act in accordance with Carter's expressed preferences, he was clearly working at cross-purposes with the president's best interests. Although Carter was in favor of a broad department, Califano advocated a much larger department than even Carter had envisioned. Such a large, umbrella department would almost assuredly be rejected by Congress. In "advocating" a strong department, Califano included many candidates for consolidation in the new Department of Education. Numbered among them were such contentious proposals as the National Science Foundation, Veterans Administration (VA) education programs, the Community Services Administration (CSA), Head Start, the Smithsonian Institute, Comprehensive Education and Training Act (CETA) programs, and some nutrition programs managed by the Department of Agriculture. By including such a vast array of seemingly disparate programs in his proposal, Califano was, according to one account of the time, trying to deliver an "intentional and lethal blow" to the president's plans for a department, regardless of its size or scope.[35] Despite repeated attempts, the administration was unable to bring Califano on board. It even failed to gain some sort of agreement that if he could not agree with the president, he would at least not try to sabotage the new department. In the end, Califano agreed to withdraw his adamant objection to a department, but he still pushed for internal reorganization "as an intermediate step."[36]

Of course, not all administrations face such serious public contagion from their political appointees. Still, these examples are illustrative of the problems that can occur and plague an administration when it is burdened with dissension. Consensus is difficult if not impossible to achieve because of the level and seriousness of disagreement and the consequent lack of coordination and effective communication among the major players, especially those in the executive branch. The impressions that these communication flaws and disjointed activities leave can have spillover effects in the political environment, poisoning the perceptions of outside groups and affected actors in the other branches and spreading into the public at large. These impressions can fuel the perception that the president and his administration are plagued by incompetence, and that the president is unable to control his own people.[37]

These examples may be extreme and concentrated within one administration, but they are symptomatic of a larger problem presidents face when trying to control and manage the information coming in from neutrally competent actors outside of the White House and the problems concentrated on the responsive elements in the White House. Organization theory teaches that large, hierarchically structured settings are susceptible to pathologies such as communication distortion (in this case scaling down the president's goals), suboptimization (in this case Califano working against the president's expressed preferences), and the like. These examples thus support the proposition that while the president is nominally in charge of the executive branch, the reality underlying these textbook interpretations may be less than accurate.[38]

Political and Policy Advice: A Closer Look

The case of the Department of Education is an interesting one regarding the tenor and types of information received by presidents. It is also useful for analysis because an organization (the PRP) designed specifically for the analysis of policy substance was also given a subordinate task, that of disseminating political information. It is further interesting in that the PRP, when it was occupied with taking the political pulse of the issue, sought to be more political than responsive. Here a distinction and clarification must be made. "Political" in this case refers to the process of pursuing possible outcomes given the perceived state of the current political environment, which includes Congress, interest groups, and civil servants. "Responsive" refers to the process of getting the president what he wants, and advocating and defending the president's interests *as he sees them*. The two are necessarily intertwined with one another, but it is important to understand that a subtle distinction existed between the role of the PRP and the DPS and WHS, which acted as policy directors and thus the responsive elements.[39] As I will demonstrate, the PRP largely failed in its effort to combine responsiveness, politics, and substance in one entity. The DPS would eventually have to step in and salvage the policy formulation process, although it proved to be too little too late.

Early on, Stuart Eizenstat worked to make the DPS an integral part of the decision-making process. Initially, Carter did not want the staff to control policy development, but Eizenstat's influence eventually won the president over. In a memo delivered to Carter in December, 1977, Eizenstat provided politically responsive information as well as substantive analysis of the type that the president initially hoped would be delivered by the PRP. Eizenstat systematically provided the president with various options and his personal concerns in the following memorandum, which is cited at length in order to illustrate all facets of the advice delivered to Carter:

> Joe Califano makes a strong case against a separate Department of Education. *If we had no campaign commitments, these arguments would deserve considerable weight. However, no commitment we made was clearer.* In addition, I am impressed with the argument made by the Vice President and by you that under the present structure, education has no advocate in the upper policy levels of the Executive Branch. Therefore, I am in favor of endorsing a separate Cabinet-level Department of Education.
>
> *I am, however, opposed to adding social services to the Department as OMB (PRP) proposes.* I support the notion of using the schools to a greater extent for the provision of social services, particular to children and families. . . . Moving social services to a Cabinet-level Education Department would support this concept. However, it would *divorce* social services from welfare, social security, medicare, and medicaid. Yet these programs presently are linked closely to social services, and in many cases share common delivery systems at the state and federal level. I do not believe that at this time we could defend, as a policy matter, separating social services from these programs. In addition, I believe such action would disturb governors, state welfare directors and the Senate Finance and House Ways and Means Committees—jeopardizing enactment of the Education Department. . . .
>
> I recommend that Jim McIntyre or Secretary Califano testify before Senator Ribicoff's committee endorsing the *general concept* of a separate Department of Education, not including social services, early next year. The statement would indicate that OMB and HEW will work closely with the appropriate Congressional committees to develop the final bill in the context of the legislative process. I would recommend *against* sending up a detailed Administration bill, in view of the long Congressional history.[40]

As evidenced in this and other memoranda, the DPS quickly advocated the idea of a narrow department based on political and analytic grounds. The creation of a narrow department would minimize the "disruption of past political and bureaucratic relations."[41] Although the PRP was in the process of developing proposals for a broad department, Eizenstat worked in earnest to modify the president's directive to get a broad department, advocating instead as broad a department as was *politically feasible.* Eizen-stat's minimally disruptive strategy was clearly responsive to the broader implications of the president's interests in that it reached for a new de-partment, but one within the boundaries of what other key political actors could accept.

While the DPS displayed policy expertise, much of the work of the PRP lacked political sophistication. Although the PRP was established as a policy organization, it worked to supplement its substantive assessments with political analysis, though that analysis often fell far short of accuracy or political usefulness. For example, PRP believed that interest groups would communicate their policy preferences explicitly, and that the mem-bers of Congress who sponsored administration legislation in their respec-tive chambers could be expected to endorse all reorganization measures. The PRP analysts overemphasized the positive consequences of organiza-tional change as it was to be carried out in accordance with the proposal's grand design. In addition, spokespersons for the PRP were not particu-larly adept at conveying technical specifics or providing penetrating analy-sis. They were generalists who emphasized the political aspects of the pro-posal. In contrast, the analysts were technically oriented and emphasized the substantive core of the initiative.[42] Here the evidence suggests there was a poor mixture of policy and politics as the PRP sought to fulfill its ad-visory function.

The DPS was not fully engaged in the education reorganization pro-cess until it became clear that political assessments, mostly advanced by PRP, sorely lacked a coordinated analysis that linked policy substance with political reality. This failure to bring the DPS on board early for coordi-nation purposes, or even to direct policy formulation, had adverse affects on the president's ability to maximize his chances for an even moderately sized department. By the time the DPS assumed the role of policy direc-tor, the possibilities for strong and purposive leadership had been lost as a consequence of diminished political capital. This was manifested most im-mediately in a loss of prestige within the Washington community. Indeed, as time went on, the DPS began to usurp the PRP's political role, and some DPS staff members criticized the PRP for its poor understanding of polit-ical factors, especially those related to various interest groups. The fol-lowing excerpt from an internal DPS memorandum clearly documents the gap in the perceptions of PRP and DPS: "The new Department of Edu-cation and Human Development recommended by OMB is essentially all of HEW except welfare, Medicare, Medicaid, and social security. . . . *In no case should we commit to such an approach before we are we are sure that this will be accepted by the education groups and others in our campaign commitment.*"[43]

In some instances political operatives within various departments stepped in to save the president political embarrassment when PRP was unable to function in its assigned capacity. The following memo from HEW's Jim Parham, the undersecretary for Human Affairs, to Jack Watson of the WHS is an example of the higher form policy competence, that which combines policy expertise with political assessment: [44]

I have been urged by friends and acquaintances from around the country to be sure that the President is aware that a decision to include Head Start and other Youth Development programs into the proposed Department of Education *will trigger a loud negative reaction from significant groups that are composed of our natural allies and supporters.*

Many of these local groups consist of minorities (especially blacks and Hispanics) who have struggled for recognition from local school systems which have been unresponsive and/or condescending toward their effective participation. Turning the fate of their hard won gains over to a Department of Education, which is bound to be dominated by the professional educational establishment and their more narrow interests, will be viewed as a lack of sensitivity to their interests—at worst as a "sell out" of loyal supporters.

It seems to me there is no need to pay such a political cost. The narrow Department of Education will satisfy the educators— and it will avoid the disruption and further fragmentation of programs that are related to education, but are primarily "restorative" and "compensatory" for more general developmental deficiencies. [45]

According to centralization theory, this type of analysis should have come from responsive elements in the White House and perhaps from the PRP. However, the analysis came from a department and, even more interestingly, from Califano's deputy at HEW. Policy competence is amenable to a responsive element by tapping institutional memory and political expertise—both of which Califano possessed but exercised in opposition to the president's position—to foresee problems that may recur over time and within policy categories.

The administration's next order of business was to maintain political sensitivity when announcing the president's intention to create a department. Eizenstat wrote to Jordan and James McIntyre in January, 1978, advising them on how such an announcement should be handled: "My own view has been that the education groups would be most pleased with a brief announcement in the State of the Union (together with a reference to our major education budget increases and new legislation). *We are doing so much for education this year that we should make a special effort to claim. . . .* We should not waste a reorganization slot on a proposal which is not broadly acceptable."[46]

Eizenstat's savvy is amply displayed in this excerpt. He was sensitive to the president's diminishing political capital, which stood to increase in the eyes of certain critical groups if the administration did a bit of trumpet blowing. At the same time, he was responsive to the likelihood that the president's capital would continue its free fall if the administration were to become embroiled in a political fight that ultimately proved to be more damaging to the president than to his opponents. It was apparent to all involved that other political crises were already on the table and that education was a relatively minor initiative in the face of energy, Camp David, and other high-profile agenda items. Eizenstat and the DPS played the part of protector of the president's interests, which is the textbook role for responsive agents within the White House and the EOP.

Political problems were intrusive, heightening the need for sophisticated political advice on how to proceed on multiple fronts. More than half the Senate had cosponsored various bills designed to create the department. More than 120 cosponsors had signed on in the House. The creation of the separate department would also mean a redistribution of power within the executive branch, as well as upsetting the relationships between interest groups and government agencies. Teachers themselves were divided on the issue. In practical terms, this meant that no single, cohesive interest could be fully mobilized in behalf of any of the president's education initiatives containing provisions for a new department.[47] The proposed legislation included transferring a number of programs that had been independent into the new department. Reshuffling programs and jurisdictions in the executive branch can cause political problems because the affected agencies and program beneficiaries resist being usurped by other departments, thus risking a loss of autonomy. The fight to transfer programs into a new Department of Education was no exception. The programs at issue included the National Science Foundation, the Arts and Humanities Foundation, Defense Department and Indian schools, school lunch programs, and Head Start. Interest groups, government agencies, and leaders of the various foundations joined forces to wage a battle to accomplish one of two things: either eliminate plans for a new department, or prevent such programs from being included in the department's jurisdiction. The concerns of the coalition members gathered mainly around the possibility of being buried in a large catchall department.[48]

Political imperatives dictated that the president handle such delicate issues with considerable care. The political advice he received focused on overcoming problems with Congress, whose members were feeling the pinch of the opposition groups. McIntyre and Frank Moore sent a memo to the president in August, 1978, that outlined a political strategy targeting key members of Congress: "[Director of Legislative Liaison] *Frank [Moore] should be authorized to call, on your specific behalf, Representative John Brademas and seek his assistance in expediting the bill in the Rules Committee and on the House floor. If he agrees, tell him that the administration will not oppose transfer of the vocational rehabilitation programs to the department."* [49]

Carter approved the strategy, but wrote in the margin: "I don't support this move." The president knew he was in a position where he had to play the political game, but this marginal note, as well as others in the same memo, indicates that he did so with considerable reluctance.

With regard to Congress more generally, there was a semicoordinated process with the DPS taking the lead. After interest groups had annihilated Sen. Abraham Ribicoff's bill proposing a broad-based department, Carter ordered the DPS to formulate a revised strategy. In early 1979, for example, he agreed to support a bill proposing a relatively narrow department. A White House task force headed by the DPS drafted the bill. The task force in turn worked closely with House and Senate Government Operations Committee staff members on the proposal's political ramifications. [50]

Political concerns and information thus dominated the advisory process and were considered mostly within the White House itself. The political considerations of the proposal were given pride of place, while broad policy goals and possible administrative effectiveness declined. Carter may have been able to achieve more in the way of his goals had he brought DPS on earlier in the process. By doing so, it is reasonable to assume that poliical opposition might have been either nullified or at least minimized. Instead, opposition forces were unwittingly given time to mobilize in response to interest group pressure and other political concerns. Policy substance might have benefited from a better mixture of policy competence and responsiveness by being coordinated and integrated into a single organization that was fully responsive to the president's realistic preferences and sensitive to the substance of the issue. This was the purpose of the PRP, but it suffered from a lack of political sophistication, whereas the DPS displayed sensitivity to both political and substantive issues.

The other side of this coin deals with substantive policy advice. When it had to deal solely with substantive advice, the PRP performed well. It was less successful when attempting to wed policy and political advice. Its method for doing so concentrated on bringing in people from within and outside the government and asking them to detail a particular policy issue,

usually a smaller issue, partitioned within the broader legislative framework. The following is an example of substantive analysis examining the
implications of administrative reorganization for government at all levels
in the federal system:

> Restructuring federal programs, whether into a new depart-
> ment or within DHEW, will not, by itself, produce constructive
> change in the delivery of education and related programs. The
> federal organization structure can be important, however, in ori-
> enting education toward some concerns rather than others and
> in determining the level and visibility of federal leadership in
> education.
>
> As in state and local government, federal education programs
> are separate in policy and practice from human service programs.
> Consequently, the two types of programs are not well coordinated
> and the development of comprehensive approaches which reach
> out to families and communities is not fostered. Moreover, fed-
> eral education programs are often criticized as burdensome with
> respect to the violence and detail of program requirements im-
> posed on state and local governments.[51]

The analysis in this memo is sensitive not so much to the political
ramifications of policy, but to the likely substantive outcome of the proposal. Digging deep beneath the surface of political maneuvering, the
analysis is consistent with the idea of advice as investment. Presidents
prosper when their policies are effective, although a symbolic element can
come into play in the president's favor.[52] Given that presidents stand to
gain from policies whose outcome mirrors their output, the president invests in policy-substantive advice. The memo just cited brings policy development and historical memory to bear on the policy process. While the
president is not bound to follow the advice, his investment risks are either
reduced or at least addressed, allowing for appropriate political and/or
policy adjustments. Such is the case in this instance.

Further analysis was forthcoming just before the main meeting between all major participants. In an appendix to a premeeting memo, the
PRP analyzed various substantive issues. These included the already well-
considered areas of what to do about education, which organizations to
include in a department, hammering out criteria for consolidating educa-
tion-related programs, and a providing a summary of tentative conclusions.[53] Careful inspection of the documents reveals that the analysis was
carried out *without reference to politics*, and with very little or no reference
to Congress, interest groups, and the like. The PRP conducted a strictly

analytic project, highlighting programmatic procedures and the likely administrative consequences of following various procedures. In this realm the PRP was more successful at providing the president cogent analysis than when it endeavored to combine politics and policy.

High-level officials in the president's overall reorganization effort supported the PRP's substantive analysis. Richard Pettigrew, who had experience with reorganizing Florida's government and was later appointed assistant to the president for reorganization, took the OMB/PRP proposal, which had suggested an extremely broad department similar to the Ribicoff bill, and added political assessment: "It most completely fulfills your campaign commitment . . . it signals the prominence of education as a Federal concern, without turning education over completely at the Federal level to a narrow, insulated, professionally dominated establishment. . . . It promises a substantively defensible and politically attractive breaking-up of HEW, the popular epitome of overgrown, unaccountable bureaucracy."[54]

His analysis was likewise couched in the dual terms of wedding policy and politics, without "selling out" policy substance to make a program more politically palatable. Indeed, the broad department plan was politically risky.

Finally, the departments provide much of what is traditionally meant by policy substance. Aside from presidential appointees at the top of the organization chart, departments are staffed with career civil servants who develop not only substantive expertise, but a feel for the politics of an issue. In dealing with the logistics and analysis of how reorganization would be played out in the executive branch, Secretary of Labor Raymond Marshall defended his department against the possibility of losing programs to a new department. After remarks indicating his opposition to transferring several youth training and employment programs to the new department because "such a transfer is based on a misunderstanding of employment and training programs in general and little understanding of the specific programs targeted for transfer," he wrote:

> Our employment and training programs, for youth and adults, have the primary purpose of providing jobs, whether through job creation, job training or the matching of workers and jobs. In contrast, education programs have the goal of teaching basic competency and some analytical skills. There are certain important interrelationships between these two types of programs. However, these missions are separate and should remain so. Transfer of programs between agencies would achieve little and would undermine the basic purpose of each. . . .

The need to establish linkages between education and employment programs at the Federal level is unavoidable. It is
tempting to think that shifts in function among cabinet agencies
can achieve this.[55]

Like the Marshall memo, Carter received substantive advice from the
departments that formed a sort of informational baseline from which he
worked. However, the policy and political seams were not well joined in
the separate streams of advice he received. Both existed in isolation from
one another, and the coordinating organizations (PRP and DPS) were not
able to provide a synthesis of the two. The inability to bring the strands
of politics and policy together in the advisory function works against a
smoothly coordinated process. Such a process is necessary for the fusion
of each type of information, which in turn contributes to the success of the
centralized decision process. No synthesis of the two types of information
can be identified in this case.

Consulting and Political Outreach

The need to pursue public outreach and consulting processes constitutes
an important opportunity for combining political and policy information.
Objectives include getting political soundings from interest groups, persuading the skeptical, solidifying supporters, and the like. In this case, the
consultative process initially fell short of expectations because interest
groups and their bureaucratic allies believed that issues were left unsettled
even after they were given the opportunity to provide input.[56] Furthermore, administrative outreach in the executive branch lacked comprehen-
siveness. The PRP, for example, was told by those close to the president to
ignore advisory input from OE careerists.[57] This systematic exclusion of
relevant information did not bode well for sustaining a coordinated process. Political and policy analysis, juxtaposed for thorough consideration
of options, cannot be entirely divorced from one another. In this instance,
interest groups had "captured" appointees and ignored careerists, and an
important source of analysis was cut off from the outset of the advisory
process.

When the PRP was unable or incapable of either public or executive
branch outreach, DPS stepped in. Beth Abramowitz crafted a strategy for
reaching crucial constituent groups, including higher education groups,
business, elected officials, private education, civil rights and womens'
groups, and Congress. When Abramowitz informed Eizenstat of her efforts, Eizenstat affirmed her strategy, and wrote in the margin of the memo:
"Beth: Anne Wexler should be given this and you should sit down and
let her work on outreach parts. She'll do more to pass bill than all of us

together."[58] The task of directing the consultation process and especially those responsible for taking political soundings for incorporation in political advice had their hands full. From the outset, the president found himself in trouble. Potential beneficiaries of the reorganization, other than the NEA, resented the prospect of being passed along to a new department. With the exception of the handicapped lobby, which received most of its benefits from HEW vocational rehab programs, no one really wanted to be included.[59]

The attempt to coordinate outreach also faltered because no precedent existed involving such heterogeneity of the interests allied around the issue. The alliance that emerged was, in Charles O. Jones's opinion, "unusual" and tested the political acumen of the Office of Public Liaison (OPL) and Anne Wexler. The American Federation of Teachers (AFT), a traditionally liberal branch of the American Federation of Labor–Congress of Industrial Organizations (AFL-CIO), joined forces with conservative groups to fight reorganization. The AFT opposed a new department because its members believed that such a department would destroy cooperative relations among education, health, and labor groups. Conservatives opposed expansion of the federal bureaucracy and the NEA favored a narrow department for reasons cited above.[60]

Outreach was thus stymied due to a number of factors not necessarily attributable to any particular organization or entity. The politics of the situation played a major role in that the PRP was given orders from above to disregard executive branch players in the OE; the groups that mobilized in favor or opposition to the department were unprecedented in their makeup, which added a sense of confusion to the strategy; and the DPS, which directed outreach with the help of OPL, was unable to effectively unite those in favor or quell those opposed. Once the bill authorizing the department passed Congress and was signed by the president, it was extremely narrow—large enough to satisfy a campaign promise but not nearly as large as Carter had originally envisioned.

A Brief Examination of the DPS Role in the Advisory Process

The new institutionalist framework suggests that individual action can affect institutions to some degree or, at a minimum, try to change the boundaries of the institution. This analysis sees institutions as at least partly endogenous. Organizational routines affect policy content, but they often must act in a reactive rather than a proactive mode. The analysis presented here is consistent with that perspective. Organizations such as the DPS had a profound impact on the nature of policy but in the end were ultimately stymied by forces outside their control, forces both within and outside the White House. The evidence suggests that although the DPS was brought in late to direct the policy formulation process, it got what it advocated: a narrow department. Still, it is possible that if the DPS had been brought in earlier and in an even more authoritative fashion, it might have been able to prevent the opposition's momentum from building. Moreover, it might have been able to mandate a clearer direction for advisory purposes.

When the DPS was finally brought in, it played a more decisive policy leadership role than in some other cases. This took place in 1978 and 1979, after the DPS had been strengthened by Carter, making explicit the role DPS would play as director of policy formulation in certain instances. In addition, because policy was heavily formulated in the PRP, over which Eizenstat felt comfortable asserting his presidentially bestowed authority, DPS began to actively gather political intelligence and broker advice and information sources for the president. The DPS began, with the president's blessing, to assert a decisive role in political information gathering, eventually becoming the domestic policy equivalent of the honest broker in a multiple advocacy process. In the end, the DPS advised in concert with the reality of what political feasibility would allow.[61]

An excellent example of DPS responsiveness to Carter, keying in on both political and substantive questions, can be drawn from the November 28, 1977, meeting in which Carter expressed his desire for as broad a department as possible.[62] According to secondary accounts, most everyone in the room assumed the president meant exactly what he had said: broad in the sense that it would include Head Start, nutrition programs, the NSF, Indian programs, vocational rehabilitation, and the like. However, after Carter left the room, Eizenstat stood and announced to those present that although the president had said he wanted a broad department, he actually wanted a department that was only as broad as was politically feasible. In this case, said Eizenstat, it meant that he actually wanted a relatively narrow department.[63] This example illustrates the DPS acting to keep the president on track by indicating to him what he "really wanted." That is, what was politically inexpensive and least damaging to the president's already fragile political capital. This preoccupation with the politics probably saved the initiative from defeat, but it also prevented Carter from getting what he had promised: a broad-based department that would house under one roof almost all programs dealing with education.

In the end, DPS, with help from the PRP and OMB, was able to get a Department of Education bill through Congress.[64] Could Carter have gotten more than what he ultimately received? As Willis Hawley aptly put it, "The only way he could have gotten more was to want less."[65] In other words, the Department of Education might have been more of a success and closer to what the president wanted if he had taken better account of the political climate during the 1976 campaign. Had he done so, he might have gotten a greater proportion of what he was after and therefore appeared more successful. However, presidential campaigns are often characterized by promises designed to court political support from key constituencies. Of course, after the election is over and the new president takes office, affected groups are only too ready to hold the new administration to its promises. Thus, Carter could not have wanted less *after* he became president because he had made commitments *before* he was elected, and those commitments were decidedly unambiguous. The hard choices constituting trade-offs between the two areas were readily apparent to those interested in the outcome, and they hindered purposeful administration policy action.

In this case, the highly centralized strategy—even after DPS was given authority to direct the advisory and policy-making processes—worked poorly. On the other hand, the administration's youth employment proposal, although burdened by preexisting fiscal burdens on the federal budget that ultimately led to its defeat in Congress, serves as a model of a well-coordinated, staff-directed policy formulation process.

Successful Policy Directorship: Youth Employment

Like many presidents, Jimmy Carter had to deal with the stubborn issue of unemployment. One of the major problems with which the administration had to contend was the related difficulty of skyrocketing youth and black unemployment, the combination of which accounted for a substantial amount of the aggregate unemployment figures. The statistics were straightforward, unambiguous, and needed to be dealt with if unemployment as a whole was to be adequately addressed.

Young people, who made up a quarter of the entire labor force, accounted for fully half of all those unemployed. Nearly four million sixteen- to twenty-four-year-olds experienced problems completing the transition from school to work. Demographic predictions held that while the total number of young people was expected to fall during the 1980s, the number of youths who were in the greatest need, such as those who were economically disadvantaged, dropouts, or minorities, was not expected to decrease. The gap between white youth employment figures and those for minorities since the mid-1950s was increasing. While white unemployment remained fairly constant, minority youth unemployment increased by 30 percent, roughly twice the rate it had been in 1955. Jobs for young people who lacked a high school diploma decreased precipitously. In 1980, their chances of finding employment were 3.3 times lower than they had been in 1950.[66]

President Carter dealt with some of these problems early in his administration. In 1977 he won passage of the Youth Employment and Demonstration Projects Act (YEDPA)—legislation that added $1 billion to employment programs—and four pilot programs aimed specifically at youth employment. Summer jobs were increased to one million and available Job Corps openings were expanded to more than forty-four thousand. In 1978 the president won the passage of the Targeted Jobs Tax Credit and the Private Sector Initiative, which together provided private sector opportunities to disadvantaged young people.[67]

Youth employment, while important in these years and consuming large chunks of the president's budgetary requests, received *special* emphasis in the fiscal year (FY) 1979 and 1980 budgets. The 1979 initiative was part of an economic stimulus package and reversed the Ford administration's desire to let youth employment programs expire.[68] The Carter proposals included the expansion of public jobs programs, local public works programs, and countercyclical revenue sharing. Carter's budget also contained provisions for a new $400 million allocation for a program designed to encourage private sector businesses to provide jobs and job training for youth and minorities. These programs were justified on the grounds that nearly half of the total number of unemployed (which registered 6.4 percent in December, 1977) were below the age of twenty-five, and more than 37 percent of teenage blacks were without work. Many of the federal jobs authorized by CETA were to expire in September, 1978, and the administration viewed this sunset provision as an opportunity to restructure a number of areas within CETA.[69]

Another related problem was that of black unemployment. The number of African Americans who were out of work consistently ran well above the number of whites who were unemployed—in some cases by as much as 300 percent. The 1977 youth employment initiative had gone some distance to narrow these differences by slightly shrinking levels of black unemployment, but the results were far short of their targeted goals. The challenge for the Carter administration was to provide job opportunities to youths in areas readily accessible by transportation, and then to retain job recipients in their positions once the terms of the plan had expired.[70]

Developing Proposals: Task Forces in the Initial Stage
In 1979 the administration launched Vice President Mondale's Task Force on Youth Employment. The task force was given the responsibility of analyzing the consequences of youth employment programs and policies. Its

initial findings were decidedly substantive. The first was hardly surprising: Employers were systematically less willing to hire young people who lacked basic literacy and computation skills and a "knowledge of the world of work" (i.e., a solid work ethic accompanied by at least a rudimentary degree of conscientiousness such as being at work on time). Second, employment and training programs could be improved or simplified by consolidating categorical programs and using financial incentives for workers rather than regulations designed to encourage good performance.[71] The findings presented in the task force report provided a clear analytical foundation upon which the administration could base policy proposals to meet these needs.

In an effort to reconcile substantive analysis and politics, the DPS, which had explicit presidential authority to direct the project from the beginning, suggested that the task force extract relevant information from two sources: Congress and affected interest groups. These, it was suggested, would be useful for accomplishing three objectives: First, analyzing existing programs and constructing demonstration programs; second, offering fresh perspectives from outside the executive branch (this would be useful for bringing in substantive and political information which was notably lacking in the Department of Education case);[72] and, finally, assisting in educating the public.[73]

The task force initially met with various interested publics. Four meetings were held in April, 1979. These included public interest groups (e.g., the League of Cities, the Conference of Mayors, and the Governors Association), community-based organizations and labor (e.g., the Urban League and the UAW), education (e.g., the NEA, the AFT, and the American Volunteer Association), and nonprofit and citizen groups (e.g., the United Way, the Council of Negro Women, and Catholic Charities).[74]

Internal DPS memoranda urged coordinating information gained in these sessions by setting up a task force advisory system. Three such task forces were recommended. These included asking selected interest groups to establish their own individual panels of advisers who would then work closely with the vice president's task force while the DPS was in the process of developing its recommendations. A second recommendation was to establish an advisory council composed of distinguished individuals representing a broad cross section of interests. This group would be "charged with developing a set of recommendations and issuing a report to the Vice President on actions the Administration should take." Finally, a panel of advisers would serve as a resource for all involved in the process, rather than as representatives or members of a formal group. The panel would meet with the vice president and members of the task force from time to time and review their work. After each recommendation, an analysis of the strengths and weaknesses, both in political and substantive terms, was offered. Eizenstat accepted the first and third recommendations.[75]

This comprehensive mode of analysis, which combined policy and politics so as to lay out recommendations sensitive to both, gave the president the benefit of a smooth and coordinated process. The honest brokering of options, with the recommendations and analysis of opposing sides dispassionately presented along with recommendations made by the various participants, is illustrative of the type of process that prevailed in this case. Furthermore, this type of action indicates a high degree of policy-making direction from within the White House, while at the same time coordinating the input of affected groups. The flow of communication, which had been obstructed in Department of Education case, was notably smoother, and all perspectives of the various issues were presented without any particular group being systematically shut out of the process. In short, the process was more effectively controlled from within the White House.

The accomplishments of the vice president's task force can be easily defined. From April to October, 1979, the task force had been in touch with nearly every sector of American politics connected in some way with youth employment. The following excerpt from an internal DPS memorandum details the activities of the task force within this timeframe:

> Five conferences were held on different aspects of the youth employment problem. Over [a thousand] representatives of business, education, labor and community organizations from around the country participated in sessions which addressed such issues as inner city youth unemployment, the role of community based organizations and education and work linkages.
>
> A series of five "Roundtable" meetings were conducted in cities around the country at which over [two-hundred] local representatives of business and education shared their views on youth employment. . . .
>
> White House briefings were conducted for local affiliates of [seventeen] national organizations. Over [350] representatives of . . . associations . . . participated.
>
> A series of seminars were conducted by leading education and employment experts for key Congressional staff and agency representatives on the major issues and questions in youth employment. Over [two hundred] young people were interviewed by representatives of the NFL Players Association on behalf of the Task Force to obtain the views of youth on federal jobs programs and the world of work.[76]

As a result, the task force was able to achieve broad consensus on policy direction both within agencies and among interest groups, as well as securing broad congressional support. This type of coordination and consensus was clearly missing in the creation of the Department of Education. Congressional support was easy to obtain because reducing unemployment and creating jobs for youth was initially seen as politically popular. The difficult issue then focused on *what level* to spend resources, not on *how* to spend them. As a result, the administration was able to fashion comprehensive proposals that integrated politics and policy.[77]

The proposals, which were assembled by Mondale's task force under the general direction of the DPS, consisted of a massive program in which the Department of Education and the Department of Labor (DOL) would cooperate to provide disadvantaged youths with work experience and training in reading and writing. The proposal was the administration's major domestic initiative. When operational, it would add $2 billion to the $4 billion DOL spent on youth employment and serve one million youths in addition to two million that were currently in related programs.[78]

Key members of the administration were "optimistic that they were able to address the youth employment program successfully for the first time," wrote Harrison Donnelly. "[It] combines education with work in the classroom and on the job site, to give young people the ability to make their own way in the world of work."[79] At the heart of the plan was a new education program, welded to a rearranged structure of preexisting programs designed to combat youth unemployment.[80]

The jobs program was to be run by state and local governments using federal monies. "Prime sponsors" would be responsible for running public service employment programs authorized by CETA. These prime sponsors would receive federal dollars to provide jobs, usually by funneling the money to local community-based organizations that promised to hire eligible youths.[81]

In short, this case serves as an example of an effective centralized staff-shift process. The major actors were executing tasks defined by presidential preferences. The process was controlled by the White House, staffed by the task force, highly consultative, and encouraged intrabranch agreement. Affected groups were brought along early so as to prevent the opposition from gaining momentum.[82] Although nowhere near the level seen in the creation of the Department of Education, the administration did have to exert some political capital in brokering intrabranch dissension.

Meeting Minor Intrabranch Dissension
There was little intrabranch dissension in the youth employment initiative. Everyone connected with the proposal was either brought along early

or eventually steered toward action agreeable to the White House. The administration had asked for $400 million for private sector jobs, but the details of how that money would be spent was the subject of minor disagreement between the Departments of Labor and Commerce. These monies involved tax credits and/or direct subsidies to participating private employers. However, these disagreements were minor and easily assuaged. No one ruffled administration feathers or subverted purposive administrative action. The reason for this, as mentioned above, seems to be that critical players who could possibly be mobilized to oppose the initiative were consulted early, quickly brought on board, or had their disagreements brokered by the DPS.

A Closer Look at the Consultation Process

Consultation is an important part of collecting and disseminating both political and policy information. If done thoroughly and comprehensively, consultation increases the quality of political information while furnishing substantive information.

The capacity of extensive outreach efforts to bring in groups and interested citizens was not lost on those responsible for the youth employment initiative. Interest groups that were previously opposed to one another coalesced. For example, the National Alliance of Businessmen and the AFL-CIO worked closely together to hammer out programmatic agreements.[83] This coalition differed from those involving liberal and conservative groups (such as the NEA and the AFT observed in the creation of the Department of Education) because the actors charged with coordinating youth employment strategies (i.e., the DPS and the OPL) were able to convince each affected organization early in the process that youth unemployment was a problem whose solution would be beneficial to both business and labor.

The DPS controlled the process of policy development while the OPL actively pursued the advice of outsiders in all major areas. In a February, 1980, memo, Eizenstat wrote the president: "A series of consultations have been conducted with key Congressional representatives, their staffs, and representatives of all the major interest groups. Every effort has been made to take account of their comments and concerns where the changes proposed did not fundamentally affect the principles of our program."[84]

Here Eizenstat was the consummate responsive agent. His efforts included consulting a broad array of individuals and groups so as to gain information, both political and analytic, and then use that information to enhance the proposals, all the while remaining true to the president's preferences. Carter wanted to consolidate and expand funding levels for existing programs, as well as add education and training components that would make black youths more attractive to prospective employers.[85]

Substantial efforts were also made to persuade key congressional leaders to support the president's initiative by supplying substantive information and by recognizing the importance of political appeals. As mentioned at the beginning of this section, one of the major reasons for consulting is to bring members on board or to at least slow or dilute the pace of the opposition. This is especially important in the congressional realm. Mobilization of early opposition can easily kill a bill or make it politically unpalatable for members to support. An example of these efforts to persuade key members can be seen in the following excerpt. The context of the memorandum is a DPS briefing of Eizenstat in preparation for a meeting with Sen. Thomas Eagleton (D-Missouri), with special reference to identifying where Eagleton's probable concerns lay: "[Eagleton] has long championed the need to do more about teaching basic skills in order to make young people employable. . . . In other times he would be one of our strong supporters. However he is running for re-election and has made opposition to new spending programs one of the planks in his campaign platform. . . . The meeting provides an opportunity to give the Senator a detailed briefing on our proposals and explain that these initiatives differ substantially from current practice.[86]

The memo continues to detail the task force's efforts, analyze the reasons why the problem was likely to worsen, and oversee various proposals concerning the Labor and Education Departments. Eagleton's concerns were addressed during his meeting with Eizenstat by explaining to him the central part of the youth employment initiative, which was to provide individuals with basic job skills. While these targeting attempts are surely not confined to "successful" advisory cases, there does seem to be a trend toward a more comprehensive and strategic process in these cases.[87]

The patterns described here explain intrabranch, interbranch, and external outreach from the White House, which increased the quality of the advisory and decision-making processes, and the quality of the information that went into administrative decisions and appeals for support.

Political and Policy Advice: A Closer Look

One of the White House's greatest responsibilities in a strategy designed to make full use of the staff to forcefully direct policy formulation is to remain informed of the politics of passage. It must carefully consider how accurately substantive analysis assesses the probable impact of a proposed program on both the problems addressed and on the political implications of probable policy impacts. As we have seen, a crucial factor for bringing politics and policy together in one coordinated process is to emphasize a single strategy and identify the groups essential for carrying it out. The following is an example: "In order to make introduction of this legislation credible and passage possible, it will be important to develop a broad *policy and political consensus*. . . . We will indicate specific strategies for working with these [previously set out] categories. Ultimately we will develop a specific strategy for each group."[88]

Consistent with the implications of the preceding quote, political advice was sought from a number of sources—a tactic similar to multiple advocacy in the foreign policy process. Chief among the myriad advisory sources for President Carter was Vice President Mondale, a political man thrust into a position of providing substantive policy advice as head of the youth employment task force. Recall that in the case of the Department of Education, the PRP was not politically aware. In contrast, Mondale was quite politically sophisticated. His political skills, coupled with knowledge of how politics and policy mixed, allowed him to provide the president with sophisticated analytical advice, carefully balancing the imperatives of these two types of information. He enjoyed a relationship with the president in which he could offer policy advice *and* political advice, and Carter often adopted the position advocated by his vice president.[89] The following is an example of Mondale giving political advice that was in opposition to the substantive analysis offered by OMB:

> I think it would be of greater benefit politically to forego increases elsewhere in the budget than to send the signal that our youth strategy is a go slow, highly cautious approach. . . . There are several problems with the OMB position:[90] it does nothing beyond the status quo on the jobs side; it will make no one happy, in fact if we come anywhere close to the OMB funding level we will be subject to severe criticism; it will appear that we are unwilling to match on the human side the productivity investments we are making for business. For $2 billion in new authority, *we can get exactly the right reaction and make this a genuine highlight of your 1980 legislative program.* Interestingly, this program has appeal for many conservatives who understand the problem of a generation of American youth who cannot read or write or count and lack solid work experience and training.[91]

The memorandum went on to include a detailed analysis of the problems with the OMB recommendation, why it was not sound politically, and why it would not attack problems on the substantive end that the president wanted to see addressed.

In bringing members of Congress along, the DPS was able to spot political problems that might otherwise have gone unnoticed. The legislative task force in the DPS took responsibility for fully monitoring legislative activity, paying close attention to members who were wavering, and identifying those who were solidly with the president. Frequent meetings were scheduled with key members of the Senate Education and Labor Committee. Both Bert Carp and Stuart Eizenstat split the duties of conferring with members.[92] The meetings were designed to accomplish three objectives: First among these was to assure committee members that the administration gave top priority to securing passage of the youth employment initiative in 1980. Second, they sought to help members understand that the content of the proposals was of particular interest to them and their constituents. Finally, the meetings sought to communicate a willingness to work with Congress to develop legislation acceptable to all participants.[93] This process is identical to that spelled out in the previous section. However, it is further evidence of how the process of giving and receiving political advice was fashioned to fully exploit the possibilities of synthesizing politics and policy in a manner that satisfied the members' policy and constituency goals.

Wedding policy and political information into a coherent analysis is not easy. Often, things done for either political or policy motives alone can backfire. Viewing advice as an investment suggests that responsive elements in the administration should be able to disabuse the president of political and/or policy mistakes and to correct those mistakes whenever possible without compromising the nature or the spirit of presidential preferences. Again, youth employment provides an example. Task force studies largely corroborated the public's opposition to cutting the eligibility of fourteen year olds from the program and further discovered that the program was thousands of jobs short of meeting the needs of large cities. At the urging of Eizenstat and others, Carter responded by asking for help from program providers. In doing so, he was able to receive policy advice pertaining to matters the providers deemed workable. This advice was often divorced from political concerns, creating a situation in which staff members had to synthesize the two streams.[94]

Such a synthesis is quite possible, though. The following illuminates an example of such a sensitive mixture of policy and political advice, one that clearly analyzes the problems endemic to both: "I believe it is imperative that we [divide] the $800 million, with $700 million for DOL and $100 million for DOE [Education], so that the $2 billion in new resources will be evenly divided between jobs and education. We must have second year DOL figures in order to explain the impact of the program in terms of job and training opportunities over the two years. The key questions that will be asked by interest groups and reporters are 'What is the split between education and employment?' and 'How many additional jobs are there in the program?' In your announcement and in testimony before Congress, we must make our intent clear."[95]

Eizenstat descriptively offered substantively informed analyses of dollar figures, based on what was workable given considerations of available resources, and in turn coordinated with the political reality of the situation. Certainly, the figures may have been targeted to meet political reality, but the memorandum leaves the distinct impression that this was the optimal strategy given the administrative, substantive possibilities, articulated in the political context, and ultimately consistent with the president's pure preferences.

A Brief Examination of the DPS Role

With DPS working as policy director, the youth employment process was comprehensive in scope, anticipated loose ends, and thus left little to chance. In this section we see the DPS role as one in which the staff combined the roles of honest broker, coordinator, director, and facilitator of the policy-making process. All of this is consistent with the staff-shift framework set out above, given that youth employment was one of the Carter's high priorities at the very end of his presidency. In previous sections we considered the coordinating role in areas such as consulting for the purpose of advising the president as to the political and policy ramifications of various proposals. This section focuses on the various hats worn by the DPS in its efforts to regulate information coming in from political and policy sources.

In April, 1979, the DPS sent a memo to a large interagency committee consisting of most cabinet officers, the DPS, and the vice president's task force. The process was coordinated by the DPS through the Presidential Review Memorandum (PRM) process. In this process, the DPS was responsible for circulating policy and politically related questions to many different individuals, mostly those within government. The questions were designed to invite substantive and/or political input from different sources, covering as many facets of whatever problem was under consideration. In accordance with this task, the DPS kicked off an extensive three-pronged study defining the dimensions of the problem and identifying potential policy options, reviewing existing efforts regarding youth employment, and developing proposals for new initiatives.[96]

The DPS coordinated policy development through the PRM process. There is evidence that responsive staff members were sensitive to political reality when formulating policy recommendations. Consider the following (which is representative of memoranda generated by the PRM process in other policy areas), taken from an appendix to the PRM submitted to

Carter for approval near the end of 1979: "This appendix describes the rationale and details of two proposed new efforts to meet the education needs of youth in high poverty, high youth unemployment areas of the country. The proposals are grounded in the evidence put together over the past year and are similar to proposals in the recent respects of the Carnegie Commission and the National Commission on Employment Policy. Each of the proposals will require new legislation and are consistent with FY 1981 funds."[97]

These proposals included, for example, rationale, analyses of strategies, proposed targeting services, estimates of clientele participation, methods of ensuring accountability, relationships to DOL programs, impacts under different budget options, and the estimated impact of the policy under alternative budget estimations.[98] This clearly illustrates the type of information synthesis that the DPS review team, in cooperation with members of the interagency committee, undertook in an effort to merge policy and political information in a comprehensive fashion.

In addition to synthesizing the political and policy realms, a role that must be played in an effective process is that of protecting the president's political interests. In short, this role constitutes the primary function of the responsive agent within the White House. This agent keeps a watchful eye on the president's political fortunes. The Carter DPS balanced these roles well in the case of youth employment, in particular combining the roles of honest broker and advocate. The balance between the two is a precarious one, and the line between them can become blurred unless the president is fortunate to have a staff that executes the appropriate role at the appropriate time. Often, the appropriateness of the role is in some sense dictated by the president, whether he wants a gatekeeper, or when he explicitly seeks the advice of staff acting in an advocacy role.

In the case of youth employment, the DPS brought policy options based primarily on political analysis to the attention of the president. Consider the following, the first paragraph of which is policy analysis, while the second estimates political reality:

> On the education side, all evidence suggests that a root problem of structural unemployment is lack of basic literacy and computation skills. OMB is persuaded—even with recent funding increases in ESEA Title I and vocational education—that some additional highly targeted resources could help to improve school performance. However, OMB believes the best way to initiate this new program is to phase it in. It would not be wise to threaten the effectiveness of the new Department of Education by asking it to mount a very large new program during this start-up year.

DPS believes that [this option] would severely disappoint key
constituencies, Congressional leaders and experts who have followed the course of the youth PRM. Two thirds of the DOL uni-
verse of need are out-of-school and are those in severest need.
DPS predicts that without roughly equal resources for employment and training it will be very difficult to achieve the program
consolidation we recommend.[99]

This synthesis is representative of other memoranda. Bringing both
modes of information together reduces the president's degree of risk
and informs his judgment as to the best way, in his opinion, to proceed
given available information. Institutional factors (e.g., existing statute)
form the basis around which decisions can be made, as is evidenced in the
excerpt. Given these institutional constraints, the president is given political "wiggle room" in trying to forge a consensus and stake his political
direction.

Similarly, in December, 1979, President Carter was presented with exceptionally detailed and comprehensive summaries of programs that the
DPS had designed and recommended in cooperation with the departments
of Labor and Education. It set out each program with budget outlays and
estimated impacts while recommending a course to take.[100] Here is observed an example of the roles of policy maker, advocate, and gatekeeper.
There is no question that the DPS directed policy focus, but it was also actively involved in policy advocacy. Moreover, the staff was also sensitive to
the substantive input of outside actors. Consequently, the DPS was able to
address both policy and political implications in its recommendations.

In short, the DPS acted as more than a coordinator as policy was directed from within the White House. There was an important additional
task to be accomplished in policy development, as evidenced by the recommendations the DPS made regarding policy advice given by outside actors. These recommendations concerned the content of policy and the extent to which it was changed so it would comport with the president's
political interests. The evidence suggests that the process was cooperative,
setting guidelines for outside actors to follow, always sensitive to the imperatives of policy substance recommended by various bureaucratic and
interest group actors.[101]

Conclusion

The administration's efforts in the areas of youth employment and the creation of the Department of Education illustrate some of the problems and
successes that can occur when using the staff as both policy director and

advisory source. Task forces were a major part of both initiatives. Whereas the PRP in the Department of Education initiative was politically unsophisticated, the interagency coordinating committee and the vice president's task force in the youth employment case were successful at combining policy and political analysis.

The Department of Education is a curious example of a process in which an organizational entity was created for the express purpose of acquiring and assessing policy information. The PRP was designed to advise the president in accordance with its policy competence, but it also tried to combine policy and political information in an integrated advisory structure. However, it was unable to accomplish what it set out to do because no mechanism existed by which PRP could realistically gauge the probable impact of policy direction on the political realm. The DPS was brought in to coordinate and direct policy making, but it was too late to accomplish much. The administration was perceived as one that could not coordinate or communicate internally, and this failure nearly doomed the president's chances of getting even a moderately broad department, owing to both institutional and political factors. Policy analysis that might have been forthcoming from the OE was systematically shut out as the PRP was told to ignore the office in pursuit of its information.

Conversely, a task force that was both responsive and sensitive to substantive policy issues marked the youth employment initiative. Key members of Congress were sought out and either convinced to come on board or kept from building momentum in opposition. This was primarily due to the administration's extensive outreach activities, both with interest groups and with the relevant bureaucratic actors. The DPS managed to juggle a number of responsibilities successfully. It was able to be an advocate, honest broker, director of policy making, and facilitator of information, all at the same time. This, of course, took place in the period after President Carter strengthened the DPS staff's authority. However, it was the ability of the staff to take political soundings and weld this information to an analysis of policy substance that was perhaps the most important aspect of this particular process.

The combination of policy and political analysis was important in the proposal stage, through the use of task forces and the role of the DPS, which was charged with collecting and coordinating information and ensuring its compatibility with presidential intent.[102]

Although the cases examined in this chapter, and indeed throughout this book, were developed in accordance with a centralized policy strategy, the analysis presented here suggests some problems endemic to a tightly centralized policy process that uses staff to direct policy. Presidents, practitioners, and scholars should be aware of them. Some are novel, whereas others support or confirm other impressionistic accounts. First, the experience with the creation of a new department clearly shows that important information relevant to a president's advisory investment portfolio can be shut out, thus greatly increasing his margin of risk. Critics who claim that a tightly centralized process is too insulated from external forces, many of which can go far to provide a president with something approximating complete information, seem to be vindicated by this example. In addition, and somewhat paradoxically, the political process can falter as well. This is at least partly paradoxical because a tightly centralized process is designed to support, protect, and enhance the presidential political preferences in accordance with their incentives. In the cases studied here, an in-house task force failed to be responsive. It was not until the staff itself, rather than the task force, claimed responsibility for policy formulation that some semblance of political and policy synthesis took place. Eizenstat standing at the November cabinet meeting to announce that the president wanted a narrow department when Carter had explicitly stated otherwise is evidence of this. That was responsiveness, but the DPS did not, at that particular time, have the authority to carry it through.

On the other hand, a staff-directed system can work if the organizational apparatus is sophisticated enough to encourage a smooth, coordinated process with open and functional lines of communication between the White House, the bureaucracy, and affected groups. The ability to forge compromises is critical if presidential policy is to have its intended impact. Stubborn adherence to unworkable political or substantive elements can be hazardous to the administration in terms of public *policy*. Although, as John Gilmour reminds us, such bullheadedness might win the president *political* points.[103] Thus, a fully centralized process can work if coordination and collegiality are the norm rather than simply closing the process, with little input from outsiders. Outside input is valuable, and if used efficiently by the staff, is consistent with the goals and incentives of centralization.

The new institutionalist perspective delivers a nuanced view of the interaction between the endogenous preferences of individuals and the exogenous forces that shape their preferences while structuring terms of conflict or consensus between the president and interested political operatives. In the cases analyzed here, Carter and his staff are faced with several constraints, including members of his own cabinet, congressional leaders, the lasting impact of campaign promises that then have to be delivered, and the like. Institutional characteristics structured the terms of debate, although Carter's preferences for some sort of reorganization in the form of a new department in order to streamline education policy were clearly his own. The youth employment issue was thrust upon him as part of a larger unemployment problem, but the specific ways in which the president could maneuver, especially in political terms via the advice of the Mondale task force, left him considerable room with which to work. The fact that the youth employment initiative did not pass was not so much attributable to individual risk assessment or advisory pathology as much as it was felled by structural (especially budgetary) factors that impacted on the political and institutional environment.

This chapter has shown that a centralized, internally directed process can be successful. It can also fail to produce intended consequences, whether anticipated or not. Staff-directed policy making is not necessarily any better or worse than a facilitated or monitored strategy. While it might be true that presidents tend to highly centralize top policy priorities, they must remain sensitive to outside input if those policies are to be politically viable. Substance and politics can be joined from the inside, but efforts to remain open in some respects may be required. Thus, in the Carter administration a staff-directed advisory system was not necessarily better or worse than other systems. Presidents may opt to use a mixed, staff-facilitated strategy when issues become complicated and cut across bureaucratic jurisdictions, suggesting that these types of issues cannot be fully controlled from the center.

CHAPTER 5

Staff as Facilitator

Welfare Reform and Energy II

The staff-facilitated strategy, which forges a middle ground between the extremes of centralization and the search for responsiveness on one hand, and delegation to civil servants in order to maximize policy analysis on the other, is the focus of this chapter. Chapter 2 described the mixed strategy as one in which presidents assign policy-making authority to their staffs as well as to executive branch agents more or less in tandem. Mixed-policy processes are likely to involve highly political issues that cut across traditional departmental or agency jurisdictions. The fact that more than one or two departments need to be consulted and considered of primary importance in policy development and implementation mandates that the White House staff play a strong coordinating role while at the same time be especially sensitive to substantive advice from career civil servants.

A synthesis between policy and political advice can be demonstrated on normative grounds. Aberbach and Rockman observe that: "Politics provides energy and revitalization while bureaucracy brings continuity, knowledge, and stability. One can exist without the other but only to the detriment of effective government. The problem for government and . . . the public interest is not to have one of these values completely dominate the other, but to provide a creative dialogue or synthesis between the two."[1]

My analysis does not suggest that the middle ground is the only strategy in which we can identify a synthesis between the contours of politics and bureaucracy. Rather, there is a special need for such a combination in a mixed strategy because of the nature of the issues involved and the fact that experts and political staff members share the burden of policy formulation.

I argue that a middle ground, with internal White House policy staffs acting as facilitators in the policy process and accommodating both policy and responsive competence, can be forged on both theoretical and empirical grounds. A middle ground exists in two senses. The first concerns differential modes of thought (i.e., the categories of politically oriented or policy-oriented knowledge) that enter into the decision framework. The second pertains to just how a fully centralized policy-making strategy can be feasibly pursued, given insights derived from the staff-shift framework that argue that conditions exist under which presidents shift the focus of policy attention in accordance with dictates of policy content or political environment. For example, if the DPS acts as a coordinator of policy and political perspectives, the effort to manufacture a middle ground is manifest in the endeavor. Responsive agents in the DPS use advice and information provided to them by neutral agents in order to construct policy substance. In this sense, there is an explicit and presidentially mandated pursuit of political and policy perspectives.[2] Presidents formulate policy priorities based upon a variety of factors. Thus, the predominant types of analysis and information flowing between and among actors in the formulation stage varies with the intensity of presidential incentives, preferences, and priorities, as well as the shifting configuration of policy brokers competing in the political environment. Some modes of advice may be politically motivated, some may have symbolic purposes, others may be truly important to a president, while still others may reflect some combination of these factors.[3]

In the staff as facilitator strategy, a pronounced tension exists between policy analysis and responsiveness. These sets of actors (the WHS and departmental employees) may see the world through different lenses. This does not, of course, always obtain, but it can be a problem for coordinated policy action.[4] It is likely that staff members and civil servants or department heads will have strong opinions regarding both the political and substantive content of policy. They may coincide, but given the different primary constituencies each serves, considerable potential for disagreement exists. This tension is partially a result of multiple actors vying for influence in the policy-making process.

While it is almost certainly true that there are vestiges of political knowledge in policy analysis, and likewise policy substance in responsiveness, the two modes of thought remain somewhat separated. One reason for the tension between policy competence and responsiveness is that very often the nature of the issue assigned to the mixed strategy will fall across two or more departmental or agency jurisdictions. The likelihood that the proposed policy is of a large scope or has the potential for broad impact makes the issue politically volatile.[5] This creates an incentive for the White House to maintain close control of the direction of policy proposals. However, the White House does not fully centralize policy development via the strategy of using staff as policy director because it is virtually impossible for members of the WHS to possess enough knowledge of the subject matter to adequately manage the policy process internally. In addition to lacking sufficient substantive knowledge, the politically volatile nature of the issue often prevents the president from delegating authority for policy development to the departments because it would be potentially politically risky for one bureaucratic agency to try and coordinate the input of all interested parties.

For all of their perceived "policy-ese," bureaucratic agencies are often burdened by myopic vision resulting from different perspectives in organizational cultures and standard operating procedures.[6] Control problems thus exist when issues are highly politicized and cut across departmental jurisdictions. The WHS, and in Carter's case the DPS, is well suited to operate as a central facilitating organization, coordinating the flow of information and the activities of relevant individuals and groups, both within and outside the government. This is especially true given its proximity to the president, its defense of the president's preferences, and the malleability of internal working procedures

The policies that fit this category are welfare reform and the second energy program (hereafter referred to as Energy II). Originally, the responsibility for developing the welfare reform proposal was delegated to HEW secretary Joseph Califano. However, by late April, 1977, after repeated requests from Califano, President Carter allowed the DPS to enter the development process. The DPS served as facilitator between the warring factions of HEW and the DOL, headed by Secretary Raymond Marshall. Much of welfare reform's failure to mirror Carter's preferences and its inability to successfully negotiate the congressional process can be attributed to several factors. These include a closed policy process, excessive presidential inflexibility in areas that hampered political negotiation, the president's failure to perceive Congress's intense opposition to another Family Assistance Plan (FAP), and, perhaps most important, uncontrolled dissension within the executive branch pertaining to the proper scope and content of the proposals. The latter contributed to a perception that Carter was unable to keep his own house in order. In short, there was no smooth, cohesive, and coordinated process. The process was faulty due to the inability to mandate a compromise and the president's own failure to accurately assess the nature and possibilities of the political situation.[7]

In contrast, Energy II is an example of organizational learning in response to the nearly disastrous Energy I process. In addition, its story is instructive in how it differs from welfare reform. The White House decentralized policy making by coordinating the input of a greater number of affected departments and interest groups than was the case in the mostly closed off Energy I negotiation process. In this manner, the DPS was able to maintain a strong facilitating role, coordinating the crucial task of developing the proposals, while at the same time benefiting from policy expertise from bureaucrats and other expert groups. Thus, Energy II is characterized as a successful mixing of responsiveness and policy competence, which was conducive to a cooperative formulation process and subsequent legislative passage.

I will take up each story in turn, focusing on a few aspects of each story and illuminating various features of the processes in order to understand the differences that led to welfare reform's demise and Energy II's triumph.[8]

Unsuccessful Staff Facilitation: Welfare Reform

Welfare reform was nothing new when Jimmy Carter assumed office in January, 1977.[9] Most observers agreed that the welfare system was a shambles. Piecemeal attempts to assuage the perceived inequities and waste in a system that seemed to invite corruption and abuse had culminated in an unwieldy organizational mess. It was a system plagued by burdensome administrative regulations that in turn created what many thought were unnecessary problems for both recipients and civil servants.[10] In order to reform the welfare system, the Carter administration would have to conquer the aggregate negative effects of differing viewpoints within the executive branch. Some wanted to curtail the system, others wanted various types of structural reforms (e.g., budgeting housing allowances), while still others lobbied for management reform.[11]

The political environment outside the executive branch appeared even less friendly to comprehensive reform. Congressional conservatives, welfare rights organizations, labor unions, academicians, welfare program administrators, and financially burdened state and local governments all wanted a voice in any process aimed at revising the system. Even in a Congress controlled by the president's own party, conservatives headed the major committees with jurisdiction over welfare reform. Senator Russell Long (D-Louisiana) was chairman of the Senate Finance Committee, and Rep. Al Ullman (D-Oregon) chaired the House Ways and Means Committee. Each was opposed to distributing cash assistance benefits to individuals capable of working. In particular, Long was opposed to a major overhaul of the system. Instead, he advocated a pilot program that would include strong work incentives and job creation. Senator Daniel Moynihan (D-New York) also promised to be a critical player as he chaired the Senate Finance Subcommittee on Public Assistance.[12] Powerful actors in the political environment would need to be courted carefully at every stage in the process. Carter thus needed not only to recognize the rocky path that lay ahead, but to have political and policy advice at his disposal that would allow him to assess his risks accurately.

Carter wanted to focus on jobs and job creation. For the most part, members of Congress were reluctant to do so. Moynihan was an exception. He was more concerned with fiscal relief for individuals on the welfare rolls. Most important, the president insisted on a welfare reform proposal that would not increase the federal budget.[13] Although he was a Democrat, Carter was a budget-balancer at heart and an advocate for reducing waste by making the welfare system more equitable.[14]

The problem with creating a new system at no extra cost was that many existing welfare recipients would be hurt by its implementation. According to some accounts, Carter never seemed to understand that. Or, if he did, he never acknowledged it. He felt he could get enough money to offset programmatic increases by windfalls gained from stopping graft and welfare cheating. However, even if this were the case, the numbers Carter relied on simply did not add up.[15] Finally, both the White House and the departments managed to edge him toward increasing programs in $1 billion increments. But even these increments were attached to constraints. For example, such increments were only to be used for increasing equity and to make proposals politically palatable. Carter's insistence on zero cost and the tenacity with which he clung to it eventually assured the failure of welfare reform.

Additionally, Carter hurt his chances for a successful process by holding Califano to an off-hand comment the latter made long before he was appointed secretary of HEW. Shortly after the 1976 election Carter sought Califano's advice on a number of issues, including welfare reform. When the president-elect asked Califano when a welfare reform plan could be completed, Califano responded that a comprehensive proposal could perhaps be developed by May 1, 1977. After he became HEW secretary, Califano recognized that May 1 was far too optimistic and did not afford him sufficient time to develop a comprehensive plan. He pleaded for a later deadline, but, as was the case with zero cost, Carter refused the extension.[16]

Developing Principles and Proposals: Task Forces, Outreach, and Advice
Employing task forces can be an effective way for presidents to gain simultaneous and systematic input from bureaucrats, affected interests, and administration officials. Carter pursued this strategy at the beginning of his term in order to get input from bureaucrats and the personnel who monitored individuals receiving welfare benefits. However, the only person in the White House delegated to help coordinate the process and act as the president's emissary was Charles Schultze, chairman of the Council of Economic Advisers (CEA).

In accordance with the president's directive, Califano formed a consulting group to study the problem of welfare and develop a set of proposals that would encompass the administration's priorities. Califano appointed Henry Aaron, an economist on leave from the Brookings Institution serving as HEW's assistant secretary for Planning and Evaluation, to chair the group. In a February 5 memorandum to Carter, Califano stated that he had instructed Aaron to conduct the "most open process possible consistent with our May 1 deadline."[17] The memo went on: "One portion of the process will involve congressional, state, and local officials. The major effort to obtain views from groups and constituencies concerned with welfare reform will focus on intensive efforts to have department staff meet personally with relevant organizations, to conduct meaningful public hearings, and solicit requests for written comments."[18]

Indeed, the effort made by the HEW group through early February was quite extensive. It had written to 350 groups, including the fifty state governors, a hundred mayors and county officials, a hundred representatives from public interest organizations, fifty academic experts, and the fifty-one members of the House Ways and Means and Senate Finance Committees. With the process in full swing, Califano was well on his way to achieving his goal that "at the conclusion of the study, no group, public or private, and no constituency will accurately be able to say that they were not fully consulted or that they were not provided a full opportunity to express their views."[19]

With Aaron's help, the welfare reform consulting group prepared five analytic papers, the purpose of which were to give Califano, and later the president, background material and elicit his views. Even so, the feeling persisted that the May 1 deadline was too rigid a timeframe within which to craft the best possible product consistent with the president's expressed preferences.[20]

In an April 15 memorandum, Jack Watson, the president's coordinator for intergovernmental affairs, and his aide James Parham, argued against imposing arbitrary deadlines. Their arguments appear ideologically passionate: "*We believe that you have an historic opportunity to establish new ideals for social and economic justice that will set the pattern in this country for the next several decades.* . . . Judgment on such a vital issue should not be rushed. Unrealistic deadlines should be tempered until you have a proposal with which you are comfortable philosophically, intellectually, and pragmatically."[21]

This advice is illustrative of the intellectual climate that pervaded debates on the efficacy of welfare reform. The appeal to historic opportunism appears meant to advise the president as to the opportunity to effect programmatic change consistent with his preferences. Nevertheless, it did little to fully examine structural considerations such as budgetary and public-oriented factors. Arguments sharing an ideological, intellectually forceful tone reinforced the advisory tactics of these and other highly

ranked advisers, but they did little to fully explore the degree to which the
president's political risk would be increased. Nonetheless, the advice was,
for its ideology and appeal to historic possibilities, promoted as a caution
regarding how best to proceed, offsetting the potential risks inherent in
falling into rhetorical hyperbole. Advice here was thus balanced, with an
implicit appeal not to move too much, too quickly. Doing so risked losing
the real possibility of creating political change in the way welfare was carried out.

Persuaded by these and similar arguments, Carter relented and agreed
to a July 1 legislative target date, but retained the May 1 deadline as one
on which to announce broad programmatic principles. In addition, there
was confusion over the proper relationship of departments to the White
House. Aaron wrote Califano: "The process presumes naively that the department will be operating more or less on its own until, say, our initial
presentation to the White House on one or a few specific options. . . . We
do not yet know the intended full extent of likely interaction."[22] This is
instructive for understanding this particular process because it provides
evidence that key administration officials realized early on that a mixed
strategy, one that implies staff facilitation, would be necessary given the
uncertainty of "likely interaction" between relevant actors, even though
the president had delegated responsibility to HEW. The White House
would have to play an active role in facilitating the coordination of advisory sources in the formulation process. The DPS staff, especially Eizenstat's deputy, Bert Carp, recognized this as well. However, the president
continued to actively oppose a staff-facilitated strategy, preferring instead
to let HEW take the lead. The process soon became cumbersome and produced no conclusions as to the direction proposals would ultimately take.

In April a series of meetings was held in an attempt to impose coherence on the process. It was not until four days before the principles were
to be announced that the first indication of any proactive White House participation surfaced. A meeting was held on April 26 between the welfare
group and the White House staff. Participants included Treasury Secretary Michael Blumenthal, Califano, OMB director Bert Lance, Schultze,
Marshall, Eizenstat, presidential assistant Hamilton Jordan, press secretary Jody Powell, OLL director Frank Moore, and Jack Watson. The next
day, Watson wrote Carter a memo describing the meeting's outcome and
general points of agreement: "Everyone agrees that it is important for us
not to give the indication that we are subordinating, or even deferring our
commitment to comprehensive welfare reform [to other proposals]. Everyone also agrees that we should not give the appearance of trying to dictate
the Congressional time table for review of Administration proposals, but

rather that we are simply informing them of our own timetable on these two major Administration initiatives."[23]

This excerpt shows a White House staff member providing the president politically responsive analysis, but without reference to synthesizing political and policy advice. The role of the president's personal advisers in this case was simply to keep him abreast of developments in the political situation. Only later, when the policy process in the relevant bureaucracies had begun to break down over a conflict between HEW and the DOL, did Carter allow his staff to play a more integral role. By that time it was too late to save a coherent proposal.

Intrabranch Dissension

If the consultative process was confused, the debate between HEW and the DOL over the "viability of a large-scale, full time jobs program" was even more so.[24] Health, Education, and Welfare, while favoring the creation of part-time minimum wage programs, opposed a massive public employment program. The department argued that it was hard to filter out employable from unemployable recipients, and that a job guarantee (i.e., "make work" jobs) would be too costly and violate the president's no-cost mandate. On the other hand, the DOL was not concerned about this provision because, in its view, work was work. Jobs would be created, sending people to work, and therefore reduce the welfare rolls.

As mentioned above, Carter decided to present only a set of principles on May 1 rather than risk releasing a flawed, incomplete plan. Sticking points centered on the issue of jobs and the continued dispute between Califano and Marshall and their staffs. No There was no White House organizational apparatus for resolving these disputes. Some of the proposed principles were agreed to by HEW and the DOL. The most important of these included simplifying administration and introducing efficient management by consolidating cash assistance programs (e.g., Supplemental Security Income [SSI], Aid to Families with Dependent Children [AFDC], food stamps, housing, the Earned Income Tax Credit [EITC], and extending unemployment benefits), redirecting CETA public service employment and job training programs for the poorest people who could work, freezing state supplements to AFDC and SSI at their existing levels, providing a universal minimum federal benefit pegged to the cost of living, and guaranteeing that working families would make more money than families with no wage earner. Marshall agreed with these principles, but this agreement only masked the underlying fundamental difference of opinion on jobs.[25]

Members of the WHS were working to provide Carter with advice on jobs and the reduction of the need for public sector employment, such as that found in the following: "Reform plans should stress maximum incentive to work, and maximum effort should be made to move employables to private sector jobs. As a general proposition, work efforts should be rewarded by higher relative income."[26]

Califano, however, continued to have trouble getting the policy analysts in HEW and the DOL to agree to provisions in the plan. Califano's staff favored income maintenance for those on welfare as well as the working poor. The DOL advocated providing jobs for the employable poor. The DOL position was based on assumptions: (1) the need to provide jobs for the employable poor was "pressing," and (2) the "belief that welfare reform without work requirements and opportunities would not be politically feasible in Congress."[27]

Through it all, Carter maintained his commitment to cash assistance, job creation, and zero cost. Owing to Carter's position, Califano was fighting a war on two fronts, one with Marshall and the other with the president on the zero-cost issue. Part of the problem with persuading Carter to change his mind on zero cost was his personal commitment to balance the budget in FY 1981 and keep federal expenditures to no more than 21 percent of the gross national product (GNP).[28] Thus, the main sticking point with the president was whether the $6–9 billion dollars from CETA programs, which were set to expire in 1979, would be included in the baseline figure when computing the base cost. Califano eventually scored a small triumph when he got Carter to agree to keep the $9 billion figure in the baseline estimate.

The Califano "victory" was only partial as Carter's no-cost mandate remained in effect. Despite warnings from Califano and Senator Moynihan that such a mandate would seriously damage the viability of the program's goals, Carter stood firm. Internally, the DPS was involved, but only sporadically. Carter's mistake was in not including costs beyond the CETA windfall to be included in the baseline figure. Califano consistently argued for increasing spending whereas Carter wanted to decrease benefit levels. In late April, at Carter's request, Charles Schultze met with the staffs of Califano and Marshall in an effort to mediate an agreement. The meeting ended without resolution and the opposing sides remained separated by fundamental disagreements. In early May, Carter gave the staffs two weeks to work out their differences. The two weeks came and went, but, despite the intensity and duration of the meetings, no agreement emerged. Califano, perhaps sensing the president's frustration, again asked the DPS to intervene. This time Carter agreed to have the DPS broker an agreement.[29]

On May 13 the two staffs met in Bert Carp's office and agreed to combine cash assistance with income maintenance. The following excerpts from a memo to Aaron from Arnold Packer clearly indicate that not all agreements had been fully worked out, and that there was still quite a way to go in forging such an agreement:

> At the meeting held in Bert Carp's office . . . we agreed only on a basic structure for the benefit system. . . . I have no authority to go beyond the compromise set out in [the May 13] memorandum from Secretary Marshall to Secretary Califano [which mapped out the agreement on jobs]. The following lists six decisions that are yet to be made. I am not sure that any but the first issue has to be decided prior to the state-by-state discussions of the proposal. . . . You should be advised, however, that the Department of Labor *has not agreed on these . . . issues.*
>
> 1. What are the rules and procedures by which those required to work are allowed to become eligible for the higher track? What rules and procedures will be followed to return to normal operating status? The arrangements as specified in your draft memo describe a single track [negative income tax] with a work test. *This is no compromise and absolutely unacceptable.* This issue is clearly crucial and should be further clarified by the two Secretaries before we go to the President.[30]

A compromise finally was reached on May 20, but three points remained unsettled: the number of jobs required; upward flexibility of minimum wage levels for those required to work versus those not required to work; and the precise allocation of funds. While these were key aspects of the plan, a range on each had been agreed upon. Analysis of the advisory process and the information reaching the president support the impression of a forceful DPS process, combining policy competence and responsiveness. This is further illustrated by the following excerpt:

> In addition [to the above-mentioned three points that remained unresolved], a broad array of second-level design problems remain—including state-local cost-sharing in the jobs programs, the administrative structure for jobs programs, rules governing state supplementation of income support, a mechanism for reflecting differences in cost-of-living among areas, and many other issues. In addition, we are not satisfied as yet that the cost and impact data derived from Labor and HEW computer models are sufficiently accurate to meet close congressional scrutiny. . . .
> We will continue to work closely with the agencies to assure that

remaining decision issues are thoroughly staffed out and presented to you. . . . You should know that as this proposal becomes
public, we will receive criticisms from some for inadequate fiscal
relief, for providing too low an income support level and for expanding welfare roles through our inclusion of singles and child-
less couples (although these persons are already covered by food
stamps and state programs).[31]

The first part of the excerpt exhibits substantive policy depth, followed
by a concern for maintaining the administration's integrity when its estimates would encounter policy scrutiny from Congress. Next, the memo
displays staff activity as facilitating by brokering an agreement that policy
areas would be "staffed out." Finally, the staff identified and briefly analyzed the potential sources and extent of criticisms that the administration
would likely receive.

In closing a memo to Carter detailing the substance of the administration's proposal, Califano called on his political acumen to supplement his
otherwise substantively oriented analysis:[32]

The politics of welfare reform are treacherous under any circumstances, and they can be impossible at no higher initial cost, because it is likely that so many people who are now receiving benefits will be hurt. . . . The States are our natural allies in welfare
reform—most members of Congress would still prefer not to
deal with the subject at all—and there is virtually no relief in this
proposal for governors and mayors. In addition, there will be
problems in cutting benefits for the aged, disabled, and the blind,
and there will be disputes over our ability to put a significant
number of the 3.4 million mothers on welfare to work. . . . I suggest that we stress to the States and to Congress that we are only
presenting a working plan and that we are engaging in this process before submitting legislation in order to assess impact and
to determine what improvements are necessary to make the plan
work fairly and effectively for all—beneficiaries, States, cities,
and tax payers.[33]

It is not surprising, of course, that Califano would couch his last-ditch appeal for abandoning zero cost in political terms given his Great Society experiences in the Johnson White House. Additionally, he was arguably the
most politically astute of Carter's cabinet advisers, especially with regard
to social policy and welfare reform.

Thus, at least tentative agreement was reached when the DPS and

WHS got involved and facilitated operations between warring factions in the administration, and between these administrative operatives and the White House itself. The analysis suggests that the advisory process was marked by better coordination of policy and political advice, as well as efforts to mediate the rift between the HEW and DOL staffs. This is not to suggest that the program would have fared better had it been centralized, but the initial impetus to delegate without a facilitator to coordinate policy direction clearly was a mistake. The DPS was brought in too late. Interest groups and Congress had already perceived administrative incompetence throughout the process. Since the DPS role was pivotal in getting agreement, I now analyze more fully its role and the implications of the mixed strategy.

A Brief Analysis of the DPS Role

One reason the DPS did not step in sooner and develop a more powerful presence was that Bert Carp, buttressed by Eizenstat's support, wanted Califano and Marshall to come to an agreement on their own. Initially, there was a standoff between HEW and the DPS. Interestingly, Califano let it be known that the staff was not to interfere and dilute his control of HEW. He did this in the same way he treated cabinet secretaries when he was in charge of domestic policy development on Lyndon Johnson's White House staff.[34] President Carter viewed welfare reform as a program that should be managed by bureaucrats and officials in the agencies of the executive branch, with Califano and Marshall the key players. However, it soon became apparent that someone would have to take the lead in brokering divisive jurisdictional and ideological disputes. The DPS was selected for this function and began to play the pivotal role in policy formulation. Later, the role of Bert Carp and the staff was amended to help clarify the president's intentions in the welfare debate to the affected agencies. Staffers mediated between departmental actors and guided debate into the arena of political feasibility.

Some in the administration insisted that having two strong and conflicting views was a positive force in the advisory process. This is, of course, reminiscent of the famous advisory strategy of Franklin Roosevelt. The theory of relying on diverse viewpoints holds that the best policy direction will emerge more or less naturally and that compromise will inevitably result. However, this did not happen in the case of Carter's welfare reform initiative. Henry Aaron blamed this state of affairs on the fact that no one took the lead in coordinating and resolving the disputes. When the DPS entered and finally took the lead, it did so only because Califano repeatedly requested it of the president. His pleas were joined by those of experts from outside the White House. Tom Joe, a Washington consultant and former

director of the University of Chicago's Center for the Study of Welfare
Policy who had also worked in HEW during the development of Nixon's
FAP, wrote to Eizenstat: "This memo is not attacking the substance of any
specific option, but is, rather, *a plea for some positive coordinated plan* within
which the President's principles can be converted into a workable plan." [35]

In order for the DPS to be effective in coordinating information
sources and synthesizing policy and political advice, it was necessary to
control the level of disagreement between the two competing departmental staffs. The major means they employed to this end was to limit membership in the group working on the compromise. Laurence Lynn and
David Whitman quote a DPS member involved with the process: "We
made sure [assistant to Califano Ben] Heineman was there because we
came to realize that he was the only person at HEW who could speak for
the secretary. We tried as much as possible to freeze OMB out of the process because we knew they were going to oppose the plan; they were concerned over its costs, so we wouldn't always invite them to meetings. Similarly, we would rather invite Schultze than [CEA member Bill] Nordhaus
because we knew that Charlie was more sympathetic to welfare reform.
We would invite [the assistant treasury secretary for tax policy Laurence]
Woodworth rather than Blumenthal, because he was more liberal with
Treasury's money, and so on." [36]

Another way that the DPS performed its coordinating role was to
simply threaten to submit the issue to the president for an immediate, authoritative decision. As Frank Raines, a DPS member, said: "It wasn't necessary to invoke our authority and we didn't see our role as that. We were
playing the honest broker, but we would also invoke the possibility that the
President might decide, and that made them more than willing to work out
compromises." [37]

This example is instructive for our purposes because it shows the DPS
striving for a compromise that had been advised by experts in the bureaucracy while remaining sensitive to political imperatives as it sought to force
the agencies into agreement. In a process not known for its successes, here
is at least one clear example of a "good" facilitated strategy in which those
responsive to the president did not directly impose substantive preferences
on bureaucrats. Rather, they looked after the president's interests by in-
ducing, through whatever means necessary, an agreement on policy substance and detail.

Early on, and continuing after its role in policy development was
strengthened, the DPS was not simply an information broker, it actively
protected the president's policy preferences and political interests. It is for
this reason that methodological problems of classification arise. For ex-

ample, only the DPS seemed aware of the political problems that haunted HEW's consolidated cash approach. The major disadvantage of such an approach, according to an April 26 memo, was the intense opposition of Senator Long and Representative Ullman. The staff contrasted the choices between a negative income tax (NIT) as easy to administer but hard to sell politically; saw the DOL's jobs/cash approach as "overly complex" but "saleable to the public and to Congress in terms of theme" because of its resemblance to Long's 1972 Workfare proposal; and described Tom Joe's three-track proposal, which was similar to the DOL proposal but based on the unemployable poor, the employable but jobless poor, and the working poor.

A DPS memo to the president put it this way: "Tom [Joe] would provide an escape from the total commitment to minimum wage jobs for these in the "work track" by removing the entitlement to work and providing a stipend for those in the work track for whom work is not supplied. Particularly in times of high unemployment this should substantially increase the feasibility of the plan."[38]

The DPS analysis was steeped in political context, but this political advice was joined with policy advocacy. The DPS in this instance brokered information coming from external policy advisers, staffed out options, and supplemented these more neutral roles with advocating one approach over the other.

The presence of a strong responsive element and the role of political advisers in the White House increased in May. Watson and Parham wrote to Carter to argue against Tom Joe's separate approaches to the working poor, the unemployed who were expected to work, and those who were not expected to work. In an excellent example of coordinating policy and political analysis, they identify the main reason such an approach would not work as the undesirability and administrative nightmare of having three departments (Treasury, HEW, and Labor) involved in administering the program. "The argument has merit, but it may be a good candidate for tradeoffs, making it more acceptable to Congress, less divisive, and less stigmatizing."[39]

This type of coordination can again be seen in a July 27 DPS memo to Carter. In it, Eizenstat and company succeeded in keeping the president apprised of the political and substantive problems, as the following excerpt shows: "We believe this reform proposal will engender both liberal and conservative opposition, and that Congressional enactment will be difficult to secure. While House response is uncertain, the Senate under Chairman Long's leadership is likely to move in the direction of reducing the benefits to recipients under this program, requiring mothers with small children to "work off" existing benefits, and investing the savings in tax incentives (of dubious real value) for employment of low-income persons both in business and in providing household and other personal services."[40]

The purpose of the memo was to sketch the political and substantive problems, and to assess the incremental additions to the basic proposal in terms of their desirability. The memo was broken up into two parts, each of which consisted of a series of objective descriptions of the problems followed by recommendations.

Finally, the DPS performed adequately in its dual roles as honest broker and facilitator of compromise. In a memo combining the perspectives of HEW, the DOL, the CEA, and the DPS, Eizenstat wrote: "CEA suggests that you issue a *strong* statement in your message that you will not let the real value of aggregate cash assistance benefits decline, but that you want to retain flexibility in distributing this increment. *On balance Treasury, CEA, HEW, Labor, and Domestic Policy Staff agree that the proposed credit provides an acceptable compromise among these conflicting objectives* [concerning the EITC and various earnings levels]."[41]

If the DPS, the White House, and to some extent the relevant bureaucracies did well, why is welfare reform considered a failure from an advisory standpoint? Why is it not broken into two parts, one classified a failure and the other a success? At least two reasons present themselves. First, Carter did not adequately perceive the political opposition that comprehensive welfare reform would engender. Interest groups, Congress, and the bureaucracy were ready for reform, but a type of reform more incremental than Carter wanted. Second, the division within the administration impeded a smooth process. The inability of Califano and Marshall to reach an agreement and manage the development of the reform proposal gave rise to the need for a facilitator to keep the relevant actors (in this case, the HEW and DOL staffs) on track, serve as an advocate for the president's preferences, and, when necessary, force compromise among warring factions. While dissension in the administrative ranks can increase the quality of the proposals, failure to control that dissension and broker an agreement can lead to policy drift, which occurred in the case of welfare reform.

Finally, the DPS and WHS were brought in too late to salvage a process that had already imparted the perception of chaos and confusion, as well as a president out of touch with political feasibility and unable or unwilling to compromise to save his program.[42] In short, much of the blame for the failure of the advisory process in the welfare reform case must be placed on Carter himself. Had he recognized the potential rift in the bureaucracy and seen that welfare reform was a highly charged political issue, he might have realized that a mixed strategy, using staff as facilitator, was the appropriate path to take from the outset, instead of delaying WHS involvement for nearly three months. The evidence suggests that the DPS performed its responsive function well. At times it played honest broker, and at other times it advocated various policy positions. In several instances, it effectively synthesized substantive and political advice, thereby offering the president both policy and responsive competence under one roof.[43] However, the process had almost spiraled out of control by the time the DPS became an active participant. When it finally did enter the process, it was too late to effectively salvage the proposal.

The staff-shift framework suggests that the variation in the role played by the staff is part and parcel of the mixed strategy. However, it also suggests that an active role be taken by staff members and encouraged by the president. Neither happened in this case, at least until near the end. The position of the presidency in a separated system illustrates how a president can be hamstrung by institutional realities—even those ostensibly within his own branch. The institutional analysis set forth in some detail has, I would argue, supported the proposition that Carter and his staff were heavily constrained by factors outside their control and were impotent in handling those problems, at least early on. The empirical description illustrates the very real constraints placed on presidential action. These constraints took many forms, including Congress, external consultants, interest groups, and administration officials. Although the various constraints might seem somewhat random, their interplay is in effect predicted by the new institutionalist approach. The degree to which the president and his staff were impeded in what they wanted to do and how they decided to go about getting it varies, depending upon individual factors such as style and so forth. However, the incentives that structured the president's preferences were almost tangible in their presence and the dampening effect they had on the conversion from his pure preferences to his grudging, realistic preferences. As John Kingdon has noted, there is a lot of structure to what might appear to be random political elements, but the predictive enterprise will always be subject to a degree of uncertainty.[44]

The Energy II case, as we will soon see, avoided many of the problems of welfare reform. The White House became involved early, the process was more open and fluid than both Energy I and welfare reform, and the consulting process was more effective.

Successful Staff Facilitation: Energy II

On April 18, 1977, President Carter addressed the nation and called on the American people to sacrifice and to become part of the solution rather than the problem when he declared that the effort to control the energy crisis would be the "moral equivalent of war."[45] It was at this press conference that Carter unveiled much of his "secret" energy proposal. James Schlesinger, who was later to become the first Energy Department secretary, developed the plan in virtual secrecy after Carter gave him ninety days from the beginning of the administration to put it together. Schlesinger had asked for more time, but Carter refused. He wanted to act boldly and early, before his popularity began to wane—a phenomenon most presidents experience over time.[46]

Several factors have been cited in the literature for why Energy I failed to pass Congress in a form even partly resembling the president's initial proposal. David Davis argues that the lack of consultation with interest groups and the resulting revolt by energy lobbies tore the plan apart and left it weak.[47] Charles O. Jones blamed the proposal's demise on the administration's failure to consult with members of Congress, who in turn complained that they had "almost no role" in developing the plan.[48] Similarly, scholars such as Erwin Hargrove and Barbara Kellerman ascribe the plan's failure to a lack of advance consultation with both administration officials and Congress. Perhaps most devastating, the plan lacked a constituency that closely identified itself with the goals of the proposal.[49] The administration avoided these pitfalls in Energy II by giving the DPS a strong coordinating role, leaving most of the substantive detail work up to civil servants.

Developing Proposals in the Outreach Process

In contrast to both welfare reform and Energy I, the White House, especially the DPS, was involved early on as an equal partner and given facilitating responsibility in policy making.[50] Additionally, the administration recognized that the scope of energy legislation cut across a number of agencies and departments, and did not affect the Department of Energy (DOE) alone. A mixed strategy with staff facilitating between groups was thus employed early in the policy development stage. Katherine "Kitty" Schirmer, Eizenstat's aide in charge of energy policy, quickly gained Carter's trust and he relied on her for substantive and political counsel, "free from the institutional bias of Department of Energy bureaucrats."[51]

Schirmer and her staff operated on two levels. First, she coordinated development of energy legislation. The proposed bills were drafted in the DOE because the DPS lacked the computer capability and substantive expertise to construct the proposals. Second, she served as an adviser to both the president and Eizenstat, offering her opinions on the shape and character of the legislation and brokering the disparate views of others as they pertained to any particular proposal.[52]

This pattern adduces an early coordinating process. But the process also combined the honest broker and advocacy roles of the DPS, which had been missing early in the welfare reform process. This allowed for the dissemination of policy competent advice and expertise (i.e., drafting legislation in the DOE) by taking work done in the departments by professional civil servants and integrating the substance of the proposals with the available political possibilities. Thus from the beginning the DPS, the WHS, and the relevant bureaucracy benefited from a kind of organizational learning in which all three became integrated early, played forceful but conciliatory roles, and contributed to a more successful process in terms of openness, collegiality, and coherence.[53]

Outreach and Consultation
In response to high prices attributable to the Iranian revolution and the consequent decrease in oil production, several groups and subnational governments pressured Washington for action. In stark contrast to other policy areas, the Carter administration was ready to act. In 1979 Carter asked Eizenstat to chair a task force charged with developing a second energy bill. Evidence suggests that the process was more systematic and open, an impression that is corroborated by Eizenstat:

> We had every single agency around a table . . . [and the meetings were] attended on the average by fifteen or twenty people every . . . afternoon for weeks and weeks. . . . *It was a very open . . . very consultative process* and we did a lot of work on the Hill, talked to Jim Wright, talked to Scoop [Jackson], talked to the people who were involved and we were clearly handling it . . . [and included] extensive discussions with the business community because the business community was key to getting the synthetic fuel corporation passed. . . . I had meeting after meeting of the chief executive officers of the major corporations and we finally got them, including the oil companies to come around, which was very important in ultimately getting it passed. . . .
>
> When we got through with that process we had a really first rate decision-memorandum for the President and we had a policy which was passed. Every single item passed except for the energy mobilization board. . . . But the synthetic fuel corporation, which was the centerpiece, was passed plus additional conservation initiatives. . . . [It was] a considerable improvement over the '77 process. And there was a lot of talk about energy being now moved to the White House and the Energy department had lost the initiative. . . . That was baloney.[54]

Eizenstat's observations support the impression of a high level of co-ordination among the White House, civil servants, Congress, and inter-ested parties—especially those in the business community. The process was enhanced by a pronounced anticipatory component; staff members re-alized that business support was crucial for the passage of the synthetic fu-els (usually referred to as "synfuels") component and worked proactively to secure industry backing. This type of facilitation, with its emphasis on coordination, was largely absent from both welfare reform and Energy I, which in turn contributed to the downfall of each program's advisory pro-cess. Nor did these program's benefit from the acquisition of public sup-port. Certainly no anticipatory measures were employed, save for consult-ing with a few members of Congress in the case of welfare reform.

As with the advisory role of the work group cited above, task force strategies followed an open process. In the initial phase of developing En-ergy II, the DPS was brought in at the beginning, coordinating substance and politics. Consultation on Capitol Hill concentrated on the affected committees, especially those dealing with synfuels. In a memo to Carter, Eizenstat assessed the consultative process with particular reference to the task force: "The task force is obviously large, but I believe it essential that all of the major agencies and individuals involved be brought together on a regular basis to *ensure that coordination occurs.* To do that, the Task Force will meet regularly."[55] To make the process more manageable, the task force was divided into jurisdictions, with most of the work being done in subcommittees dealing with specific legislative issues. Each subcommittee consisted of participants from the White House and affected departments. For example, the Legislation Subcommittee, which was responsible for co-ordinating various drafts of the legislation as well as regulating lobbying efforts on behalf of the proposal, consisted of members of Frank Raines's staff, Eizenstat's staff, and representatives from OMB, DOE, and Treasury. The subcommittee met for one to two hours each day and did so for some time afterward.[56]

Although the task force system appeared to work well, it did receive some criticism, especially from the media. For example, the group that put together the energy package "raised eyebrows" because it appeared to usurp the DOE's role in policy formulation. The perception was that Eiz-enstat was undercutting the authority of Energy Secretary Schlesinger. As one journalist put it: "Eizenstat reputedly was displeased with Schlesin-ger's performance and urged Carter to replace him. The ultimate effect was to give more agencies a crack at energy."[57] However, the evidence sug-gests otherwise. Internal memoranda from this period include a number of dual memos to the president from Eizenstat and Schlesinger, and the texts exhibit overarching agreement on strategy, tactics, and substance.

Also, Schlesinger and his staff forwarded a number of memos that offered substantive policy advice and analysis to which both Carter and Eizenstat agreed.

Policy and Political Advice: A Closer Look

Of the many procedural and political problems with Energy I, perhaps the most daunting was that it lacked a vocal, mobilized constituency to politically sustain it. Without the continued support from the public and affected communities, Congress could not be expected to develop much interest, much less to pass the program fully intact. The reason it failed to mobilize such a constituency was that Schlesinger had developed the program in isolation from much of the executive branch, and had even less contact with interested publics. The same problem plagued welfare reform.

In June, 1978, Gerald Rafshoon, director of Carter's Office of Communications, assumed responsibility for developing a comprehensive outreach program in support of Energy II. Rafshoon ordained a citizens committee, chaired by Anne Wexler of the Office of Public Liaison (OPL), to examine energy policy and forge a base of operations in the White House until such time that a more comprehensive committee could be convened. In a series of memos, Rafshoon displayed a high degree of responsiveness in that his analyses reflected sensitivity to the White House headquarters, was receptive to substantive issues, and sought to convince various publics of the efficacy of the president's program. These memos detail a comprehensive political plan that included several committees, including the Themes and Tone, Citizens, Media, Speakers Bureau (which provided speeches to participants and a systematic identification of key administration, congressional, and outside spokespersons), Interest Group Contacts, Democratic National, and Congressional Liaison Committees.[58]

Such an effort was desperately needed because by the time Rafshoon assumed command of policy direction, Congress had passed much of Energy I. However, the closed process carried with it the consequence that the legislation bore little resemblance to the policy originally envisioned by the president. A comprehensive plan was needed because acquiring and maintaining a high degree of public support and continued interest was critical for securing congressional passage. However, keeping public interest high would not be easy. To achieve this goal, Carter himself got involved by "going public." He bypassed Congress and went directly to the people in an attempt to advertise the issue, make the problem salient, and pressure Congress to keep it on what John Kingdon has called the "decision agenda" (i.e., the point at which an issue item is being acted upon).[59] The White House implemented a National Energy Hotline that provided citizens updates on the energy crisis. It also began incorporating the advisory views of various groups, especially environmentalists, directly into the president's speeches.[60] All of these things were done in an attempt to maintain a high level of public interest in the energy program.

The DPS facilitated political strategy meetings to bring along those individuals and groups whose support would either be crucial for the plan's success or whose opposition the administration wanted to avoid. For example, in an April 19, 1979, memo to Eizenstat, Wexler explained her strategic program, a strategy that included anticipatory and reactive elements. In the following excerpt, she lays out a plan to bring along groups in support of the windfall profits tax. Since it is representative of the overall strategy, which included energy conservation and four standby plans, the memo is worth quoting at length:

> The tax must be approached positively—new, reliable sources of energy, benefits for urban areas and the poor—rather than negatively as a penalty on the oil companies.
>
> A range of groups are possible members of a supporting coalition:
> —Business: General reaction will be opposition from big business; however, if business is approached selectively based on who benefits, an initial threshold in the business community might be developed—e.g., coal industry, bus manufacturers, utilities, solar industry, building industry, etc.
> —The Poor Coalition: Essentially the full employment coalition which supported Humphrey-Hawkins; includes minorities, labor, liberals, etc.
> —Oil Industry: Majors are opposed; might be able to break off independents, particularly if royalties are deducted before taxes are computed. . . .
> —Grass Roots Leadership: Drawn from high quality leadership on other issues. This is a "strong national interest issue" and many Carter supporters and leaders on other issues without a specific interest will want to help with it. . . .
>
> In addition, it might be possible to get the support of some of the environmental groups depending on the use of the funds. Consumer groups will be more difficult although there are some indications that consumer leaders outside Washington might be more supportive.[61]

This memo, and others like it, adduce evidence that the process was at once comprehensive and thorough. The level of political sophistication far outflanked the processes in welfare reform and Energy I. One of the problems in welfare reform, for example, was that Carter felt he was blindsided by the large number of groups opposing the plan. As can be seen in her memo, Wexler identified the oil industry as hostile, indicating that there was little hope for compromise (the implication being to not waste valuable time or capital trying to bring them aboard). Nevertheless, she suggested that a possible compromise might be worked out with small, independent oil producers. The process kept Carter informed of the political ramifications of pushing the plan to certain groups and heading off another potential blindsiding. The president, of course, was personally involved in this political process from time to time. For example, on September 1, 1978, at the suggestion of Hamilton Jordan, Carter telephoned a number of high-level members of the business community. These business moguls included David Rockefeller, chairman of the board of Chase Manhattan Bank; Robert Wingenster, chairman of Libby and Owens-Ford Company; William Klopman, chairman of Burlington Industries; George Stinson, chairman of National Steel; Irving Shapiro of DuPont; and Robert Anderson, chairman of the Atlantic Richfield Company.[62]

The process was also much more effective in tracking congressional opinion than other efforts analyzed in this book. Memos from this period show staff members carefully identifying congressional support and opposition, placing congressmen and senators into one of three categories: those who favored the program, those firmly opposed, and those who could be persuaded to support it. The strategy of congressional tracking was similar to that employed with interest groups in that the administration used an approach designed to maximize efficiency in targeting resource allocation. By concentrating on uncommitted members of Congress and taking care to retain the support of those already in favor of the program, the WHS, with the cooperation of the DOE staff, avoided the problems with Congress that they experienced in Energy I and welfare reform. As a result, the quality of the political advice from responsive agents, tempered by the substantive expertise flowing from the departments, was more refined and served the president's interests in a way that it had not in other policy processes.[63]

In short, those involved with the advisory process, as well as the design of the process itself, yielded insights to Carter that had been lacking in the welfare reform process. Even if Carter could do little to change congressional views and opinions, he was at least prepared to counter opposing ideas and was thus protected from the possibility of being overwhelmed by the scope, nature, and intensity of some congressional resistance. For example, when the Senate voted in June to repeal the president's authority to impose oil import fees, Eizenstat convened a meeting of the interested parties and brokered an agreement on strategy. This entailed synthesizing the political views of the DPS and National Security Council (NSC), bolstered by the expertise of the CEA, and the substantive knowledge of bureaucrats in the State, Treasury, and Energy Departments.

In short, the White House did not stifle the bureaucracy's *policy expertise* in favor of *political expertise*. Eizenstat and his staff were clearly charged with presenting both to the president in a coherent, evenhanded manner. Just as political views were freely aired, so was the incorporation of substantive expertise, a pattern similar to that found in welfare reform. However, the difference between the two processes lies in the manner in which policy advice was presented to the president.[64] The DPS played a strong facilitating role, but some members, especially Schirmer, brought an additional brand of political feasibility to an otherwise coordinating and synthesizing role.

Conclusion

In examining the advisory strategy of using the staff as a facilitator coordinating the advice of disparate groups in the policy development process, we have considered the dynamics of one successful and one failed case. The first, the failed case, was the administration's effort to promulgate comprehensive welfare reform. Other observers of welfare reform, such as Lynn and Whitman, argue that the traditional criticism of policy analysts (i.e., that they tend to ignore politics in their own technocratic way) does not seem to hold in this case. They observe that if "Carter's advisers been forced to show a little less 'political savvy' and a bit more allegiance to what Carter wanted, they might well have helped the President as well as themselves."[65] They further note that:

> At no time did the President's advisers seem to be doing what he really wanted them to do. A proposal and an adviser Carter really liked . . . played minor parts in the process; the "no additional cost" restriction was neither understood nor accepted by those developing the proposal; as the days grew short before the May 1 deadline, a high-level presidential adviser could not persuade two cabinet officers and their presidentially appointed subordinates to resolve their differences so that Carter could meet his commitment. There was something wrong with the way the President and his staff were communicating his decision to Califano . . . who [was] systematically kept at arms distance from the White House.[66]

My analysis largely corroborates Lynn and Whitman's interpretation. However, my analysis of documents used to reconstruct the advisory process, some of which were not available at the time Lynn and Whitman completed their study, extend and modify their judgments. First, more so than they recognized, achieving welfare reform was a political problem. The administration would have done well to learn from previous attempts to reform the system, perhaps using Nixon's Family Assistance Plan as a blueprint.[67] The few systematic discussions of political options tended to be analytical and technical rather than responsive. While such advice is certainly not undesirable, more politically open and realistic discussions earlier in the process almost certainly would have alerted the administration to the location of myriad pitfalls. Indeed, such politically sensitive discussions did eventually materialize, but not before the DPS was brought in as policy facilitator. Even after the DPS assumed control, there remained several problems concerning technical expertise, including using erroneous cost estimates as the basis for forecasting, and an inability to resolve technical disputes concerning the jobs program.

My analysis also suggests that President Carter must assume even more of the blame than Lynn and Whitman ascribe to him. Carter was rightly counseled that the zero-cost provisions would have to be scrapped in order to achieve the type of reform he wanted, owing mostly to the high probability that many individuals would be hurt if the no-cost dictum was preserved. The president's stalwart position fostered alienation in Congress and even within the administration itself by tying the hands of the various staffs in order to reconcile the actual numbers with the plan's stated goals. In addition, the president was far too reluctant to grant active White House involvement in a process that should have been DPS facilitated from the very beginning.

Why did Energy II succeed when welfare reform failed? The development phase in Energy II succeeded largely because of a collegial advisory process. Bureaucrats fed substantive advice and policy analysis into the White House. The WHS, especially the DPS, played a strong coordinating role that secured a unified administration perspective. This in turn culminated in a high degree of coordination among the political and policy actors. The DPS was instrumental in clearly communicating the White House view to the department, acting as honest broker in bringing substance to the president through Schirmer, and in brokering agreements both among bureaucrats and Congress. Perhaps most important was that the staff was brought in early, at the beginning of the development process rather than after it had spiraled out of control. It thus played a pivotal role in making the process more open, coherent, and comprehensive than it had been in Energy I.

In turn, bureaucrats in the DOE and other affected agencies provided the White House with policy expertise and substantive critiques, with special regard to simplifying the extremely complicated concepts accompanying natural gas deregulation and synfuels. This suggests that policy outcome is at one level both a matter of process and information dissemination. The crucial support of executive branch officials is cemented in a collegial, coordinated, and coherent process. As Eizenstat himself said: "We [DPS] were not initiators, we were *coordinators*, we were pushing, we were mediating, we were arbitrating, we were getting agencies together. But the *substantive work was done by the energy experts in each of the agencies involved*."[68]

In sum, political operatives outside the White House were involved in a staff-facilitated process more so than had been the case in welfare reform. Similarly, the president was more flexible to political realities than he had been previously. Overall, the process was highly integrated, blending the incremental nature of securing support of a number of key players, including Congress and interest groups, thereby facilitating policy input from relevant bureaucracies. The execution of process compares favorably to that of welfare reform, which used only one narrowly focused task force, while Congress was largely ignored.[69] The major point concerning Energy II is that, after Carter scolded Schlesinger early in the Energy I process,[70] policy making included the active participation of experts in various parts of the executive branch. The DPS facilitated *strong* bureaucratic input. Political life was easier for the president in that a more explicit *political* dimension emerged, a dimension seemingly absent during the welfare reform process.

Additionally, the cases examined here provide evidence of what Bert Rockman has called "termcycles"—cycles that rise and fall or ebb and flow with the changing dynamics during a president's term.[71] President Carter had to deal with declining overall support, independent of his policy proposals, and a growing effectiveness within the governing community. His efforts in youth employment speak most directly to this dynamic, illustrating a president more effectively dealing with the realities of the institutional structure while fighting the debilitating effects of declining support. A full specification and explanation of this is outside the scope of this discussion, but I note it here as a suggestion for future research on advisory patterns, namely that the confluence of termcycle factors enforce the endeavor to understand intra-administration variation in how presidents go about doing their jobs.

What does the new institutionalist framework illuminate with regard to the cases discussed in this chapter? First, we see evidence of presidential preferences shifting with the realization that the incentives structured

by the political system were intransigent. Not only do substantive preferences shift within one case (welfare reform), but also across cases. The
president's political strategy changed, sometimes dramatically, in the face
of institutional pressures that proved intractable. Carter's initial refusal to
revise his stance on items such as zero cost indicate that institutional realities provided a context-based set of structures that proved impossible for
Carter to penetrate. The fact that Carter's modus operandi shifted does
not mean that he was simply accommodating seemingly intractable institutional boundaries. Some of his advisory revisionism can be attributed to
this, to be sure, but not all. It is quite clear that Carter chose to pursue political and policy priorities regardless of what the institutional structure
held. His pursuit of policy on his own terms ultimately led to failure in the
welfare reform case. However, his refusal to budge on the zero-cost issue,
among other things, illustrates the propensity of presidents more generally to capture their individual preferences in a policy context, at least initially, in a way that accounts for institutional parameters while operating
on them independently. No doubt the administration enjoyed political advantages in pursuing youth employment as a domestic policy prescriptive
for the larger problem of unemployment. Nevertheless, the success Carter
enjoyed in bringing national health insurance to a national audience and
getting both mass and elite audiences to take notice and act in response to
a presidential initiative lends credence to the idea that presidents are not
simply reflections of the larger institutional setting. The president is capable of transforming that setting, making it at least partly a reflection of
him and his priorities, preferences, and pursuits.

This chapter has provided a theoretical and empirical exposition of
what the middle ground between political and policy competence might
look like in the form of a staff-facilitated strategy of information collection
and synthesis. The major findings demonstrate that the middle ground can
be identified empirically, and that using the staff as policy facilitator is not
necessarily better than using it as director or monitor, relying instead on
civil servants in the bureaucracy. In the facilitated strategy, a tension exists
between policy competent and responsive advice. In the cases considered
here, the impact of the proposals fell across agency jurisdictions. The fact
that these proposals required departmental cooperation was a strong reason for the White House to maintain control, although it did not unduly
centralize because it was unrealistic to expect to completely control policy
development on these types of issues. A facilitating role for staff was more
appropriate under these conditions than other advisory strategies. Problems of control still existed because issues were highly politicized precisely
because they transcended clear-cut bureaucratic domains. Too much centralization forfeits needed substantive expertise, whereas delegation might

prove to be chaotic or, worse, fail to serve the president's interests (as was the case in Energy I). Like all policies examined in this book, I do not argue that advisory systems or informational advantages are directly responsible for the success or failure of any one particular policy. Still, advice did contribute to the terms and definition of turf from which the president came to be judged.

Another situation in which presidents run the risk of having their interests poorly served is when they choose to delegate policy-making responsibility to external actors in the bureaucracy. One way presidents can minimize that risk is by using their staff to monitor the degree to which externally promulgated policy priorities are faithful to the their articulated preferences. The advisory strategy of using staff as monitor carries with it the danger that the White House role can become diminished by definition. The key is to make agencies or departments responsive by maintaining a degree of staff involvement that is not as active as in the director or facilitator strategies.

Chapter 6

Staff as Monitor

National Health Insurance and Civil Service Reform

Scholars who analyze a decentralized mode of policy making most frequently base their appraisals on normative claims concerning the utility of good government, the value of expertise, and the dissociated and analytical perspective that accompanies policy competence.[1] The staff-shift framework developed and applied throughout this book holds that such a strategy has the benefit of using presidential staff, specifically the DPS, to monitor policy development in the executive branch's departments and bureaus. Policy can be formulated in the departments, even those issues that have presidential priority. Furthermore, the staff-shift framework suggests that such delegation is consistent with the broader tendency of presidents to centralize policy in the White House so as to maximize policy responsiveness to their domestic program. It does so by viewing advisory sources through lenses of institutional memory and technical expertise. Civil servants in the departments or agencies, long reputed to be repositories of policy competence, are seen as capable of providing advice separate from political trappings and pressures.

To some degree, advising in a decentralized strategy is different from the advisory processes dealt with in the preceding chapters. Advice is not part and parcel of the White House day, and comes to it from delegated agents at various intervals after components of policy substance have been completed. The staff-shift framework suggests that advisory patterns will closely resemble a system in which broad discretionary decision-making authority is given to the delegated department or agency, which formulates proposals or variants of proposals, then sends them to the White House for approval. Thus we obtain the monitoring label given to staff in this strategy. More generally, the theoretical thrust of using the staff to monitor policy formulation is straightforward: The president and his staff can rely on the expertise of civil servants and appointees in the bureaucracy to formulate policy. In doing so, internal resources (staff time and energy) are directed toward policies that require a facilitating or directing role by staff members. Policy makers are left largely unattended, free to enter into negotiations with others within broad parameters set by the White House, while the president's staff monitors the progress and content of the policy under question, using external advice to cement, modify, or reject various political or policy strategies. This assures the product of the process will be acceptable to the White House. Staff is involved, to be sure, but as a supervisor rather than an active participant in the policy formulation process.[2] The staff-shift framework maintains that this monitoring role is consistent with centralization in that the president's staff plays a critical role, but its activity is less in both degree and kind from the role it plays in other advisory strategies.[3]

Policy competence can and often does have a political component. Without entering debates as to whether or not individuals can be neutral with regard to anything, much less policy formulation, it is possible to give advice based on what is politically acceptable because institutional memory is not limited to technical specifics. Few policy innovations are new, and programs are often recycled when political climates and/or administrations change.[4] The identification and analysis of pure policy competence is made difficult because politically informed information can drift in from outside the White House walls. Just as in chapter 2, policy competence or responsiveness is not the exclusive jurisdiction of either the departments or the White House staff, respectively.

Still, just because the analysis of policy competence in a decentralized strategy is difficult does not imply that it is impossible. Policies ripe for delegation are likely to be clearly within the purview of one of the delegated bureaucratic entities. Moreover, the type of policy under development is important both for the degree of coordination between the agency and the White House and the prospects for presidential success as defined.[5] Finally, for a policy to be considered delegated, with the staff serving as monitor rather than facilitator or director, the president must give a bureaucratic organization primary, if not exclusive, responsibility for developing the proposal.

In the Carter administration, this turned out to be quite simple. Two policies were easily identified. The creation of a national health insurance (NHI) plan is the unsuccessful case considered here. Secretary Joseph Califano and the HEW were given authority to develop a plan in consultation with other affected agencies. This authority was reaffirmed several times, even when the HEW proposal did not jibe with what the White House would have preferred.[6] The successful case we will consider is civil service reform, which fit neatly into the jurisdiction of Alan Campbell at the Civil Service Commission (CSC). He and his staff were directed to develop a policy proposal and manage the advisory process. In both cases, the president's staff served as monitor.

Unsuccessful Monitoring:
National Health Insurance

Jimmy Carter's 1976 presidential campaign resurrected the controversial issues surrounding NHI. Carter promised that, if elected, he would propose a health insurance program comprehensive in coverage and national in scope. The emerging campaign brought the differences between Republican president Gerald Ford and Democratic candidate Carter clearly into focus: Simply put, Carter favored such a program whereas Ford was opposed to the idea. Carter's enthusiasm for the program was directed against the status quo, which was burdened by rising health costs and uneven care.[7] As with welfare reform, many policy makers perceived a need for a program, citing several lingering problems, including gaps in protection and 22 million individuals with no health insurance. However, there was never a great *political* imperative, if one employs public opinion as the benchmark. Polls from this period do not reflect strong popular support for NHI, nor was there a widespread perception that health insurance was a public priority. With the exception of labor unions and other similarly affected groups, there was no readily identifiable, broad-based constituency that could potentially be mobilized to strongly support any proposed legislation. For example, a late September, 1976, Gallup poll shows that the public ranked national health insurance ninth out of ten issues in terms of their perceived importance.[8] Indeed, through 1978, when the health insurance controversy reached its peak, Gallup periodically asked respondents a question designed to identify pressing public issues. National health insurance never made the list.[9]

Carter promised during the campaign to propose a NHI plan soon after assuming office. His plan centered on a multistage process designed to "minimize cost impact." He was allied with labor groups that wanted to make health insurance a critical issue in the campaign, in effect locking the candidate into a position in a way reminiscent of how education groups forced his hand on the creation of a new department. This signaled that health was an issue that had to receive priority attention should Carter win the presidency.

The UAW's president, Leonard Woodcock, was Candidate Carter's most visible early supporter. Indeed, two facets of the labor health care plan, a compulsory program with mandatory benefits and payroll taxes supplemented by general revenues from the federal government, were co-opted by the Carter people.[10] Clearly, Carter owed the labor movement a debt of gratitude.

External pressures, both for and against the proposal, came from a variety of sources. Opposition forces mobilized quickly once it became clear

Carter decided to make national health insurance a presidential priority. Objections from the various groups ran the gamut between political, social, and economic aspects of public policy. Journalist John K. Inglehart put it this way: "Given the awesome social program budget pressures, the medical system's massive resistance to controls, the lack of a congressional consensus on the shape of or even the need for national health insurance and the President's preoccupation with a host of other issues, any changes in federal health policy will come not through a great leap forward but rather in a series of much smaller steps." [11]

Carter had practical policy problems in addition to political troubles. He enjoyed the support of few, whether they were inside or outside the executive branch. Several reasons can be cited for this lack of public and governmental support, including the widespread perception that too many proposals were already on the agenda, that Congress was "virtually unanimous in its lack of enthusiasm" for national health insurance (save for Sen. Edward Kennedy), and that there were few administration NHI advocates. Those who did favor the proposal—including Hamilton Jordan, his deputy Landon Butler, and Peter Bourne, special assistant to the president for health issues—based their support on the crush of political imperatives and the necessity of maintaining a positive relationship with UAW and the AFL-CIO. [12]

The initial justifications for pursuing NHI were couched in terms of controlling rising health care costs. Some analysts, though, said that incremental steps had to be taken and hospital cost containment had to be implemented first. Others, like Senator Kennedy and Douglas Fraser, the new UAW president, argued that the only way to control sources and forms of payment was to have a unitary national system. [13] The problems of health care would not be resolved easily given the multiple and very different proposals the administration was getting for both incremental, cost-effective steps and a long-term, comprehensive, more immediate plan. Attempting to fight the battle on two fronts, Carter labored to keep the issue on the government's agenda. In May, 1977, he addressed the UAW and reiterated his support for NHI. "It is not difficult," he said, "to guess which union made NHI a national issue." He faced harsh criticism, however, when Senator Kennedy told the same convention that NHI had been left out of the administration's legislative program. [14]

In the early, crucial stages of planning, Carter had to decide how best to handle the dynamics of policy delegation. On one hand, health insurance fit neatly into HEW's purview. However, the consequences flowing from any program of national scope, especially health insurance, would cut across a variety of agencies and departments. Still, the bulk of policy formulation, as well as the task of assessing consequent implications, would be centered in HEW. Thus, Secretary Califano and his staff were given responsibility for developing the proposal, but with the understanding that the White House would monitor policy progress. A further reason for Carter's decision to delegate is most assuredly that he had pledged his allegiance to the concept of cabinet government. To have something as vitally important as NHI controlled from the White House would have violated both the spirit and letter of that advisory strategy. In light of all these factors, Carter directed Califano to lead the policy formulation process, but to report often to the DPS.

Early on, Carter experienced in-house dissension of a different sort than that described in previous chapters. Instead of having to deal with outside mavericks or battle departmental appointees, Carter had to contend with dissenters much closer to home (literally). The DPS tried to take control of the plan by stripping HEW of the control Carter had delegated to it. Memos circulated within the DPS indicate there was a perception that the HEW staff, Secretary Califano in particular, was not effectively presenting proposals. This is clearly consistent with a monitoring strategy, which suggests that its purpose is to utilize the expertise of civil servants but to be able to quickly identify problem areas. However, in this particular case the staff overstepped its bounds. In a memo to his WHS superiors, Peter Bourne wrote, "What is necessary is a tighter, direct control from the White House."[15] His request went unheeded, and nearly a year later President Carter reaffirmed his commitment to HEW by again directing Califano to formally prepare the proposals. Throughout this period the DPS monitored HEW's progress.[16]

Outreach

Theoretically, a president's active personal involvement in outreach and consulting during a delegated, staff-monitored policy process is necessarily more limited than in either the facilitated or directed strategies. The very fact that a particular policy is developed outside the White House indicates that much of the consulting that is done is carried out in and by the affected departments and agencies. But NHI was such a massive issue, penetrating a number of jurisdictions, that one could reasonably expect the president and his staff to have more personal input.[17] Such was not the case, however. For example, whereas Carter himself met with a number of groups in the mixed (staff-facilitated) and fully centralized (staff-directed) categories, he personally met with a comparatively small number of individuals involved with NHI, including only three high-ranking officials of major health insurance companies.[18]

Several prominent interest groups were consulted by task forces run from outside the White House, and ultimately enjoyed great influence in developing the plan. At a hearing on NHI, UAW president Douglas Fraser pushed for a plan modeled on the Canadian health program. Fraser argued that UAW members in Canada paid half the amount their American counterparts spent on health insurance.[19] Although not entirely clear, Califano's use of task force operatives was perhaps an attempt to "pad" his position in the manner of agency administrators when presenting their budgets to congressional authorizing committees. This strategy entails increasing or "padding" agency budget requests in an attempt to minimize losses in the appropriations process.[20] Califano thus assumed a position at the extreme end of the ideological spectrum by advocating the UAW's position so as to increase its chances of being favorably represented in a compromise version of the plan.

Congressional outreach efforts were handled by Califano's office, in most cases by the secretary himself. In May, 1978, Califano reported to the president that he had met extensively with key players in Congress, including Reps. Al Ullman, Dan Rostenkowski, James Corman, and Paul Rogers, as well as Sens. Russell Long, Herman Talmadge, Abraham Ribicoff, and Edward Kennedy. After listing each name, he attached a paragraph describing their current state of interest, the direction they were leaning, and the prospects for either changing a negative vote or maintaining support. At the end of the memo Califano identified each of them as extremely important to the administration's chances and recommended that Carter meet with them before announcing his set of principles. This was especially true for everyone *except* Kennedy, as each member had criticized the administration for overestimating the aggregate impact Kennedy would have on the legislative outcome, saying that the president had neglected other important players while concentrating his efforts on securing Kennedy's support.[21]

In retrospect, this may bolster the argument that Carter erred by assigning NHI development to the decentralized category. Critically placed members of Congress regarded NHI as a highly salient, high-impact issue. Had Carter been more personally involved, actively consulting with a broad array of congressional actors, it may have enhanced the possibilities for presidential success. Califano was clearly in charge of developing the policy proposal, but Carter probably erred in not developing a more extensive network of personal contacts regarding the legislation. National health insurance was extremely important to the president, and it is highly possible that although it was an issue of technical complexity, it might have benefited from having staff act as facilitator rather than as monitor. As to outreach, though, Califano consulted widely with members of Congress and interest groups as well as counseling Carter of the potential problems that accompanied the specter of an overly active president. Such activity at the personal level, burdened as it was by the declining capital of the Carter presidency, might have further impeded the proposal's chances in Congress.

Developing Principles

One of the first items of business in policy making is to settle on a set of principles describing the general goals and objectives that an administration desires for incorporation into the final policy proposal. Fidelity to these principles then guides the process of policy development.

In order to gain as much input in the development of principles, Califano had initially agreed to hold intrabranch meetings with affected agencies such as Treasury, the VA, Defense, Labor, Commerce, the CEA, OMB, and DPS. Califano had also agreed to provide the product of HEW's labor to OMB and the DPS in time to insure adequate analysis prior to presidential and interagency meetings.[22]

However, long before principles had been established, the president was having trouble controlling administrative resistance in forging NHI leadership. As several DPS members put it, "The spirit of detente with HEW seems to have broken down."[23] Several pitfalls plagued interagency coordination, which presumably would have led to a set of principles capable of gaining broad administration support. For example, although Undersecretary Hale Champion of HEW had agreed that the president would be briefed as to the contour of the policy, no such briefing was in the preparation stages, much less scheduled, even as the calendar turned to late September. Additionally, Champion had informed OMB's Sue Woolsey that the bureau could delegate a staff member to work full time with HEW's cost experts. However, Champion later withdrew his promise and allowed no such coordination between OMB and HEW. Finally, the following statement suggests that HEW took its role as lead agency to the extreme: "HEW has made clear to both Sue Woolsey and us that there will be no informal interchange between staffs, and that we will see nothing other than formal submissions to the President and other agencies."[24]

In the days and months following these events, the president was able to restore a degree of leadership by publicly asserting that while HEW was charged with taking the lead in developing NHI policy, the process was to be a cooperative venture in which other affected agencies would have direct input—especially with reference to how they would be affected by NHI, how their constituencies were likely to react, and so forth.

The early phases of policy development are often prone to obstacles, especially when the scope of policy is as broad as NHI promised to be. One indicator of this is that it was nearly fifteen months from the time Carter announced that NHI was an official presidential priority before principles were articulated. Other policies, whether successful or not, had been proposed, passed, and even implemented in the same time span. Finally, in July, 1978, the guiding principles were publicly announced by Califano, with DPS chief Stuart Eizenstat in attendance. The overarching theme was the desirability of having cost control elements as the functional basis for the health plan. Individual goals, still in abstract form, included quality health care, freedom of consumers to choose doctors and hospitals, "aggressive" cost containment that would be vehemently anti-inflationary, multiple-source financing, a significant role for private insurers with "appropriate" government regulations, and, finally, NHI was to be phased in rather than made immediately comprehensive at the time of its implementation.[25]

In order to facilitate the process of collecting, synthesizing, and disseminating the advice and information he had collected, Califano established the Secretary's Advisory Committee on National Health Issues (SACNHI). In late February the committee sent Undersecretary Champion a letter detailing its concerns regarding the substance of the deliberations to be carried out in formulating the principles. Their concerns included, among other things, the need to provide broad access to health care, the need for a universal health care system, universal eligibility, and to argue that comprehensive benefits should include preventive and primary care services. The committee held meetings in a variety of locations, including such divergent places as rural communities, youth centers, and state administrative offices.[26]

It was crucial for the principles to be firm, but with some degree of flexibility, so that Carter could position himself to offer a viable alternative to Kennedy's plan, which he was in the process of developing and promoting in the Congress and around the country. However, in a memo commenting on these principles, DPS member Joe Onek observed that the spirit of the principles did not go far enough, nor were they specific enough in general substantive areas (e.g., benefits, phasing requirements, co-payments, and the "leanness" of the benefit package) in order to distinguish the administration's plan from the Kennedy proposal.[27] These concerns proved prescient when Kennedy and the labor constituency, especially AFL-CIO boss George Meany, objected immediately after the public announcement of the administration's NHI principles. At the same time critics were distinguishing *their* plan from the administration's, they berated Carter for his lack of leadership on the issue.[28]

Yet another problem area that promised to directly impact the proposals derivative of the principles was the fact that NHI might run into the same trouble that had hindered welfare reform and Energy I, namely it lacked an identifiable and mobilized constituency. This became abundantly clear when Rep. Dan Rostenkowsi (D-Illinois), chairman of the House Ways and Means Subcommittee on Health, asked to identify where the constituency for NHI was, said flatly, "I don't see it."[29]

Ironically, in November the administration received a much-needed boost from HEW. In his efforts to develop principles, Califano and HEW experts were quite active in bringing together as many divergent views as possible. In so doing, they labored to integrate policy and political concerns. Not only did the department consult with affected interest groups, it conducted information-gathering meetings with the general public outside the Beltway. "We have . . . sought to incorporate into our decision making," Califano wrote the president, "lessons to be learned from our experience with health care financing both in this country and abroad."[30]

The activities to which Califano referred included soliciting the views of all members of Congress, governors, mayors of the larger cities, other state and local health officials, and more than two thousand experts and organizations with knowledge of NHI. By November the department had conducted more than a hundred regional hearings, including at least one in each state, in order to obtain advisory input from organizations and interested citizens throughout the country. In addition, an Advisory Committee on National Health Insurance Issues, established under the chairmanship of Undersecretary Hale Champion, had been operating since April, also exploring a range of NHI issues. The committee, composed of individuals from business, labor, consumer groups, the health industry, and state and local governments, held public hearings and made site visits to underserved communities. Finally, Califano had traveled to Canada in September to assess the problem of NHI in comparative perspective, and to gain ideas from the Canadian system. He later made similar trips to Britain and Germany.[31]

There is little doubt, then, that HEW was extremely active in the development of NHI policy. However, the degree to which this aggressive leadership lent itself to a smooth, coordinated process is debatable. Relations among the actors involved were surely strained, due in no small measure to HEW's initially dictatorial management of the process.[32] Theoretically, even when such situations are eased, there are lingering questions as to the degree to which advisory input from affected actors is legitimately heeded. I see this as an innate problem of the delegated strategy.[33] The delegated agent will sometimes ignore the advice of other agencies or presidential advisers when formulating either principles or proposals. And, as we saw in the strategy of using staff as director, communication flows can break down, depriving the president and the policy process of needed policy or political information. In the initial stages, at least, this appears to have been the case with NHI. The HEW staff shut out affected groups and departments, although it eventually opened up lines of communication when it came under pressure from the White House to do so.

Developing Proposals

In early 1978 Eizenstat recommended that the Presidential Review Memorandum process be implemented in order to develop the substantive NHI proposals. The PRM process originated under Henry Kissinger when he was Nixon's national security adviser. The process entailed canvassing various departments and agencies, requiring each unit to submit working drafts of policy proposals. These would be written and rewritten a number of times until Kissinger was satisfied as to the direction and content of the particular policy being considered. A similar process was implemented in the Carter White House, but it was not confined to national security policy. Having such a process in place increases the probability of successfully collecting and synthesizing policy expertise and advice. In the case of NHI, Eizenstat felt that the policy area would be ideal for the process, but emphasized that HEW would be the lead agency responsible for policy development rather than agents within the White House. Carter approved the implementation of the PRM process.[34] The purpose, as DPS members put it, was to "assure that when there are issues affecting many agencies, all agencies have an opportunity to present their views and influence the President's decision."[35]

Eizenstat announced the details of the process to the secretaries and administrators of the various departments and agencies on February 6. He reiterated that HEW would be the lead agency and that HEW would also chair the Domestic Policy Review committee staffed by the heads of the various agencies. In addition, he required every department and agency to appoint at least one staff member to serve as a point of contact HEW could consult directly for information regarding any concerns that might crop up.[36] This arrangement is significant for our purposes because it marks a rather sharp break with precedent. Other Domestic Policy Review committees were normally chaired by either the DPS or some organizational entity ostensibly outside of the formal bureaucratic structure.[37] In this case a department was given the explicit power to chair the committee. This is further evidence of the administration's commitment to let NHI be formulated outside of the White House, supporting the impressions of using staff to monitor the process from a decidedly reactive position. Instead of requiring agencies to send working drafts of policy proposals to the DPS or others in the White House, drafts were to be sent directly to HEW. Califano and his staff would then determine how best to use the various types of policy information collected from agencies and departments, eventually integrating that information with the president's political concerns.

The thorn that continually plagued Carter was the steady decline of copartisans who supported his position on NHI. The decline was most likely accounted for by the lack of a mobilized constituency, whether in the country or inside the government. Furthermore, whatever momentum could be gained from NHI was preempted by Kennedy, who had rekindled his career-long partnership with labor and joined with it to craft an alternative NHI proposal. During the course of policy development, several problems emerged as HEW was developing the administration's plan. Many of the specific suggestions put forth in the Kennedy/Labor (K/L) plan were politically more palatable for members of Congress than suggestions in the administration's plan. For example, the K/L plan insisted there be no patient cost sharing but compromised by acceding to small co-payments. Costs were to be assessed to employers through a mandated system, and a nonrestricted benefits package was to be implemented. The administration, on the other hand, sought to protect political interests favorable to business by not requiring employers to carry the cost for high-risk employees, instead mandating only that they pay premiums for their own employees (i.e., an "experience rated premium") as opposed to paying premiums for other people in society (i.e., "community rates premium").[38] Still, it was obvious that the political strength accruing to an NHI bill and the different types of proposals being offered targeted different constituencies. Kennedy courted Democratic groups who felt that the president had abandoned them. Their perception was that Carter was deserting them by seeking out a moderate or conservative course they felt was more favorable to business than labor interests.

On May 24, 1978, a meeting was held that included the principal actors in the NHI process, including representatives of the K/L proposal. In a memo summarizing the meeting, DPS member Joe Onek provided Eizenstat with an ultimately balanced and thorough analysis of the differences between the two proposals, and a description of labor's flip-flop. Labor constituencies had shifted their support for a public plan to a private one. The following excerpts illustrate the problems, as well as the options facing the White House staff, in trying to monitor progress on a large-program delegated to an external actor:

> [The] meeting illuminated the issues on a large public plan vs. an all private plan. Kennedy/labor believes that a separate public plan for the power and the elderly will deteriorate into a two-class system. I believe that they agree that technically it is possible to eliminate the two-class system danger by legislating uniform

reimbursement, etc. Their fear is that politically there will be constant pressure to reduce the support of the public plan. The only way to prevent this, they believe, is to have the public plan include significant numbers of non-poor, elderly Americans.

HEW is perfectly willing to have the public plan include significant numbers of the non-poor and non-elderly, for two reasons. First, to reduce the danger of a two-class system and second, to increase leverage over private insurance by making the public plan an attractive alternative for many non-poor.

Needless to say, the insurance industry will oppose any public plan which could attract many of their actual or potential customers. The insurance companies fear that the government will provide substantial general revenue subsidies to the public plan and thereby compete unfairly. . . .

[L]abor's all-private position appears to be an 180 [degree] flip from their previous position. It is possible that they will modify their stand somewhat when we discuss the form which a private plan will take, including such issues as community vs. experience rating.[39]

The above analysis shows that the DPS kept a watchful eye on processes going on outside of the White House, even though the plan had been delegated to HEW. Although HEW unquestionably maintained authority, the thinking going on in the White House sought to mix policy and political imperatives at the proposal stage. Califano was doing the same, while suboptimizing the president's political agenda.

The final problem the administration encountered centered around inflationary concerns and the voter disquiet Califano believed would accompany the proposals as they stood, which he felt would exacerbate the problems of inflation and fiscal shortages. One of the major principles of the policy held that it would not place undue stress on the economy, which would then create upward pressure on prices. Califano had stressed that as the proposals stood in late June, 1978, they would create precisely the inflationary circumstances the president desired to avoid. To avert these conditions Califano proposed holding off on announcing the plan at least until fall. In the following memo to Carter, which was designed to brief the president on his upcoming meeting with Kennedy, Califano played the dual roles of policy adviser and political analyst:

The combination of inflation and taxpayer disquiet means that the NHI issue will be hurt if baldly presented in the present climate. . . . Although you personally believe deeply in the

comprehensive approach, you too could suffer adverse consequences if you go forward with unqualified support for such an
approach at this time. . . .We all must acknowledge—by putting
the tentative plan off until fall—that this is simply not the right
time to air the issue. We risk repudiation of the issue by candidates in the fall, given the present mood. . . . The debate needs to
be focused on the intolerable costs and failings of the present
health care system. . . . Organized labor and . . . Kennedy should
work closely with HEW in making the economic and budgetary
case for a broad NHI plan. . . . You are under tremendous pressure to abandon NHI or to accept a targeted approach. You will
stick with the broad approach—but you will only do it in this
manner.

Califano ended the memo with the punch line, "This approach should
effectively send the issue back to HEW for from 8 to 10 months."[40] The
analysis, punctuated by the last line, was consistent with Califano's overall
concern, shared by other administration officials, that the plan should not
be put forward in its present form. The timetable originally proposed was
slipping. Anecdotal evidence indicates that most of the principal operatives hoped to delay the public announcement of a plan, basing their ap-
prehension on lingering questions as to the plan's financial viability. In addition, there was quite a bit of hand wringing over the administration's
reputation, both within and outside the Beltway. There were already in-
dications that Carter had overloaded his policy plate, and the ordeals of
energy and welfare reform had fueled a widespread perception that the
administration was politically amateurish. The last thing the president
needed was to expend large amounts of political capital on a policy that
would most likely prove to be too expensive, enjoy no committed congressional constituency, and cost the administration more in political goodwill
than waiting would.[41]

Compounding the already considerable problems, speculation arose as
to the extent that Califano, acting as the delegated agent on NHI, would
go beyond the policy limits Carter wanted. In a memo to Vice President
Mondale, Eizenstat raised concerns about Califano's political savvy: "We
should not end up with a strategy in which we have no friends—neither
Kennedy and labor on the left nor Long, Ribicoff, and others on the right.
I also agree that Secretary Califano would be a major problem here since
he remains committed to have a very comprehensive package with all types
of fancy trigger mechanisms. This would be a mistake now that Kennedy
has made a break with us on this issue. We can never satisfy him and can
only drive away support for the type of approach (Richard Moe) is talking

about."[42] Eizenstat finished the memo by recommending that a meeting with the principal actors (i.e., Califano, Mondale, Eizenstat, Hamilton Jordan, and Moe) be held in order to try and "steer Califano in the right direction on this issue."[43]

The concerns discussed regarding Califano's handling of the issue as the administration's delegated agent raise interesting questions regarding employment of the strategy of staff as policy monitor. Without question it raises the rather apparent necessity of inspiring administration loyalty in the delegated agent. A related issue, from an advice as investment perspective, illustrates the emerging incentives and changing preferences inherent in choosing to delegate, and the prospective trade-offs, cast in cost-benefit terms, of using the White House too loosely. By definition, the strategy of staff as monitor makes fewer demands on staff resources than the other strategies discussed in this book. But it does not, or should not, imply that the White House can be largely aloof. The analysis in the memo just cited brings that point into specific relief. By keeping policy development firmly in the hands of HEW, the White House began to lose control and ran the risk that the department would enter into coalitions with objectives counter to the president's. Using the staff as a monitor has its advantages both in terms of policy and politics, but by definition it is most susceptible to losing much needed political ground, as the NHI story has thus far suggested.

With concerns such as these tied to the political and policy stakes they implied, the balance between policy competence and responsiveness was crucial to the advancement of NHI. Political considerations such as the need to appease Democratic constituencies as well as business and employer interests took precedence over other matters. But policy stakes were high as well and included the necessity of fashioning a feasible plan that was both cost effective and would carry the desired impact.

Policy Competence and Responsiveness: A Closer Look
The staff-shift framework, drawing on the notion of advice as investment, suggests that in an advisory strategy in which a delegated agent is responsible for the bulk of policy development pursuant to monitoring parameters constructed by the White House, policy competence takes precedence over (but certainly does not quash) responsiveness. Indeed, to expect otherwise would cause one to ask, "Why delegate at all?" This strategy in and of itself connotes the pursuit of policy competence as James Fesler proposed.[44] We will now consider the means by which policy competence was sought, or not sought, and the trade-off between policy and political information as it was played out in the case of NHI.

As has been shown, Secretary Califano, acting as the White House's delegated agent for NHI policy development, gave at least cursory attention to policy as both political and policy analyst. However, these distinctions broke down, and the task of synthesizing policy was best performed by the DPS, breaching and ultimately extending beyond the monitoring role it was originally assigned in the initial phases of policy strategy. On the surface, this seems like a paradox because the DPS is, first and foremost, a White House support organization. But it should be remembered that the DPS engaged a *synthesizing* role, along with HEW. Although the delegated strategy was certainly in effect, this organizational role lends credence to the proposition that a strong and effective White House role is necessary regardless of the location of policy formation, and is therefore consistent with the pattern of policy centralization in the presidency.

Unlike in some of the cases described in this book (e.g., creation of the Department of Education, Energy I, and welfare reform), the DPS was actively ensconced in its role (in this case, monitoring) from the beginning. The major difference from the other cases is that in the monitoring strategy it was active initially in order to keep NHI *out* of the White House. Given its ethos as responsive to the president's goals, the DPS relied heavily on its political savvy to save the plan from excessive scrutiny that might have killed it before it ever had a chance to be even discussed. For example, Peter Bourne suggested to Hamilton Jordan that the administration establish a formal link with Kennedy and his forces in order to portray a united front when it came to presenting NHI. But Eizenstat recommended against such action on grounds that to do so would violate political sensitivity. The following excerpt shows the degree to which staff operatives worked to maintain responsiveness to the president's objectives:

> *It would pull a sensitive issue into the White House at an early stage.*
> Discussions such as Peter describes would immediately be known,
> and undercut both Joe Califano's credibility and his ability to
> serve as a buffer. . . . *Kennedy is not the only key member of Congress
> on this issue, and the others will be offended.* A number of the other
> key actors—such as Senator Long, Senator Talmadge, Representatives Ullman and Rostenkowski—will be equally or more important. . . . Kennedy is likely to represent the labor-liberal coalition in the ongoing NHI debate—and to preserve differences
> with the Administration until late in the game. . . . However,
> we tend to doubt that he will criticize us again on the *timing* of
> our proposals, since the President and Califano have said our
> proposals will be out early next year.[45]

Eizenstat strongly argued against bringing NHI into the White House, opting instead to use Califano and HEW as go-betweens with congressional leaders and, more important, continue to use the staff for monitoring purposes, steering clear of sensitive issues, which would, in turn, allow Califano to maintain credibility by acting as the White House's delegated agent.

As the above memo suggests, responsiveness, as always, was the central task of the agents located within the White House. In May, 1978, Califano advised the president on the relative merits of adopting a targeted approach as opposed to a broader one. Califano, who himself had recommended a broad plan, divided his analysis into several subheadings. These included previous presidential commitments, health system considerations, economic and budgetary considerations, and political considerations, as well as an analysis on the timing of the proposals. The timing section cautioned in favor of proceeding incrementally and for waiting until autumn to put forth the tentative HEW plan. Each point in his analysis strongly reiterated why a broad approach was, in his opinion, the most prudent course for the administration to follow.[46] The next day, CEA chairman Charles Schultze and OMB director James McIntyre blasted Califano's analysis on both political and substantive grounds. They attacked several perceived problems, including what they considered to be Califano's naivete concerning the plan's true impact, the inadequacy of the various counting methods proposed, and the mathematical calculations of the program estimates, upon which Califano's analysis was based. Indeed, they went so far as to propose that the administration reject NHI altogether on the grounds that it was too costly (which it did some two years later).[47]

This is an example, then, of the different modes of analysis that lie at the heart of the policy competence–responsiveness debate. One interesting twist is that an administration department head was offering explicitly political advice while engaging in policy substance. This particular case is not so surprising given that the secretary was Califano, a politically shrewd and experienced individual. Still, he was challenged by White House operatives representing entities such as the CEA and OMB, both of which are traditionally linked to technical expertise.[48]

The problem of classifying policy competence and responsiveness lies in where to look for advisory sources. In the classic theoretical sense, policy competence should come from bureaucrats and responsiveness from within the WHS or the EOP. But this is problematic when analyzing administrations such as Carter's. Califano, a shrewd political tactician who served on President Johnson's White House staff, was in the habit of attaching political advice along with substantive analysis in an attempt to attain the higher form of policy competence. This higher form is at least partially, if not mostly, defined as the ability of the advisor to combine substantive expertise with political assessment.[49] Sometimes that advice was heeded. Other times, Califano's particular political stance, which often shone through in his memoranda, was discounted by the WHS. Joe Onek, writing to Eizenstat, expressed reservations about the character and accuracy of Califano's advice:

> HEW is likely to continue to insist that its tentative plan . . . be a comprehensive one. HEW's position appears to be that neither a comprehensive plan nor a Phase I plan is likely to pass next session and that for political reasons it is best to leave open the option of a comprehensive plan. HEW also believes that a Phase I program consisting largely of catastrophic benefits is programmatically wrong . . . We believe, by contrast, that a Phase I package could pass and that, particularly if we are successful in our hospital cost containment efforts, a catastrophic program is not programmatically objectionable. We note that over half of all Americans already have catastrophic coverage and that many others incur catastrophic expenses but are unable to pay them. Therefore, catastrophic insurance should not lead to a dramatic increase in hospital expenditures for catastrophic programs. Finally, it is widely conceded that even under a comprehensive plan, catastrophic benefits would be phased in first because of their political appeal.[50]

In order to clarify the above point further, consider the following example. Internal memos from late in the development stage support withdrawing the national health plan in general and NHI in particular because the administration would "look at best a little stupid" for arguing for a $17 billion increase in spending when it had announced only a week before that it would take unprecedented actions to decrease federal expenditures. This analysis combined substance and estimated policy impact, counseling the president to let Kennedy take the blame for pushing an inflationary program rather than let the inevitable criticisms descend on Carter.[51] Substantively, pursuing the president's NHI proposal would not have promoted a credible public goods philosophy because of the virtual impossibility of enacting such a broad plan, to say nothing of the potentially devastating effects on the economy if it was implemented. Politically, to withdraw the plan and let Kennedy draw fire for hurting an already sagging economy would have been beneficial to the president's political goals. In this case at least, substantive information emanating from the White House could be considered both responsive and substantively competent, based as it was on estimates of the plan's fiscal impact. It is not new, of course, to note that White House operatives are capable of and expected to provide sound policy advice. Indeed, the CEA and OMB were set up for just that purpose, although the degree to which they are faithful to their appointed endeavors is the source of some debate.[52] The Carter DPS, made up as it was of generalists, was able to bridge both, acting as either an honest broker or policy advocate, depending on how Carter chose to use it.

Analysis of the DPS Role

Perhaps the most surprising thing to note about the monitoring strategy is just how much activity is undertaken by the DPS and how much work is involved even within a framework that relegates the staff to a reactive role. Its first responsibility was to provide the president with a synthesis of policy and political advice while remaining sensitive to presidential inter-ests both substantive and political. The staff-shift framework employed throughout this book suggests that the DPS would play an active role in keeping the delegated agents in line with the president's broad program-matic goals. The role of the staff was different in degree and kind than in other strategies described in previous chapters, but the level of activity was hardly passive.

The DPS kept the president informed of both lingering and potential problems in Congress. Primary responsibility fell to staff members Jim Mongan, Joe Onek, and Peter Bourne. On the policy side, immediate concerns included controlling hospital costs and the persistent lack of physician fee guidelines. Political dimensions focused on the differences between the administration's proposals and Kennedy's, Carter's public posture, and the need to keep in close touch with key congressional mem-bers, especially Senators Long and Ribicoff.

A sort of comprehensive responsiveness was fashioned around the political and policy dimensions, the core of which can be clearly seen in a background memo from Peter Bourne to Eizenstat and Joe Onek. The memo relates the analysis to Carter's previously taken public positions:

> [Citing public documents from the 1976 campaign] The Presi-dent clearly committed himself to using the national health in-surance plan to encourage needed reforms in the health care system. . . . *Resource development cannot be separated out from financ-ing.* . . . Recent experience suggests that the trend toward physi-cian specialization can partially be reversed by exposing medi-cal students to patient care in preceptorship programs. . . . We agree that it may well be more appropriate to fund long term

care services through a grant program rather than have them included as a benefit under NHI. I believe that prevention efforts are a key to eventual long term cost reduction. . . . I suspect that the cost of administering cost-sharing mechanisms would exceed the revenues to the system. The President is on record favoring the use of NHI as a tool to influence the supply of physician and other health care services. We reiterate our point that resource development cannot be segregated from financing.[53]

The political imperatives, coupled with policy content analysis, are clearly laid out and in turn suggest only one course of possible action: the need to forge ahead given the level of campaign commitments, but within a balanced fiscal approach to physician and resource development. By late December, 1977, this comprehensive responsiveness had become institutionalized in internal DPS memoranda regarding NHI. The following is an example of the identification and analysis of political and substantive proposals, with a hint of policy advocacy on the part of the DPS:

Peter (Bourne) may well be right that no NHI proposal can pass without the support of the UAW and organized labor generally. Most of the other interest groups, although may have introduced NHI proposals, are happiest with the status quo and would not really push our any NHI legislation. Peter is almost certainly wrong, however, that opposition to NHI is inelastic. A Kennedy-Corman type bill will be far more strongly opposed by business and insurance companies, as well as by organized medicine, than alternative proposals. In addition, it is probably incompatible with the Congress' present anti-regulatory, anti-government mood. . . . Now for the bad news. Beyond the political uncertainty there is wide disagreement on what the substance of a NHI plan should be. Peter says we should "accept a plan that is relatively comprehensive, and inevitably quite similar to the Kennedy-Corman bill." There is not much dispute about the need to phase-in comprehensive benefits. There is enormous dispute on how to achieve a less costly, more efficient health delivery system. The premise of Kennedy-Corman is that federal financing and administration is the only answer. Kennedy-Corman reduces the incentive for business, labor, state governments, etc., to care about delivery system reform. Many experts (e.g. Schultze . . .) doubt the efficacy of federal regulation and would prefer greater involvement of the private sector and greater reliance on market mechanisms.[54]

As the memo implies, if the administration were to achieve programmatic success, it would have to secure private-sector support linked to the
"market mechanisms." Included in this categorization was organized labor, which had played a significant role in Carter's election. As such, the
administration could not afford to neglect labor's input on a measure of
such immense size and potential impact. When preparing the president
for a meeting with UAW president Douglas Fraser, Eizenstat's analysis of
advisory streams was based on the timing of the program, and he conve-
niently divided his analysis into factors affecting politics and those that
were primarily substantive. Some brief examples from the background
memo follow:

> *Substance*. Labor has traditionally called for a NHI plan funded
> entirely by general revenues and payroll taxes. However, reac-
> tion to the rise in social security must therefore look carefully
> at the possibility of using private insurance premiums for our
> NHI plan. . . . This may necessitate a significant role for private
> health insurance companies. In addition, the UAW has tradition-
> ally opposed any patient cost-sharing for covered services. But
> as Secretary Califano's NHI memorandum to you indicated,
> even modest cost-sharing can reduce the budget costs of NHI
> by almost $20 billion. DPS, HEW staff, and Senator Kennedy
> have been meeting with UAW officials and other labor leaders.
> The response suggests that labor's flexibility on these issues is
> growing.

> *Politics*. While the Administration remains committed to the
> broad NHI concepts you announced during the campaign, we
> have been making it clear that we are ultimately committed to
> introducing the best passable bill we can. We have been stress-
> ing that even if the Administration, labor, Senator Kennedy, and
> other strong Congressional supporters of NHI are in agreement
> on the NHI bill submitted, securing passage will still be ex-
> tremely difficult. If labor is not supportive of our package, passage
> will be impossible from the start, probably ending the chance for
> NHI for a generation. You might stress the importance of labor
> flexibility on NHI (on the need for which Fraser agrees, we be-
> lieve). You might point out that the situation is analogous to labor
> law reform, in which compromise in advance of introduction was
> necessary to diffuse congressional antipathy and to enhance the
> effectiveness of the President's support.[55]

Even in this subdivision schema, references to politics and substance could not be maintained in isolation from one another. Political imperatives were informed by substantive necessities, while the substantive section was littered with references to important political groups, such as labor. In light of the DPS endeavor to comprehensive responsiveness, its priority was the president's political well-being. Several memos indicate the need to offer various types of policy in order to fulfill political obligations and campaign pledges:[56] a defensive strategy to protect the administration when Kennedy released his bill, which constituted a "breakthrough" for labor,[57] and providing another point of view to balance information coming in from HEW.[58] The DPS kept up its role throughout the duration of the development process. For example, it addressed the importance of offering Phase I legislation rather than a comprehensive plan because of the political climate (i.e., it would not pass) and the possibility that others in the Congress (such as Senator Long) might opportunistically step in and introduce similar legislation, thus taking credit for it while denying the president any political benefits that might otherwise have been his.[59]

In yet another example, we encounter the DPS playing the role of synthesizer. At the time NHI was proposed there was a need to increase expenditures for the Environmental Protection Agency and the Occupational Safety and Health Administration, along with other regulatory agencies. Analyzing the broad impact of this strategy in an internal DPS memorandum, the following appraisal was offered: "This suggestion may have political as well as substantive advantages. It may appease liberals and labor, who feel we are not spending enough federal dollars on NHI, if we spend some of the money we've saved on environmental or OSHA projects dear to their hearts. Of course, we do not want to throw money into environmental protection or occupational safety before we are ready to spend it wisely. Therefore, if we decide to present the American people with a broader national health policy, we need to make a careful assessment of where increased expenditures in the environment, occupation, and related areas are really justified, and we need to do so on the same time table as NHI."[60]

Eizenstat wrote in the margin: "I agree but time is short—urge that we not publicly commit to more [dollars] for prevention ti'l we see the options."[61]

In the end, NHI failed. Like all policies in this study, its failure cannot be attributed solely to advisory problems. Neither the economy nor the polity was ready for it. The financial costs were too high, and the amount of political capital that would have to be spent to secure some type of program was simply too great. Other more pressing issues commanded the government's attention, including the state of the economy and the Iranian hostage crisis. Thus, with the presidential campaign in full swing, the administration abandoned NHI in mid-1980.[62] External considerations predominated, but advisory strategies were suspect, not the least of which is the real possibility (illuminated by the clarity hindsight provides) that perhaps NHI would have fared better had it been assigned to the staff-as-facilitator strategy.

Given the problems of NHI and the administration's failure to recognize the political futility of pushing too hard in the face of stalwart opposition, another major policy, civil service reform, faced problems similar to those encountered in the NHI process. It too lacked a clear and mobilized constituency. Still, it was largely successful in spite of these problems.

SUCCESSFUL STAFF MONITORING: CIVIL SERVICE REFORM

The details of early bureaucratic reform are well known to students of the American executive branch. Andrew Jackson begat the political spoils system, which was characterized by patronage and graft and was viewed by many as the corrupting influence of partisan politics. Reform attempts were discussed but rarely if ever acted upon. Finally, the reform movement found an unlikely opportunity for change with the assassination of Pres. James A. Garfield. Using the assassination as a leverage point, given that the president's killer was a disillusioned and disappointed office seeker, reformers mounted an ultimately successful campaign to replace the spoils system with one based on merit. The Pendleton Act of 1883, which was a direct response to the perceived evils of a corrupt, patronage-based bureaucracy, has long been cited as the beginning of modern public administration. The purpose of the act was to link all civil service jobs, both acquisition and promotion, to merit-based rather than partisan-based criteria. As a consequence both of design and circumstance, the act afforded government employees virtual lifetime job security. The intent of the merit system was clear. It was to make government service an attractive career option, which would in turn give rise to recruitment and retention of highly qualified applicants into the career civil service. The federal executive branch, then, would become a bastion of competence in the finest tradition of modern public administration theory advanced at that time, with its emphasis on rationality, efficiency, and hierarchy.[63] But critics of the act claimed just the opposite. Where reformers expected to see a Weberian, ideal-type system based on expertise, efficiency, advancement based on merit, and a specialized division of labor, critics envisioned mediocrity, inefficiency, tedious and arbitrary rules and regulations, and a system incapable of handling its governmental burden in a coherent fashion.[64]

Although the critics may have exaggerated their case by generalizing to the greater population based on a few cases, their basic claims, whether true or not, were given credence in public circles. Ever since then, attacks on the bureaucracy and bureaucrats have been a favorite rhetorical tactic of politicians.[65] Public perception held that government employees were incompetent, lazy, or both, and that they could hold onto their jobs as long as they desired because of the difficulty of terminating their employment. In addition, appraisal systems were incomplete, and advancement could be attained without convincing evidence of merit independent of longevity of employment, which was all but guaranteed by the structural constraints of the federal bureaucracy.

Reorganization of the federal bureaucracy was often pursued as a means by which public officials could achieve greater governmental rationality and efficiency by making bureaucrats more accountable to those they served. With the creation of the Keep Commission in 1905, Theodore Roosevelt became the first president to lead the reform effort. In 1932, Congress gave Herbert Hoover authority to reorganize the executive branch. This authority meant that the president could take whatever action he deemed necessary or appropriate, and would be binding within sixty days of the reorganization mandate unless either chamber of Congress disapproved. In 1937, Franklin Roosevelt asked Congress to renew presidential reorganization authority, and the President's Committee on Executive Management, better known as the Brownlow Committee, was born. Several other commissions have been used to meet the needs of presidential reorganization, including the first and second Hoover Commissions (the first under the Truman administration, the second under Eisenhower), the President's Task Force on Governmental Administration in the Johnson presidency (known as the Seidman Commission), the Ash Council under President Nixon, and most recently the National Performance Review, part of the Reinventing Government movement spearheaded by the Clinton administration.[66] Given the history of reform efforts to that time, executive reorganization and civil service reform were not novel ideas in the mid-1970s. Such was the historical context that Jimmy Carter, as a candidate for the presidency, decided to address the issue in his quest to capitalize on what was a general disaffection with bureaucracy and politics as usual in Washington.

Carter attained the presidency by portraying himself as a political outsider untainted by Washington's corrupting forces.[67] When he was governor of Georgia, he had reformed that state's bureaucracy. Indeed, during the 1970s, many states were reorganizing their executive branches.[68] During his 1976 presidential campaign Carter strongly advocated a commitment to reorganization and reform of the federal bureaucracy. Later, in his 1978 State of the Union message, he again addressed the issue, this time as president. He called civil service reform "absolutely vital" to a "government that is efficient, open, and truly trustworthy of our people's understanding and respect . . . civil service reform will be the centerpiece of government reorganization during my term of office."[69]

Although his predecessors' reorganization efforts had met with mixed success, there was good reason for Carter to take interest in the reorganization of the government's bureaucratic structure. Public opinion in 1978 reflected a distinctly antigovernment mood, punctuated by a high level of distrust in America's political institutions. In 1964, 47 percent of the American people said they thought government wasted a lot of money. That number soared to 78 percent by 1978—most likely due to the lingering experience with governmental abuses propagated during Watergate. Polls conducted in 1978 also showed that just 10 percent of Americans believed the government was free of corruption, and that only 18 percent thought the "best" people were in government. Less than a quarter of the public felt that people in government placed the good of the country above that of special-interest groups, and only 24 percent believed the government would be an exciting place to work. Attitude surveys of federal managers revealed that they were themselves disillusioned about how well the system worked.[70]

It thus was clear that government reform would not be an unpopular endeavor. However, it was not clear that it would be a *politically* popular issue in the conventional sense of the term. While civil service reform may have been the right thing to do, it was not likely to gain and hold a great deal of public interest. It should be noted that there is a distinction between public support and public interest. An issue may have latent or tacit appeal that might hold some promise for a general sense of public satisfaction. I define this as public *support*. Public *interest* is more consistent with broadly based and possibly conflictual appeal. It involves issues that pique the public's interest and may, at least for some constituency or group, hold immediate potential for political reward for policy makers (i.e., electoral payoffs for those involved in the process, such as members of Congress and the president). In light of this, it would be hard for the White House to generate congressional enthusiasm for broad civil service reform as the issue held no perceptible electoral benefits for either Congress or the president.[71] This is not to suggest that the Carter administration considered it impossible to garner the requisite congressional votes once the bill got to the final stages. On the contrary, many expected the effort to clean up government to enjoy popular support (if not generate public fervor). The most likely thing to cause the greatest number of political headaches was the daunting effort that would be required to get the issue on the public agenda in the first place, given the lack of tangible benefits attached to spearheading reform. Like NHI, there was no discernible constituency that could be mobilized for reform of the civil service based on positive calculations for accruing political advantage. There was little doubt that the entire country would benefit from reform, but that did not itself offer an immediately clear and perceptible way to navigate a path from principles to proposals and finally to the passed legislation. Furthermore, since the benefits of reform would be dispersed and its costs concentrated, those groups that would bear the lion's share of the costs, such as government unions and powerful veterans groups, would have an incentive to mobilize against civil service reform. Conversely, the distributed nature of reform benefits promised to erect considerable collective action problems, presenting reform supporters with difficult obstacles to overcome in organizing and mobilizing.

Yet another problem lay in organizational reform. The president sought to abolish a ninety-five-year-old agency, the Civil Service Commission (CSC), "one identified with the principle of merit instead of spoils, and making drastic changes in long established personnel policies."[72] Indeed, many of Carter's proposals were not new. Several integral elements of civil service reform had been proposed before. Also, the recent and lingering political lessons were anything but discrete. In the aftermath of the Nixon years, it was commonly thought that agency managers should have limited discretion. There was a strong suspicion of White House and agency management systems given the perception that the White House had become a fortress of the "imperial" or "administrative" presidency. Career civil servants were several layers beneath the top levels of departments and agencies and, where possible, had been replaced with partisan appointees.[73] The Eisenhower and Nixon administrations both introduced plans similar to what would later become the Senior Executive Service, and earlier efforts to disperse personnel functions by splitting the Civil Service Commission into two agencies had failed. It was commonly held that employee groups and trade unions had enough political influence to block such attempts in Congress. In the event this failed, there was a contingent recommendation to curtail or eliminate veterans preference, which would likely kill the bill by itself.[74]

In retrospect, it is clear that the political environment in the early stages of civil service reform did not hold much promise for successful policy enactment, even though it was hardly an unpopular issue. However, Carter's commitment to its core provisions, coupled with the possibility of influencing a seemingly predisposed public to lend support to the initiative, compelled the administration to try.

Erwin Hargrove asserts that President Carter's political experiences and worldview suggest a strong desire to achieve broad and systemic change in the form of public goods, which are geared to no specific constituency but whose benefits can be shared by all.[75] Civil service reform fits easily within the parameters of this definition. Hargrove also notes that "Carter sought to achieve public goods in the form of comprehensive programs through political appeals to diffuse goals rather than to specific interests and coalitions, and he developed such programs in a decision-making process that placed the highest priority on study and collegiality. . . . [Thus] he sought a combination of new and old elements that would bring broad approval."[76]

Regardless of the political implications or lack thereof, Carter pushed civil service reform, and in doing so provided the nation with more competent governing institutions. As a consequence, he devoted time and energy, two important components of political capital, to ensuring successful policy making and passage of civil service reform legislation.[77]

Still, the environment was at best an unsure one in which to risk such innovations. Innovations, as Nelson Polsby reminds us, have "institutional or societal effects that are, in a sense, lasting."[78] In short, they have a history. This is especially true of what he calls "incubative" policies. Policy incubations are those that have developed over time and around which no enduring consensus develops.[79] Yet Carter chose to move in the direction of comprehensive reform, and he and his staff developed, through the efforts of ad hoc task forces, a set of proposals that he eventually sent to Congress.

Outreach: Groups and Task Forces

As is the case with many of the cases analyzed in this book, Jimmy Carter's introduction of policy areas for public consumption show up in the rhetoric and strategies of the 1976 presidential campaign. During the campaign, Carter strongly urged the reorganization of the executive branch for the purpose of instilling economy and efficiency in the government. He argued that the civil service system was mostly effective, but that it could be improved upon. The upshot of the proposed system would be to rationalize hiring and firing functions by making it easier to dismiss employees for incompetence or insubordination. After his election, civil service reform continued to be an important, if not politically rewarding, focus of his administration. In March, 1978, the president sent Congress a nine-point package that included detailed proposals calling for replacing the CSC with an Office of Personnel Management (OPM) answering directly to the president and subject to executive oversight by a Merit Systems Protection Board (MSPB). The objective was to split the CSC into two parts, separating out the agency's conflicting roles as personnel manager on one hand and protector of employee rights on the other. The bill also provided for, among other things, continued veterans preference in hiring, whistle-blower protection, employee appeal rights, a Senior Executive Service (SES), merit pay, and guidelines for labor-management relations.[80]

Of the several innovations pursued was the creation of the SES. The SES proposal affected only high-ranking civil service managers above General Schedule grade fifteen and below Level III of the Executive Schedule. No more than 10 percent of the entire civil service was to be admitted to the SES, and those who were would be mobile. That is, they could be placed in any agency or department depending on the particular needs at that time, and they would be highly compensated in return for their mobility. Pay increases were to be based on performance merit, and there were further incentives for "excellence" on the job in that those managers deemed to be "distinguished" could expect bonuses of as much as 20 percent of their base pay. This was to assuage any concern that mediocre executives received the same pay and bonuses as more productive ones. In addition, executives who were initially chosen for SES membership could choose whether or not to join and would not have to endure extensive inquiries regarding their qualifications. Future executives who aspired to SES status would have to undergo qualification reviews. High performance standards were to be expected of SES executives, who would undergo yearly appraisals. Those who consistently performed at less than satisfactory levels would be weeded out of the SES. Justification for the SES was based on the articulated need for executive branch leaders to be able to move managers entrenched in their jobs to other agencies as the need arose. In return, executives chosen for service would be afforded greater job security and increased compensation.[81]

Long before legislation could be proposed, Carter created a number of administrative committees and task forces to determine the degree of program support and to study various aspects of the issue that he considered central to his reform objectives. These included task forces on the composition and dynamics of the federal workforce; the SES; staffing processes; equal employment opportunity and affirmative action; job evaluation, pay, and benefit systems; and the development of employees, supervisors, managers, and executives.[82] The purpose of these task forces was three-fold. First, they were the means of mobilizing White House support and departmental lobbying on Capitol Hill. Second, they served as reactive mechanisms to developments on the Hill, garnering an impressive array of facts and figures to counter any objections arising from members of Congress. Finally, and perhaps most important, they were critical for stimulating public support. This support was especially important given the lack of tangible political benefits to be derived from civil service reform.[83] Indeed, the bulk of the work done on the project up until November, 1977, had been achieved by a total of nine task forces consisting of 110 people from inside and outside the government.[84]

The administration's basic strategy was to build support in the executive branch, in the country, and in Congress. Alan Campbell, chairman of the CSC, was a pivotal actor and one of the administration's key operatives, along with Frank Moore, head of the OLL, and Stuart Eizenstat. Soon after he was inaugurated, the president ordered Campbell to start working with the OMB on developing plans for civil service reform, and stressed his desire that most of the consultants be career federal employees. The rationale for including them was that careerists would be more intimately familiar with civil service problems than anyone else, and their participation would enhance the plan's credibility. In this manner, it was reasoned, the administration could construct a proposal that was politically more feasible than those produced by Eisenhower and, later, Nixon.[85]

In accordance with Carter's directive, Campbell and Wayne Granquist, OMB's associate director for management, became coleaders of a Personnel Reorganization Project, with Campbell clearly serving as the driving force.[86] They led what was essentially a super task force responsible for coordinating outreach activities and consolidating the recommendations of the other task forces. The project held seventeen hearings at field locations all across the country. Testimony by agency personnel yielded a database of opinion as to their perception of the nature of the problems and the scope of change needed to address them. A detailed summary of these views was then forwarded to the project headquarters in Washington, where the task forces further distilled this information and prepared option papers that were sent to more than fifteen hundred groups and individuals for comment. Thus, when the task forces presented their findings to Campbell and Granquist, the collective opinions of federal employees and the positions of various interest groups had already been integrated into the reports.[87] Additionally, Campbell kept close tabs on the status of groups that supported and opposed reform. Discernible changes in group positions were tracked, as were the changing positions of uncommitted groups. The records indicate that the administration enjoyed a high level of support, but that the opposition it did encounter promised to be vocal, whereas those who supported reform had no real incentive to get involved. Some examples of the groups supporting reform, although far from complete, include Common Cause, the Business Roundtable, the

Chamber of Commerce (although it opposed the reorganization plan in general), the National Civil Service League, the International Personnel Management Association, the Ripon Society, the National Association of Commissions for Women, the American Bar Association, the National Governors Association, and the National Conference of State Legislators. Those that opposed reform were the National Association of Government Employees, the National Treasury Employees Union, the National Federation of Federal Employees, the Professional Air Traffic Controllers Association, Ralph Nader (who withheld support based on the perception that the administration had not gone far enough on whistle-blower protection), and the National Association of Supervisors.[88]

In Washington, Campbell established a legislative task group that was responsible for coordinating contacts with Congress. Members of the group included Richard Pettigrew, the assistant to the president for reorganization; members of the OLL, the White House Press Office, and the DPS; and designated members of the OMB and CSC. The group worked closely with congressional committee staffs, providing them with vital and little understood information on federal personnel management, as well as other background materials. It also coordinated meetings between particular members of Congress and the president.[89] Again, all of these coordinating functions were essential to the administration's strategy because of the dual problems of congressional unfamiliarity with the intricacies of civil service reform and the lukewarm enthusiasm Congress exhibited for the legislation. In addition, coordination was instrumental for both monitoring policy making and assuring a balanced view of policy-specific information. Of particular importance is the notion that because civil service reform held few political advantages, it was important for the administration to minimize negative reactions from political actors affected by reform. The administration thus could garner political information and avoid costly political mistakes while assuring that when political conflict was necessary it had the most reliable information so as to cushion potential repercussions and defend its position.

Although there was little outright hostility toward civil service reform, it did not mean that the program was free from controversy. Several potentially dangerous groups almost immediately opposed the idea of reform, either in whole or in part. Most endorsements were subject to some qualification, and some groups criticized single aspects of the proposal. Unions, such as the AFL-CIO, attacked reform as being too management oriented. Other groups, including some consumer groups, objected to the real possibility of the legislation becoming a "Christmas tree" bill, carrying with it several undesired or unnecessary provisions. For example, when the bill finally came to the floor, a proposal to cut the firefighters' workweek—which Carter had vetoed in June, 1977—was attached but defeated on a point of order. Another was the attachment of Hatch Act provisions, which would have gone far toward eliminating political restrictions on federal employees. This, too, was defeated on a point of order. Only merit pay provided the elements of what could be a considered a classic political positive-sum game. Merit pay was seen as offering something for everyone. One analyst put it best when he wrote: "the promise of neutral measurement produced a merit pay coalition among normally contentious parties by allowing each to see in 'merit pay' what it most wanted: the public would get a better workforce without additional cost; employees would get the recognition and rewards they deserved; and politicians would get credit for bringing efficiency into government."[90] The development of proposals thus promised to be an exercise in synthesizing information from affected groups while being responsive to the president and his reform efforts. Such a task would prove self-contradictory at many points given that, while civil service reform lacked a truly mobilized constituency in support of its goals, the administration would have to deal with opponents who favored the status quo.

Developing Proposals

Unlike some of the other policies examined in this book, there was no protracted period of abstract principle development. The principles guiding policy direction were relatively clear and in place from the beginning: Reform the civil service by making employees more accountable and responsible, and cut back on veterans preference. The process of developing proposals began immediately under the direction of Campbell in the CSC. Campbell and his staff were given carte blanche to develop the proposals, just as Califano had been entrusted with NHI. In addition, much of civil service reform was largely free of controversy, although it was not politically profitable. Because most of the other policies analyzed in this book were highly controversial, I have chosen to focus on the proposal to limit veterans preference primarily because it, more than the nine other components of civil service reform, promised to be the most politically volatile component of the reform process.[91]

The issue of veterans preference has a long and sacred history. Its origins can be traced to just after the Revolutionary War, and was a means to reward veterans for service to their country. The practice became institutionalized in status when, in 1944, Congress approved the Veterans Preference Act, which extended hiring advantages to those veterans who suffered no injury in order to compensate them for "career interruption." There was some controversy, though, over the long-term intent of the act. Some argued that it was meant to be a temporary mechanism by which military personnel could adjust to citizen life, whereas others defended it as a system of lifetime reward for veterans who chose to make government their career.[92]

Carter, himself a veteran, strongly supported curtailing the preference system. Under the system, nondisabled veterans received five extra points on any merit service examination while those who were disabled received ten. Thus on almost any test in which veterans performed even marginally well, they were assured of scoring higher than those who did not receive the compensatory points.

In January, 1978, the administration won a small victory when VA director Max Cleland grudgingly endorsed limiting veterans preference. "While we are still not convinced that the operation of the veterans preference law results in inefficiency in the Federal personnel system," Cleland wrote, "we are aware of the pressures to make several modifications to accommodate the goal of Equal Employment Opportunity. Accordingly, we can reluctantly accept the proposed changes."[93]

The administration actively sought the advice and counsel of executive agencies and departments, which would be directly affected by limitations on veterans preference, in preparing proposals and estimating the impact reform would have on employment issues and hiring practices. The agencies responded with detailed analyses, often combining political assessments with policy expertise. For example, EPA director Barbara Blum gave detailed analyses of staff reductions in force, a termination date after discharge when preference would no longer apply, and the possibility of retaining preference for veterans who had served for more than twenty years. Included throughout were political observations on these and other elements of veterans preference.[94]

As the proposals went to the floor of Congress, the administration continued to push preference reductions. In June, 1978, Eizenstat reminded the president that Carter had made limiting veterans preference a central part of civil service reform, and if Congress deleted it, it would essentially "gut" the program. Yet, in an interesting twist of responsive analysis, Hamilton Jordan, the de facto chief of staff, advised Carter to seek out feasible political limits so as to avoid unnecessarily losing civil service reform, something that was directly related to Carter's sense of the public good. Thus, within the limits of political reasonableness, he urged Carter to continue the fight for preference limitation: "Substantively, veterans preference is a matter of access to the system. It is a critical issue but has nothing to do with actual management of the government. Politically, it would be disastrous for us to get everything else we want in civil service reform (which would give us about 90% of the total package), yet have it said that we 'lost' or have a 'weak' bill if the veterans preference issue is lost."[95]

Indeed, just the day before Carter had written to Robert Nix, chairman of the House Post Office and Civil Service Committee, stating his reasons for cutting back on veterans preference. In his letter, the president stated that "veterans preference as it presently operates severely interferes with employment opportunities for women and other minorities, discriminates against younger veterans who are outnumbered by veterans who served before, and greatly hampers managerial flexibility."[96] He gave special focus to this reality, making it a crucial point when pursuing the now well-known strategy of going public, as he set forth his reasoning in a series of press conferences.[97] For example, at a July 28 press conference, he stated: "To have a veterans preference retained, say, for a naval officer who served twenty-years, who has a good pension, and who comes here (Washington) and bumps . . . literally hundreds of other people who might do better than he does in a competitive exam, I think is ill advised. . . . It's been expanded from year to year into such a state that it discriminates against both other veterans, like the Vietnam veterans, and disabled veterans on the one hand, and women, blacks, and others who have to be competitive."[98]

Not surprisingly, the president was criticized immediately by veterans groups that had been mobilized in a far-reaching grass roots effort. Led by the American Legion, veterans mounted an intense lobbying effort in opposition to the bill, or at least to those sections pertaining to veterans preference.[99] Congress was besieged by angry veterans, especially when its members returned to their districts during the Labor Day recess. Veteran after veteran filed into members' offices, threatening electoral repercussions if the member supported the administration proposals as they stood. The American Legion went so far as to label its opposition to veterans preference reduction as a "test of strength." Lobbyist Phil Riggin stated, "We are labeling this as a testing ground of our ability to persuade Congress to do what we want them to do." The American Legion, which was the largest of the veterans groups, boasted a membership of better than 2.6 million. Grasping the obvious, Riggin aptly stated, "That's a lot of votes."[100]

Predictably, Congress agreed with the veterans, especially in the election year of 1978. Many of the veteran-related proposals were dropped, but the administration was able to cut back somewhat on narrowly defined preference initiatives, albeit to a limited extent. The major defeat for the administration came on September 11, when the House voted to drop almost all of the proposed changes. The Senate, which had voted to keep most of the administration's language, deferred in conference. The bill's final provision eliminated veterans preference in federal hiring for nondisabled retired officers at or above the rank of major (lieutenant commander in the navy). It permitted noncompetitive appointment of veterans with at least a 30 percent service-related disability to certain federal jobs. It further required an agency to notify a veteran with at least a 30 percent disability if the agency decided that the veteran was not eligible for appointment because of a physical disability, and it allowed veterans to ask the OPM to review the agency's decision.[101]

Policy Competence and Responsiveness: A Closer Look

Combining political and policy substance is often difficult in a delegated advisory strategy—where the staff acts more as a monitor than as a guiding hand in the policy process—unless, of course, the delegated agent is capable of providing the higher form of policy competence.[102] However, even if the delegated agent is possessed of a political background (which is quite often the case given the politicization tendencies of recent presidents), the problems of capture and parochialism described in the public administration literature may serve to impede the exercise of not only neutral analysis (however that may be defined and subsequently approximated) but awareness of what the real political environment might hold in the way of possibilities and obstacles or constraints. Depending on the perspective of the policy maker, this can add to or subtract from the acquisition of optimal advice and information, in turn cutting or increasing the president's risk factor. The theoretically motivated perspective applied here holds that whether a president chooses to delegate policy making to an external political actor, no matter what the degree of authority granted to the designated department or agency, there exists the need for White House agents to play a strong role. As I have argued, that strong role is consistent with policy centralization as suggested by the staff-shift framework.[103] Civil service reform serves as a model of the coordinated, delegated advisory process, with the staff monitoring policy direction and synthesizing political and policy imperatives.

Early on, the administration identified government unions as probable sources of opposition to comprehensive reform. In a memorandum to the president, Eizenstat and McIntyre reflected the concept of wedding information proffered by Campbell (the delegated agent) with the political necessity of deferring to unions on certain points and at certain junctures. These included, among other things, a concern for incorporating a federal labor relations authority in the reorganization plan, a pledge to develop a section on labor-management relations in order to establish collectively bargained arbitration procedures in cases involving the resolution of employee grievances, and rhetoric to the effect that a new labor-management section would improve collective bargaining in the federal sector. These items were not antagonistic to the president's plan, so the recommendations to include them in negotiations with unions served political as well as policy ends. The president accepted all facets of Eizenstat's advice and approved the recommendations.[104] The memo in general suggests the existence of a coordinated process, synthesizing information developed by Campbell in consultation with agents from OMB, Defense Department, DPS, and labor representatives.

Campbell himself sought to achieve the higher level of policy competence in a vein reminiscent of Califano, who was able to draw on his substantive expertise as well as political experience. However, Campbell's efforts did not bear the signature of the seemingly personal political agenda Califano was accused of advancing. For example, when writing about the "competitiveness" system, in which individuals would be paid according to performance and not simply on a scale "comparable" to private sector employees, Campbell wrote: "Let me simply say that no one, to my knowledge, has devised such a system. At this point, it is nothing more than a theoretical abstraction without any evidence that it could really wash. From a *political* point of view, I believe you must consider that expectations are already very high that corrective measures will be recommended to meet criticisms of the comparability system; and these criticisms could bring down the present system in favor of congressional determination of salary levels. That route, if it parallels prior experience, would be disastrous."[105]

This quotation reflects Campbell's dualism in that he advocates a particular policy direction focusing on policy specifics, but tempered by an assessment of the political environment within which the administration was placing civil service reform. The advice was thus promulgated by a delegated agent within the general framework of policy analysis, tempered by the possibilities present in the political environment, and submitted for policy perusal by the monitoring agent within the White House.

Another example of this higher form of policy competence is shown in Campbell's analysis of whether the Federal Bureau of Investigation (FBI) should be exempted from reform provisions. Note especially the combination of an astute political sense for dealing with congressional questions while displaying policy acumen in detailing substantive concerns:

> When looking at whether the FBI should be exempt, [Mo Udall] *may* be inclined to accede to the attorney general's position on one issue—coverage of the FBI by Titles I and II specifying merit principles and prohibited personnel practices—though this is not at all certain; but he strongly opposes the Attorney General's position on the second issue—placement of FBI supergrade (SES) positions in government-wide super-grade pool, rather than giving the FBI statutory authority for its current 140 supergrades.

> *For strategic and substantive reasons, I believe the administration should defer to Mo on this as we have on substantially all other questions about the bill,* and support his position.[106]

Eizenstat, the primary monitoring agent in the White House, agreed fully with the political imperatives Campbell's analysis raised and recommended that Carter heed the advice, which the president did.[107]

The responsibility for wedding policy competence with responsiveness did not fall simply within the provincial jurisdiction of the DPS. Hamilton Jordan, although not yet officially the White House chief of staff, was instrumental in advising the president of the dangers of mounting a concerted effort on behalf of veterans preference, alerting him to the real possibility of placing the entire reform effort in jeopardy. In an advisory memorandum, Jordan wrote: "Right now, the odds are against us [keeping veterans preference reduction]. We should go all out on the floor to have it reinstated, but we should avoid characterizing it as "central" or "critical" to our entire [civil service reform] package. We should say that it is an important provision to the package that relates to the basic fairness and equity of the civil service system."[108] This type of advice emphasized political imperatives, noting that the substantive aspects of civil service reform did not rely on veterans preference in order to be largely successful.

In terms of the responsiveness of the delegated agent, it cannot be denied that the WHS in general and the DPS in particular benefited from having Campbell as that agent. As the case of NHI and others suggest, presidents cannot count on having agents of high loyalty (although appointees are often chosen for their ideological compatibility with presidential policy preferences) in place at all times when delegating policy. Indeed, this problem is a primary reason that presidents resort to politicization as a strategy compatible with centralization. In this case, though, the evidence clearly suggests that Campbell was an honest broker, a role similar to that of the responsive agents, such as Eizenstat and his staff, in other policy areas. This is interesting in an analytical sense because political scientists do not normally think in terms of having this particular role played by department heads or officials, although their selection, as mentioned, is usually politicized. For example, Campbell prepared a decision memorandum discussing the relative merits of conferring cabinet status on the new OPM director—a proposition he favored given that he stood to be the one named to the cabinet post. Still, he was careful to set out the positions in support of such a proposal (i.e., those of the Departments of Agriculture, Commerce, and HEW), and was equally careful to note the source and substance of the opposition (i.e., from Defense and Interior). Indeed, his style was akin to the better journalistic accounts in his attempt to address both sides of the issue.[109] The president rejected Campbell's suggestion, opting against extending cabinet status to the OPM director. However, he noted in the margins that the rejection was "no reflection on Scotty [Campbell]." Rather, it was based on his concern for keeping the cabinet at a manageable size.[110] Indeed, Carter showed that he was willing and able to make independent decisions. Eizenstat had agreed with Campbell's desire to give the position cabinet status, but for different reasons. He argued that to keep OPM in the cabinet would be to protect against the director from going too far astray or gaining too much independence. Carter thus rejected the advice of his two closest civil service reform advisers.[111]

The facts of the veterans preference issue and NHI distinctly argue for a strong White House role in monitoring policy direction, even in the delegated strategy. I will next briefly examine this role and its contribution to the initiative's success.

Analysis of the DPS Role

For staff to play the role of honest broker is only slightly less important in the monitoring strategy than in the director or facilitated strategy. Presumably, policy-making authority is delegated for a reason, probably to maximize input from outside sources. The job of the WHS is made easier if the delegated agent plays an honest broker role. Still, honest brokering must remain in the White House as well because, when all is said and done, policy that is formulated outside the White House becomes a presidential proposal. Even more so than in the other advisory strategies I have described, it is in the president's best interest to get as many sides of the issue as possible, distilled by an honest broker.

This pattern is readily apparent in the case of civil service reform. The decision memo, for example, was a prototype of interagency coordination. The memo's structure was both comprehensive in scope and exhaustive in detail. Carter did not need to consult the entire memorandum for particular information, of course, but he could easily get any type of information he desired. The memo started with a brief substantive memo from Campbell, a synthesis of political and policy advice from the DPS (which also summarized all memos put forth previous to the decision memo), and an appendix, marked by a series of tabs, which included comments from every affected agency.[112]

During most of the reform effort, the DPS stayed out of policy making except to facilitate discussion between Campbell, veterans, labor, and affected departments and agencies. For example, Campbell disagreed with HEW "on whether the proposed changes in the comparability pay process for federal employees should sent to Congress as part of the CSR [civil service reform] package." [113] The DPS brokered the disagreement between HEW and CSC, but brought both sets of objections to the president. It also advocated a particular policy direction, but only in response to Carter's specific requests for such advocacy. [114]

The delegated strategy does not mean that policy-making authority rests completely with departments or agencies. Indeed, as I have consistently argued throughout this book, all strategies, including the delegated strategy (staff as monitor), are consistent with policy centralization when seen through the lens of the staff-shift framework. The White House must ultimately approve policy. Thus, the honest broker role in the monitoring strategy often entails combining policy advocacy with analysis, as long as objections to the particular positions or arguments advocated are duly noted and given fair treatment or consideration. This in turn implies that the responsive agents within the White House will sometimes take positions opposite those of the delegated agents. Indeed, this is the essence of responsiveness. Eizenstat and Moore took such a position in opposition to Campbell and the comments put forth by the Departments of Labor, Defense, and HEW regarding the comparability formula and refining the General Schedule with regard to the implementation of civil service reform. While noting that the approach advocated by the CSC might "well prove the best policy response to public perceptions that federal workers are overpaid," they also agreed with OMB "that this decision should not be made now and that *these proposals should not be included in the [CSR] package.*" [115] Moreover, although advocating a particular and specific position, the DPS was meticulous in articulating all of the comments, pro and con, and registering disagreements with their position, as the following excerpt illustrates:

> Harrison Wellford and Wayne Granquist state that they share Campbell's concerns about federal pay comparability, but that they strongly recommend against including these pay proposals in the [CSR] package. . . . Ray Marshall agrees with Campbell that these pay proposals should be part of the [CSR] package. He also points out that if the pay proposals are included, unions will want a more substantive involvement in the pay setting process. Harold Brown strongly agrees that the federal pay comparability changes should be included in the [CSR] package. He believes that Campbell's proposals will assure that the process of determining the comparability is as accurate as possible and believes that the proposals will result in lower federal pay costs. . . . Joe

Califano strongly concurs with Campbell. He believes that the proposals are sound and are necessary to meet public criticism about federal employees being paid too much.

Recommendation The Labor, Defense, and HEW comments above appear to have ignored the political problems involved in sending the pay proposals to Congress at this time and the important substantive problems raised by OMB. The agencies' objectives of improving the comparability process are sound, but action now is premature pending further study of the proposals. We have the most significant Civil Service package proposed by any President this century *without* these pay proposals, and a reasonable chance of passage this session. We think separate legislation to improve the comparability pay process should be submitted at a *later* date.[116]

All relevant objections were noted fairly, it seems, and policy advocacy weighing the advice of the delegated agent, the affected constituencies, and the president's stated interests characterize this mode of advisory monitoring. Of course, it is not simply a case of staff monitoring policy direction. It is also a strong advisory role, but one executed after most of the work was done by a loyal delegated agent external to the White House.

In sum, part of civil service reform's success was that it fostered coordination in the advisory process. To be sure, there was policy advocacy and turf protection, but the important point is that there was a reciprocal process of collegiality and coordination that was not present in the case of NHI.

CONCLUSION

This chapter has examined national health insurance and civil service reform from the perspective of using the presidential staff as policy monitors. The staff-shift framework employed here holds that presidents, under various conditions, will delegate policy-making authority to agents outside the White House. This holds for priority as much as for nonpriority agenda items. Modern perspectives on presidential policy management argue that presidents centralize policy making in the White House and politicize the bureaucracy by fully exploiting the appointment process, thereby maximizing responsiveness to presidential goals as filtered through preferences. Delegation to an external agent is consistent with centralization because, as the staff-shift framework suggests, the presidential staff has a forceful role, although it is as monitor of policy progress, advising the agent as to the general direction (and changes thereof) of presidential preferences for policy formulation. This role is different in degree and, to an extent, kind from the more hands-on approach described in previous chapters, where the staff acted proactively, leading or coordinating policy decisions. In the monitoring strategy, the staff acts in a more or less reactive mode (after the initial laying out of alternatives), letting the delegated agency take the lead in policy formulation. In this sense, the WHS still has a strong role to play in guiding policy direction, but it allocates its resources more immediately to other policy areas.

Emerging from the case of national health insurance is a description of a kind of comprehensive responsiveness and a high level of monitoring activity on the part of the WHS. The president and the DPS repeatedly reaffirmed HEW's role as the lead agency, delegated with policy formation authority, but with DPS in the more or less reactive role of policy monitor. The DPS's responsiveness was often couched in the language of policy substance, but this is explainable given Carter's ideological predisposition toward public goods. The role was responsive yet substantive mainly because Carter had grand plans for NHI. The DPS responded by incorporating substantive analysis into an already volatile political environment, thereby responding to Carter's wishes. At the same time, it provided a type of substantively oriented responsiveness that steered policy objectives toward political ends.

The development of NHI legislation was characterized by a process that was often coordinated and even reasonably smooth. So why is NHI considered a failure? It is undoubtedly less so than the other "failures" in this study. I believe the central reason for its failure is that neither the economy nor the public was ready for NHI, and it took a long time for the administration to finally realize this. In the meantime, a great deal of political capital was spent unnecessarily. This precious capital was already in jeopardy because of other domestic and foreign policy problems, the economy and the Iranian hostage crisis being just two examples. The delegated agent in charge of developing NHI, HEW secretary Joseph Califano, was aligned too closely with the administration's issue-specific nemesis, Sen. Edward Kennedy. Califano, an individual with formidable political skills, brought various groups on board, but it is not clear that he systematically accounted for the diverse viewpoints he was getting from the outside. Those perspectives thus were missing from the advice he forwarded to the White House. Instead, he tended to resist political imperatives identified by the White House, thus compromising the president's political interests.

Given the problems of the delegated, staff-monitored strategy identified here, it must be noted that many of the pathologies attached to the delegated strategy either did not materialize or had negligible impact. In the initial stages of NHI, there is evidence that political advice was systematically shut out. Califano and the HEW staff failed to consult with politically responsive operatives in the OMB and DPS. This is, of course, broadly consistent with theoretical reservations of employing such an advisory strategy. However, these problems were rectified by the end of the process, which may have been due to the stronger role played by the DPS. The point is that politics and diverse political viewpoints were not strangled, but, ironically, thrived. That it took the administration too long to recognize the extent of the political reality of the day and withdraw NHI as a priority is certainly one reason that it failed.

A series of counterfactuals is worth considering. If the had administration had backed off sooner, say in late 1978 or early 1979, it might have been able to save face and even take credit for trying to put NHI together as the right thing to do. It thus would have preserved its reputation by displaying the political sophistication to know when to back off. As in the welfare reform case, the president himself deserves a good share of the blame for failing to recognize this even when he was advised that spending a great deal of political capital on NHI would not be in his best interests. In addition, it is possible that NHI would have fared better had a mixed strategy been employed. Because NHI spanned the jurisdictions of myriad agencies and the technical specifics of the plan were so complex, the administration might have done better to implement a mixed strategy with DPS as the base, in partnership with HEW and Labor. They in turn could have coordinated the input of a variety of groups, departments, and agencies. A process similar to the one followed in Energy II might have been more conducive to getting a greater proportion of what the president wanted at least in symbolic terms, since the legislation was not likely to pass regardless of its content.

Other reasons for failure lend themselves to consideration. Advisory strategies are rarely the sole reason for a policy's failure, even if the criteria for success or failure rests on grounds other than whether or not the proposal passed and was enacted into law. National health insurance is no exception. But the advisory strategy must bear some of the blame, for if those steering the advisory course had done a better job of recognizing the problems inherent in the contextual environment within which the administration tried to move the proposal, they could have protected the president from political fallout. In addition, as I suggested earlier, it was probably a mistake to assign NHI to a staff-monitored strategy given that it has the conditional attributes identified as consistent with policies that are staff facilitated or even staff directed. Assigning it to staff facilitation would almost certainly have secured broader input from a host of organizations. Although the White House executed its function well, as did HEW, too much political capital was spent that might otherwise have been conserved in a facilitated strategy.

A new institutionalist perspective suggests that, in this case, the president and his advisers were constrained by external considerations, the lingering ghosts of past attempts to reform health care, the inability to shake the charge that health care constituted a step toward socialism, and intransigent institutions. In this regard, the failure to achieve the president's programmatic goals and the loss of political capital were consequences of institutional context. This is perhaps an unshakable risk when delegating a priority assignment to an external department, bureau, or agency. Although the internal staff apparatus acts as monitor, it appears that a president and his administration risk losing control of what they are trying to do when the primary responsibility for designing the specifics of policy is relegated to those outside the White House

In the case of civil service reform the DPS still played an important role in coordinating policy and political advice, as well as mediating between departments and the White House. Like the successful cases of Energy II and youth employment, using the staff as an honest broker was the key to the policy's success. Monitoring the policy development process conducted by the CSC, which acted in accordance with broad program parameters established early by the administration, appears to have served the president well. In this case, the role of honest broker was fulfilled by the delegated agent as well as the proximal agents in the White House, making it easier for the DPS to be responsive as monitoring, brokering, and policy advocacy went along unencumbered. The evidence indicates the DPS engaged in a coordination and advisory role based largely on information coming in from the departments, and that its advice took the form of advocacy consistent with the monitoring role. This advocacy was part and parcel of the DPS role, but not to the extent that it suppressed other equally legitimate and concerned perspectives from other participants. This pattern of staff activity is similar to traditional descriptions of the organizational virtues of centralization. Nevertheless, it lacked the control and hierarchical characteristics prevalent in some descriptions.[117] The monitoring activity described here, although less driven from the White House, is consistent with Moe's observation regarding policy centralization in the presidency in that the presidential staff implemented a strong, advice-driven, coordinated policy strategy. This strategy maintained policy responsiveness to presidential preferences even though the bulk of policy formulation was accomplished outside the executive mansion.

Part III

Conclusions and Theoretical Implications

CHAPTER 7

Presidents and the Political Use of Policy Information

In this book we have examined the advisory processes the White House employs to obtain and utilize political and policy information.[1] Presidents turn to a number of sources for advice and information. These include, but are not limited to, politically responsive operatives in the White House (most notably staff members), political appointees located throughout a politicized executive branch, and various task forces and study groups that seek information from a variety of sources outside the Beltway. In this chapter I set out some of the major empirical findings that emerged throughout the analysis and, even more important, address in broad general terms the direction of presidency theory as it is informed by the study of institutions, individuals, and processes. This is a tall order, so I restrict my comments to those aspects of theory that have special relevance to presidents' advisory and information concerns in a larger, systemic sense.

Throughout, a distinction can be made, sometimes clear, other times more ambiguous, between politically responsive advice that provides information and perspective on the likely impact of various policy pursuits on the president's political fortunes, and that which puts the focus on the substantive and/or technical aspects of policy concerns. These are distinct, but they need not be considered false dichotomies. The two perspectives are not of necessity antagonistic, and they can be as much complementary as conflictual. Many presidential policy priorities are formulated outside of the White House. On its face this seems to contradict the trend toward policy centralization in the presidency cited by many White House observers.[2] At the same time, it cannot be denied that presidents, in one way or another, have sought to maximize their control over policy formulation. There exists a discrepancy in our theoretical and empirical worlds, one that this book has not fully bridged. Instead, what I have tried to do is construct a modest theoretical framework of staff advisory roles and apply it to data from the Carter administration. The application of the framework indicates that it holds promise for explaining the disjunction currently illuminated by the literature. The framework, which I call staff shift, stresses that the president and his staff have precious little time and resources with which to fully elaborate a policy program. To minimize the impact of this state of affairs on presidential policy making, presidential staff roles shift depending on circumstances such as the character and scope of the policy, the priority level assigned by the president, the expected impacts on various constituencies, and the compatibility of policy with political actors placed within the White House or throughout the executive branch (or further).

Staff shift builds on a variant of the new institutionalism. The new institutionalism is essentially an organization-based theory of politics, and such has been the case with the analysis presented in this study. But while institutions have consequences for decisions and the shape of policy proposals, individuals have some discretion in pursuing various policy or political agendas. This may be the case more so for the presidency than other institutions with rigid structural rules and sequential decision processes. The main difference between these institutions and the presidency is, to my mind, that rules, sequences, and processes are often endogenously determined, whereas the organizational factors that impinge on presidential activity are often exogenously determined by a host of factors, including the masses, competing institutions, group pressures, and the like. This set of external actors formulates a political context within which the president operates. In turn, that context fashions positive and negative incentives for presidential action, which then influences (although it probably does not determine) presidential preferences for policy and political pursuits.

Presidents and their supporting organizations thus have various degrees of latitude for maneuver in whatever way they choose, but the likely consequences and impacts are conditioned by the political and policy contexts within which they move. Advice is seen as akin to an investment strategy, whose goal is to reduce the uncertainty manifest in such a potentially volatile system. Thus, one of the efforts of this book has been to try and show where one president had a relatively wide choice space within which to work, but where structural and institutional features constrained choice or, at the other extreme, played a determinative role. Finally, I have tried to show that policy "success" or "failure" was *never* purely a consequence of the advisory strategy employed. Some programs that Congress passed were deemed a failure given that they were stripped of the president's intention as stated at the beginning of the process. Others that were defeated were considered successes because the president and his staff were able to regulate the content of policy for both policy and political purposes, and did not cede to others the definition of what they were trying to accomplish.[3] Thus, success and failure are seen in relative terms, that is, relative to what they were trying to accomplish consistent with their political and policy goals.

The bulk of the book has shown how advice is filtered through organizational resources in the White House, specifically the DPS. I find that, consistent with recent accounts of presidential policy making, the staff plays an integral role in formulating and managing policy information while protecting the president's political interests. I have argued consistently that the staff advisory role is dependent upon factors such as presidential interest and activity, the scope of the policy in question, political considerations, and technical feasibility. In general, I contend that policy making can be delegated to agents outside the White House, but the staff is essential to policy success, although its role is different than when it formulates policy within the EOP. Instead of arguing that the policy making process is centered in the White House, I maintain that the staff is sensitive to these considerations. I identify three very different strategies for staff advisory activity: *director* of policy making (when the staff is primarily responsible for policy output), *facilitator* (when staff is actively involved in give-and-take with bureaucratic departments or agencies), and *monitor* (when staff is involved in overseeing work done mostly in the departments or agencies). I further supplement the analysis with considerations of the role of interest groups and congressional responses.

Thus, the White House staff is an active participant in policy making, regardless of where policy originates or is fashioned. As the framework suggests, the level of activity differs in both degree and in kind. The staff-shift advisory framework is able, then, to account for policy proposals being made in the White House, mixed with the staff acting in concert with external actors, or delegated to bureaucratic agents. Through the lens of the staff-shift framework, all are made consistent with the overarching tendency to centralize policy making in the White House.

I have tried to illuminate these distinctions by systematically exploring the three advisory perspectives detailed earlier in order to understand better the extent to which theory reflects practice. I selected the Carter administration for study because it used all three strategies and experienced policy successes and failures in each. In the sections that follow I recapitulate the major empirical findings relating to the use of political and policy advice, suggest theoretical refinements, and suggest areas for future research that may aid in the attempt to arrive at deeper insights and further generalizations in presidential policy making.

STAFF AS DIRECTOR

The Carter administration's efforts in two areas, youth employment and the creation of the Department of Education, illustrate the problems and promise of the fully centralized strategy with staff directing policy formulation. Characterizing both initiatives is the extensive use of task forces as advisory sources. The difference between success and failure lay in the how successful the task forces were in executing their functions. The PRP, which was responsible for the creation of the Department of Education, was largely successful in providing policy advice, but proved incapable of taking political soundings when it tried to do so. Conversely, the interagency coordinating committee and the vice president's task force, both used in the youth employment initiative, were largely effective in combining policy and political analysis into one coherent advisory framework.

The creation of the Department of Education was brought about in large part by a process in which an organization (i.e., the PRP) was created to provide the White House with policy information regarding technical substance. However, when trying to cross over into the political realm, the project was largely unsuccessful. Its inability to provide adequate political analysis stemmed from the fact that it lacked a reliable mechanism by which to gauge the probable impact of policy on the various constituencies. But politics, as stated, was not the primary concern of the PRP. Once it became clear that a systematic political component was missing, the DPS was brought in to coordinate and direct policy making. However, the late hour of the DPS's entrance precluded accomplishing what the president wanted, namely creating a broad, far-reaching department. Instead, the DPS was able to broker an accommodation leading to its own objective, which was much narrower in scope than what the president desired.

The process was further hindered by the failure of politicization (although virtually none of Carter's appointments were politicized in the sense we have come to understand the term, but were instead more policy oriented). Secretary Joseph Califano, the head of HEW, opposed the creation of a new department and instead advocated elevating the status of education within HEW. This was in sharp contrast to Carter's stated preference. Califano fought the administration at nearly every turn, even to the extent of recommending the creation of a *broad* department because he knew that such a proposal would be politically unacceptable and would ultimately fail if it reached a vote in Congress. Consequently, the president was unable to get the large, powerful department he wanted and, instead, had to settle for one that was really nothing more than the OE surgically removed from HEW and given cabinet status. It is entirely conceivable that if the DPS had been brought in earlier to defend the president's position and provide a responsive advisory element to the process, Carter might have been able to get more of what he wanted. Instead, the administration suffered from the appearance of policy drift, unable to communicate and coordinate policy making internally. This helped scuttle Carter's chances of securing even a moderately broad department. Policy oriented advice, which might have been forthcoming from OE, was systematically shut out as PRP was instructed to ignore the input of careerists in the agency.

The youth employment initiative, on the other hand, benefited from a task force system directed by DPS, which proved to be both politically responsive *and* sensitive to substantive policy issues. Key members of Congress were courted early and convinced to join in the administration's effort, or were kept in line due to extensive administration outreach efforts, targeting interest groups and bureaucrats. In contrast to the Department of Education advisory process, the DPS was an early participant and managed to juggle a number of competing responsibilities. It directed policy from the inside by variously playing the role of advocate, honest broker, director of policy decisions, and facilitator of the flow of information. All this took place after Carter had strengthened the DPS's authority, but it was the ability of the staff to solicit political readings and then weld this information to an analysis of policy substance that constituted the most important aspect of this particular advisory process. The character of the partnership between the White House and the bureaucracy—with the White House directing the departments to provide the staff important substantive information, which the staff converted into workable policy proposals and then advised the president—was the defining characteristic of this successful case of centralized policy making using the staff as policy director.

The analysis of the staff-directed strategy suggests the need to rethink some of the existing theory about a centralized process. First, the analysis of the creation of a new department illustrates the problem of vital information being kept from political operatives. Critics of centralizing policy in the White House identify this as a by-product of a closed system. An excessively centralized process can lead to the undue insulation of policy makers from important advisory sources, a view that is generally supported by the analysis presented in this book. In addition, political advisory processes faltered as well and an in-house task force proved unsuccessful when it endeavored to be responsive. It was not until the DPS took over and directed the process that political and policy synthesis was accomplished. This is evidenced by Eizenstat standing at the November cabinet meeting to announce that a narrow department was what the president *really* wanted, even though Carter had explicitly stated his preference for a broad department.

Nevertheless, a centralized, policy-directed advisory operation can work if the organizational apparatus is able to secure a coordinated process. Again, the character of the partnership between the White House and career civil servants emerged as most important. If lines of communication between the White House, affected groups, and the departments remain fluid, the chance for presidents to get most of what they want from a policy process increase. An obvious observation deserves noting, though: The process participants need to remain willing to compromise. Stubborn adherence to unworkable political or substantive components is detrimental to an administration's efforts. However, as the case of Califano's intransigence illustrates, political appointees are subject to bureaucratic parochialism. Such narrow perspectives diminish the usefulness of appointments as a tool of policy control in addition to its traditional use for implementation purposes.[4] Attempts to politicize the bureaucracy via the appointment process may enhance responsiveness in some cases, but it is not a panacea when parochial forces work their magic on appointees. A centralized process thus works best if coordination and collegiality remain the norm, rather than being squeezed out in a more closed system. The staff-shift framework indicates that such can be the case.

A centralized strategy can succeed or it can fail; seeking responsiveness does not itself determine policy success. It is not necessarily better or worse than either a mixed or decentralized strategy, with the staff employed as facilitator or monitor, respectively. While it appears that recent presidents have tended to prefer responsiveness, their successors must remain sensitive to input from not only outside the White House but also from sources other than their politicized loyalists. Substance and politics can be joined from the inside, but efforts to remain open to outsiders with differing views are sometimes required. The staff can handle a large amount of information and advice from the outside, but it directs the use of advisory content in response to presidential preferences. When issues become complicated to the extent that they cut across bureaucratic jurisdictions, presidents may choose a staff as facilitator strategy, finding that these types of issues cannot be adequately controlled from the inside.

STAFF AS FACILITATOR

A recent strand of the literature on presidential organization argues the need for presidents to mix policy-making functions between the bureaucracy and the White House, and is largely in response to the shortcomings of overreliance on either policy competence or responsiveness.⁵ A middle ground approach is recommended in an attempt to combine the best of both worlds. While it is true that using the staff as a facilitator can empir-ically identify the middle ground, the analysis presented in this study in-dicates that this approach is not immune to failure and is neither better nor worse than either centralizing or decentralizing policy development au-thority. Policies that fall into this category are likely to be large, complex issues that do not fit neatly into the jurisdiction of any particular depart-ment or agency. When initiatives fall broadly across departmental jurisdic-tions, it creates incentives for the White House to maintain some control. Nevertheless, it is unwise to centralize because it is unrealistic to expect to be able to control policy development from inside the White House on is-sues of such complexity and, to some extent, political volatility. Using the staff to facilitate policy formulation in such situations is a more appropri-ate choice.

The failed policy in this category, welfare reform, was hampered by the lack of institutional memory, a problem for which the advisory strategy could not compensate. The players in the advisory process might have done well to take lessons from previous attempts at welfare reform. The DPS was not brought in until late in the development stage. Consequently, little discussion concerning the relationship between policy substance and political feasibility occurred. Even after the DPS was brought in (at HEW's request), several problems concerning both political and technical infor-mation remained. These included using erroneous cost estimates to es-timate program viability and the inability to resolve technical disputes relating to the scope of the jobs program. In addition, President Carter in-correctly read the political landscape. For example, his stubborn adher-ence to a zero-cost framework failed to produce an accurate analysis of the political sacrifices that would be required, including internal quarrels in the executive branch that ultimately led to the alienation of Congress and others in the administration itself.

Energy II succeeded where welfare reform failed. A highly coordinated advisory process functioned smoothly, due in no small measure to the co-operative efforts between the White House (especially the DPS) and the DOE. The DPS, charged with the responsibility of coordinating policy advice and information, was quite active in communicating to the depart-ments the nature of the administration's preferences. It fulfilled the role of honest broker by bringing *all* affected viewpoints to the president's atten-tion and brokered crucial agreements both in Congress and the depart-ments. The most important feature was that the DPS was brought in at the beginning of the development process, and thus played a pivotal role in se-curing an open process amenable to several advisory points of view. This was most definitely *not* the case with Energy I. Civil servants in DOE and other affected agencies provided policy expertise and substantive advice. The outcome thus was less a matter of process than it was of effective information distribution helped by a close, productive partnership between the White House and the departments.

One of the most interesting findings concerned the process by which the DPS provided both *anticipatory* and *reactive* components to the process. It is important in a mixed strategy (but also to greater or lesser degrees in the other strategies) for the DPS (or a similar advisory organization) to anticipate potential problems that might arise. In doing so, it can take action to preempt opposition or, if that proves impossible, prepare appropriate political responses in the face of intractable opposition. Similarly, it must be able to *react* to unanticipated situations. In the case of Energy II, the DPS constructed a subsystem within the broader advisory process in which unexpected developments were detected early and the staff in turn formulated appropriate responses. This helped minimize the impact of political problems and prevented a host of others from crippling the policy process, as happened with Energy I. The administration's professional reputation and stature in the eyes of the general public improved as a result of this anticipatory and reactive framework.

A mixed strategy can work if it is characterized by a strong alliance between the participants. Dissension might exist, and indeed might enhance the caliber of advice and information, but an active partnership between the participants can settle disagreements and ensure the process remains controllable. A resourceful partnership between the departments and the White House emerges as the most reliable guarantee that a mixed strategy will succeed.

STAFF AS MONITOR

In pursuing neutral or policy competence, the White House can maintain control over policy content—although to a lesser degree perhaps—by using the staff to monitor policy formulation in the departments or agencies of the executive branch. This entails delegating responsibility for policy development, whenever possible, to political appointees and, by extension, bureaucrats located in the departments. It is here, some assert, that institutional memory and policy expertise—both of which are essential ingredients for making effective policy—abound. The analysis presented here suggests that the delegated strategy can succeed, but that it runs a high risk of failure if presidents do not encourage open networks of communication, information, and advice, between the WHS and the departments. Politicized appointments are not enough for advisory purposes. Perhaps the most surprising finding pertaining to the staff-as-monitor strategy was the high level of DPS activity in both the failed and successful cases. While the type of activity differed in both degree and kind from other strategies, it was nonetheless quite present.

In the case of formulating a national health insurance plan, comprehensive responsiveness and a high level of activity on the part of the WHS, particularly the DPS, was the order of the day. In a delegated strategy, theory decrees that most policy making takes place in the departments, and that the WHS plays the role of gatekeeper, examining and regulating the flow of information to the Oval Office. This was not the case, however, in the development of NHI. Although the White House repeatedly reaffirmed that HEW was the lead agency and had full authority to formulate a plan, the DPS played an extremely active role in monitoring the process. Responsiveness was couched in language more commonly associated with policy competence. This is explainable given Carter's ideological predisposition in favor of a public goods approach to governance. The implications of this will be explained in detail in the section on theory building below.

In the NHI process, many of the pathologies commonly associated with a delegated strategy either did not exist or were of little importance. In the initial stage, political advice was systematically shut off with Secretary Califano, who was hardly neutral, preventing access to most major policy perspectives. This outcome is consistent with reservations voiced by many of ceding too much authority to those outside the White House. However, these problems were alleviated at the end of the process and a more systematic discussion of political imperatives was fostered. Nevertheless, NHI failed because it was too large an initiative to be delegated to one agent, be that agent politicized or expert. In hindsight, NHI might have fared better had it been assigned to the mixed category, as was the case with Energy II, with the staff playing a more hands-on role, facilitating the advisory information that flowed between affected persons and groups.

In the case of civil service reform, we again see an important and active role for the DPS in coordinating policy and political advice, monitoring its progress. As was the case in NHI, this is somewhat surprising because presidential memoranda clearly show the president's preference for keeping most of the authority for policy development took place in the CSC. As in the successful cases of Energy II and youth employment, the role of the honest broker surfaced as the key to success in civil service reform. The reader might object to my classification of this strategy as monitoring given the high level of staff activity. However, I would argue that monitoring is the best classification for the process because the substance of what the staff did and the manner in which it coordinated advice differed in many ways from the other strategies. Those are detailed in chapter 6, but one example is worth noting here. The president's staff originally laid out parameters within which the CSC was more or less given carte blanche to pursue different policy options, and then basically pursued a reactive strategy by responding to directions forged by Alan Campbell and his staff at CSC. It is this reactive element that sets the DPS role apart from that which it played in the other strategies.

Another theoretically interesting finding is that the role of honest broker was not just the immediate jurisdiction of the DPS, but also of the CSC as the delegated agent responsible for policy development. This is not the same as politicizing the executive branch. We would not necessarily expect a politicized agent to act as an honest broker, but to be responsive to the president's perspective, especially at the implementation level. While this strategy is not precluded in a staff-as-facilitator strategy, an agent chosen for its policy expertise and perspective, not for political expediency, is probably more capable of executing the honest broker function than a politicized agent. It is when the agent is chosen both for political expertise and loyalty that this strategy can work best. In this case, the DPS played an active role in coordinating and advising the bureaucracy, but it was advice based more on information coming from the bureaucracy.

Thus, a staff-as-facilitator strategy can work if the partnership between the White House and the bureaucracy benefits from the mutual understanding of each role as they relate to the president's preference for administrative structure. In the case of the Carter administration, those roles in the delegated strategy were coordination for the WHS and a policy promulgating and advisory function for the bureaucracy. Although the analysis presented here was limited to one administration, it does offer strong support for the proposition that, to the extent these are achieved, the delegated strategy can be successful in giving the president most of what he wants.

Commonalities in the Successful Cases

Several common themes emerge in the successful cases described in this book. The first is that the pursuit of policy competence or responsiveness is not necessarily the most important component to study when trying to understand the advisory process in successful policy making. Indeed, policy competence and responsiveness are important elements in *all* categories. Rather, what emerges from this study is that the quality of the partnership between the White House and the bureaucracy is important in any strategy. On one level, this is an obvious conclusion. But the character of the relationship between policy and political operatives needs to be given systematic attention. Any such relationship is especially crucial to the literature on presidential policy making. In terms of centralization, many studies look at intrabranch relations, but works on advisory dynamics in presidential policy making often assume that bureaucrats will not play a decisive or even influential role in crafting the character and content of policy. They are seen as important players in a broader policy-making dynamic, critical mostly for implementation purposes or to provide the White House with technical advice. In each of the successful cases cited here there was a cooperative process due in large part to a collegial alliance between the White House and other participants.[6] Related to this was a clear understanding by each set of actors as to the nature of their role within the particular strategy being employed. For example, in the delegated strategy the DPS did not try to usurp policy development by undercutting the CSC. The DPS coordinated information coming in from the CSC and advised it of the president's preferences; at no time did it seek to control policy development per se.

The role of honest broker was, according to the evidence considered here, fulfilled in all the successful cases, usually by the DPS but on occasion by bureaucrats in the executive branch. An honest broker in this instance is loosely defined as an individual or organization that not only acts as gatekeeper in processing and filtering information and advice brought to the president, but it does so in such a way that all relevant viewpoints are represented. Honest broker is a term that is often applied to the chief of staff. In the cases presented here, it was the DPS that brought all relevant perspectives to the president's attention. One reason, of course, is that Carter did not designate an official chief of staff until late in his term. Although Hamilton Jordan acted as de facto chief until his appointment was made official, the DPS performed in that role as well. On occasion, the DPS assumed the role of policy advocate, but more often it was directed to do so by the president. In the case of civil service reform, responsibility was delegated to Alan Campbell, director of the CSC. Campbell brought all perspectives to the president's desk, including those that ran counter to his own. When a president has the benefit of a delegated agent, particularly one who heads a department or agency, to act as an honest broker and not just as an advocate for presidential political perspectives, the White House's job of coordinating information is made easier. While that is basically self-evident; what might not be so clear is that it may not happen very often, even though the appointment process is often used to politicize the bureaucracy, thus maximizing the likelihood of securing responsiveness to presidential preferences.

The ability to accurately read and assess both the possibilities and obstacles embedded in the political landscape was another element common to the successful cases. While "accurately" is a subjective judgment based on impressionistic evidence, several plausible instances of such accuracy or political astuteness present themselves. Even in the case if the youth employment initiative, which ultimately failed to pass Congress, the president was able to garner a great deal of credit for his efforts from the public and many members of Congress. This is at least partially due to the fact that the administration correctly read the political landscape. It understood that the issue of unemployment in general needed particular attention, and realized that attacking youth and minority unemployment would be a positive way to deal with the problem while acting on its own convictions. The fact that budgetary conditions precluded such a large initiative did not hurt the president given that he eventually dropped all efforts to push through a huge program and instead focused on maintaining existing programs. In this way he was able to legitimately claim that he had faced the problems and presented viable solutions for them, but that he was unable to follow through because of the structural budgetary conditions.

In all three successful cases the administration was able to assess the political possibilities and act on them in such a way as to enhance the president's chance of getting what he wanted. This in turn elevated the administration's stature and prestige in the eyes of the media, the public, and the Washington community. Advisory structures were open, so that a large amount of information reached the president's desk, although in distilled versions.

There is one important note of interest here. This relatively large amount of information is welcome in the presidency, especially one that seeks open-ended advisory processes, because presidents presumably wish to reduce the uncertainty factor in the political arena by reducing the level of uncertainty. Of course, time constraints and bounded rationality present natural limits within which to pursue and synthesize information, but given these constraints presidents and their staffs seek more rather than less information so as to minimize their risk factor.

Other commonalities in the successful cases include involvement of the DPS at the beginning of the policy formulation process, and the fact that the policy issues under consideration came up later in the president's term. The latter suggests that lessons learned from less successful cases of policy development make their way into the presidential calculus regarding subsequent policy formulation.[7] This pattern is evidence of a type of "term cycle" that supports Paul Light's notion of "increasing presidential effectiveness."[8] Simply put, a president is more successful later in his term because he and his staff are more comfortable and familiar with their jobs.

COMMONALITIES IN THE FAILED CASES

In a sense, the commonalities emerging in the failed cases are opposites of the common elements in the successful cases. One of the commonalities of the failed cases was the administration's *failure* to assess the political landscape properly. In all three cases, political problems contributed to the downfall of the proposals or, at the very least, hindered Carter's attempts to get most of what he wanted. Perhaps all, or certainly most, presidential agenda items run into political problems, but the failed cases analyzed here seem to have all suffered from the administration's inability (or in some cases unwillingness) to systematically address and thus overcome political pitfalls. For example, Carter's failure to see the political implications of not backing off his zero-cost stance in the case of welfare reform proved harmful to him by contributing to his loss of political capital and the broader systemic problem of declining public confidence in American institutions. Similar dynamics—whether they were perpetuated by Carter himself, members of his staff, or actors in the agencies or departments—surfaced in all three failed cases.

The three failed cases also suffered from some policy makers encroaching on the turf of others, which contributed to failed or incoherent advisory processes. For example, the PRP, which was designed as a policy committee, tried on several occasions during the creation of the Department of Education to supplement its substantive perspective with political assessments. While this is certainly not a bad thing in a normative sense, it was unable to do so to the extent other similarly charged organizations could. The consequence was that political perspectives became muddled or were patently incorrect, and the more politically astute operatives in the White House and elsewhere expended considerable resources to sort out the situation. But the damage had been done. In each of the failed cases policy actors in both the political and policy realms overstepped the boundaries of their jurisdiction as Carter defined them, causing the various set processes to be less coordinated and consequently lessening the president's chances of being able to meet his policy objectives.

Finally, all three categories were burdened with intrabranch dissension that either could not be controlled or efforts to control it came too late in the game to be effective. Intrabranch dissension is often seen as a positive for the president to the extent that it fosters productive debate over multiple policy options. It is when it cannot be controlled or the dissenting parties cannot be brought on board that dissension can wreck policy direction. It does this in a number of ways, not the least of which is by doing harm to the president's professional reputation when it is perceived that he cannot govern his own house. In the case of welfare reform, Secretaries

Marshall at the DOL and Califano at HEW were continuously at odds over the provisions of a jobs program. The two secretaries' staffs were deeply divided as well. This dissension cut broadly into the administration's comity and severely hampered its efforts to construct a welfare reform proposal that was at once comprehensive and cost effective. In all three categories, uncontrollable intrabranch dissension plagued policy progress to varying degrees, frustrating Carter's attempts to get very much of what he wanted from the advisory process and, ultimately, in policy substance. In at least two of the successful cases (youth employment and especially Energy II) there was some dissension, but an active DPS moved quickly to mitigate the problems and bring all participants on board. Thus, the best-case scenario for an administration is to try and avoid deep divisions among its members, even if it means losing some of the positive attributes that might come from such disagreements. It is then incumbent on the staff to assure that a reasonably broad range of viewpoints come to the attention of those charged with crafting policy substance. If controlling policy dissension is not possible, the second best alternative is to assure that the WHS plays an active role in brokering the disagreements, including identifying the location of the dissension and then mediating an agreement, even if it must be imposed upon the participants. Such a role is crucial to preserving both the integrity of the president's wishes and the administration's public stature. It is not clear from existing theory that politicization can guard against dissension. It is also not clear that dissension is necessarily bad for an administration. In fact, dissension is often a useful springboard to further discussion. But politicization may not be able to minimize conflict when it is time for compromise. Too much dissension, as we have seen, can ultimately hurt the administration's image.

THE NEW INSTITUTIONALISM AND IMPLICATIONS FOR THEORY BUILDING AND FURTHER RESEARCH

Throughout this book I have argued that to understand the complexities of presidential policy making writ large, one needs to understand the nature, content, and consequences of the advice a president receives. Armed with this understanding, one is in a better position to explore other elements of policy making and the many factors that impinge upon the larger decision-making process. I have further argued that the relative successes and failures of the cases analyzed in this study are related to the dynamics of the information the president received, how it came to him in the first place, from what sources, what he did with it, and how it played out in the political arena. But it is also the case that advisory elements are only part of the story. There is more to the presidency than information processing. This process is best understood by looking at the factors that affected the advisory mechanism through which presidents come to understand the vagaries of policy substance and the likely impact on their political fortunes. Other elements—many located primarily outside the White House—are important, to be sure. I have tried to note these whenever possible, but for the most part kept my focus on how presidents (in this study, only one president) might utilize an information base by which to decrease their uncertainty in a complex political system.

My theoretical framework suggests that although presidents begin as only one of several competing institutions in a separated system, this does not necessarily mean they are weak.[9] The new institutionalism perspective I adopted is summarized below, but here it is necessary to note that institutions do impinge upon and constrain a president's choice space. Within those parameters presidents enjoy varying degrees of autonomy, both symbolic and substantive. However, that autonomy is exercised within an institutional framework that largely sets the character of incentives the president works from, and from which he derives, builds, and modifies his "pure" preferences into "realistic" ones. This was certainly the case with Carter, and for reasons spelled out earlier, Carter's presidency is sufficiently similar to (and different from) other presidencies that there is little reason to doubt that many of the larger conclusions generated by this study would not be borne out in studies of other administrations. There are individual idiosyncrasies (the stuff of nonsystematic variance) to be sure, but the larger conclusions can be cast in a broader institutional framework.

Giving rise to this theoretical concern is the susceptibility of presidency research to criticisms that it either tries to base generalizations on one or a few cases, or worse, for not trying to generalize at all. Thus the perception has been that knowledge about the presidency is noncumulative, ad hoc, and good only for understanding one or a few presidencies and/or the nature of the times in which they served.[10] The analysis presented in this book is guilty of examining only one president. However, the study was designed and executed in a manner designed to discern the nature of presidential advice, the dynamics of information usage, the constraints of institutions versus the impact of personal factors, and the character of White House–bureaucratic relations. In examining only the Carter administration, my objective was to get deep beneath the surface of one presidency so as to better understand how institutional dynamics identified as important in longitudinal studies were played out in an administration that defies easy categorization in a number of crucial areas. Thus, the purpose of the study is to delve into an area of inquiry that has enjoyed a great deal of theoretical speculation but has lacked empirical refine-ment.[11] This book serves as a complement to more longitudinal studies examining the evolutionary development of the White House staff. Where those studies have looked at presidencies over time, I have tried to explore problems of presidential pursuit of information and disentangle the mix-ture of policy and politics in presidential policy making.

Advisory Patterns and the Study of the Presidency
Although institutions are fairly rigid entities, encompassing their own boundaries, temporal order, and rules of procedure constraining the abil-ity of actors to move autonomously within them, there is a great deal of evidence presented in this study that demonstrates that, within the param-eters of organizational boundaries, individuals exercise a certain amount of latitude, sometimes restricted and other times less so.[12] Indeed, it is very likely the case that formal structures greatly influences the type of policy one gets. The presidency is no exception, and the case studies presented in this book largely support this claim. But individuals form varieties of for-mal and informal networks and the perspectives that filter through these networks to the president condition the kind of policy that results. The new institutionalism is burdened by a lack of conceptual clarity from which to guide analysis. Is it formal rules and processes that guide decisions? Is it informal policy networks? What about the role of individuals, especially in an institution so clearly demarcated at any one time by the occupant of the Oval Office? While this study has done little to clarify, and has perhaps muddied the concept further, I have found the idea that individuals have constrained autonomy within organizational and institutional boundaries to be particularly helpful, especially when thinking about the presidency. This becomes even clearer when comparing the presidency to other insti-tutions such as Congress, which is run more by the dictates of formal rules than is the presidency. However, a perspective similar to the one I have adopted here might provide some insight into legislative politics given the fact that informal networks of individuals with more or less formal agenda-setting powers (such as caucuses) more and more govern congressional politics.[13] Of course, an institutionalist view can only take us so far, as I dis-cuss below, but it does offer a useful model for thinking about the bound-aries between individual and institution.

A potential impediment to theorizing is the fact that individuals shift from administration to administration. This relatively high level of turn-over (relative to many other organizations, where members of the organi-zation usually enjoy longer tenures than those found in the presidency) can make generalization, or even identifying long-term structural patterns difficult. However, this may not be as big a problem as it appears on its face. Although individuals shift, the networks they form may conform, albeit roughly, to recurring patterns of advisory processes, exhibiting organizational and, ultimately, institutional properties.[14] Researchers would do well to continue their quest to construct typologies or categories of presidential organization patterns. This study has identified three patterns of advisory dynamics consistent with policy centralization in the White House. However, they are broad. A number of advisory patterns may manifest themselves within each. To refine and clarify the different types of processes found within the greater categorical patterns is a challenge that remains. However, typologies and models must not be too inflexible. Rather, they should be suggestive of possible interactive patterns and the prospects for success or failure that accompany each. Any attempt to be too rigid in categorizing exclusive patterns risks losing sight of the several layers of interaction and the vicissitudes of informal processes that lie beneath the surface of formalized operations.[15]

One of the major findings of this study is the conclusion that the quality of the partnership between the White House and the bureaucracy is more important for the attainment of a policy proposal conducive to presidential preferences than is the pursuit of either responsiveness or policy competence. In each category the White House played an active role, regardless of the location of policy development. Further thought and study should be devoted to the problem of determining whether this is constant across administrations and, if not, whether it has any consequences for policy success. The new institutionalism has for me proven quite useful in sorting out these individual and institutional patterns.

Prospects for Presidential Control of Policy Processes
The findings of this study suggest that presidential control of policy processes may in part be a function of how deeply the president himself becomes personally involved. Even President Carter, who allegedly became deeply involved in policy development, tended to back away from issues as they ebbed and flowed with the tide of politics. On those issues where he showed personal involvement, he tended to get more of what he wanted. While it is true that presidents can pay only so much attention to any one issue, they can get more of what they want if they are able to effectively prioritize issues and personally act on those priorities. Once they have determined priorities, presidents can spend personal time on those issues while delegating other tasks to others. Further research thus might focus on presidential involvement with policy development and not just with the articulation of a presidential agenda.

WHITHER POLICY COMPETENCE AND RESPONSIVENESS?

Policy competence and responsiveness are important parts of the political and policy lives of presidents. They need both if policy is to have the maximum chance for securing most of what they want from *either* a political or substantive perspective. Given the experience of the Carter administration, it seems more important to correctly perceive the politics of the issue, the content of the policy initiative, and advice as to the likely impact on and reactions by affected groups, constituencies, and departments than to pursue one type of analysis to the detriment of the other. This offers further support to the overriding importance of the character of the partnership between the departments and the White House in understanding policy development.[16]

Policy competence and responsiveness are important components of presidential policy making, but the pursuit of each may in part be a function of the type of policy being pursued and the possibilities manifest in the prevailing political environment. The conceptualization of responsiveness and policy competence may be best thought of in terms of a seamless web. My analysis implies that it is possible that presidents have a choice as to the location of policy development, and they may tend to fully centralize more than they engage in mixed or delegated strategies. However, the identification of process variables remains relatively constant, although their values may rise or fall with differing circumstances in different modes of political time. The measure of policy competence or responsiveness thus is not so much its presence or absence as much as it is a matter of the degree. Success or failure thus might be a result of an intermediate consideration. That is, what matters most is whether institutional/organizational entities are engaged in open politics with a fluid exchange of information. Closed politics, mostly played out in the centralized process, can work against the attainment of a successful policy proposal unless the president, or more likely, his staff, is sufficiently attuned to external perspectives and incorporates these in what is otherwise a staff-directed advisory mode of policy development.

For example, in the centralized, staff-directed strategy, the White House must have input from outside actors in the bureaucracy while *control* of the process can remain in the hands of the WHS. When the boundaries of individual roles are violated or disappear altogether, then well-known organizational pathologies, such as uncoordinated action, stifled communication, suboptimization, and the like, will likely poison the process. With roles clearly defined and understood (e.g., the White House controls policy development while understanding the need to receive crucial input from outside), then procedural mechanisms function smoothly.

Presidents can then get most of what they want *regardless* of the strategy employed. However, roles must be clearly defined (most likely by the president) and adhered to, and pains must be taken to determine the most appropriate strategy to be employed.[17]

One point must be made about the staff-shift framework as it relates to other advisory approaches, most notably that of multiple advocacy. The emphasis on the honest broker and cooperative relations that the staff-shift framework emphasizes has much in common with multiple advocacy. However, it differs in significant ways and, to some extent, can ameliorate shortcomings of the multiple-advocacy framework. Not withstanding the fact that multiple advocacy tends to be elided with foreign policy, my case analyses have shown that it can be applied with modification to domestic policy. Both staff shift and multiple advocacy stress the importance of bringing presidents as much information as possible. Both stress the need to draw information from a broad array of advisers. But multiple advocacy is hindered both by the enormous demands it makes on presidential time and energy, and the dampening effect of a highly, perhaps overly, structured decision hierarchy.

An advisory system that is based on the concept of staff shift addresses these issues. First, it does not tax a president's resources to nearly the extent that multiple advocacy does. If the president has a responsive staff (as is the case most of the time), then he need only be highly involved in setting policy parameters consistent with his preferences. Any further direct involvement on his part is then a function of his degree of personal interest, but staff shift minimizes the necessity to be personally involved at every stage of the process, as is implied with multiple advocacy. Second, advisory arrangements need not be overly structured. Hierarchy is most likely the desired mode of operations if for no other reason than to insert efficiency into the process. But hierarchy within a staff-shift framework fosters collegial, informal relations and thus captures the positive benefits of multiple advocacy—namely innovation and responsiveness to the president's preferences. There is also the likelihood that staff shift is more likely to be capable of absorbing the multitude of different perspectives that domestic policy engenders, as well as the tendency for competing institutions to be involved more directly in making domestic policy. Thus, while staff shift and multiple advocacy have some underlying similarities, their methods for absorbing and integrating information differ substantially, and the likely consequences of those distinctions imply that presidential activity will differ as well.

From a methodological standpoint, it is still important to study policy competence and responsiveness, but to do so as variables affecting policy quality rather than as the units of analysis themselves. The analysis presented in this study suggests the need to refine our conception of responsiveness. As Graham Wilson has pointed out, policy competence can contain a higher conception of the role of expertise by supplementing policy substance with political assessment.[18] Similarly, my analysis shows that responsiveness can have a substantive component: Responsiveness to the president's program was often supplemented with a substantive assessment in the Carter administration. This is especially important when the policy initiatives include large, new programs, whose aggregate impact is unknown.

Another methodological problem arises when trying to analyze information such as that presented here. Responsiveness and policy competence do not always conform to the operational definitions that have been offered so as to classify the types of data the president relies on. That is to say, policy competence may be responsive, and responsiveness may contain substantial substantive content. Given a president with Jimmy Carter's public goods perspective it can be difficult to classify information based primarily on short-term political criteria, in the case of responsiveness, or on long-term policy measures, as is often the case with policy competence. But the researcher need not fall prey to this red herring. Policy components are often coupled with policy analysis, and vice versa. That is not to say that the two are of a kind. Rather, it is not unusual for the two to be interwoven. Nevertheless, it is the presidential staff that is most often responsible for picking, choosing, synthesizing, rejecting, accepting, modifying, confirming, and ultimately presenting policy options along with the expected concomitant political consequences. For purposes of scholarly analysis, it is incumbent upon the researcher to examine the source and likely impact of such information. A president with Carter's large-scale, public-goods-oriented goals may receive *responsive* information couched in *substantive* language. In other words, responding to the president in substantive terms may not always indicate policy competence. If the analysis centers on the types of policy alternatives that can best satisfy the president's objectives, then the analysis may be couched in substantive terms but might more rightly be classified as responsive. Again, location may turn out to be less important as policy competence may come from the White House, and responsiveness from the bureaucracy. But to analyze this fully, one would need a broader theory of presidential style and a president's orientation toward governing. Lacking that, one can make only speculative judgments. Context is important, to be sure. Political and institutional variables are to be noted. So while we can continue to think in broad analytic terms about the nature of policy and political advice and how it is digested and used in the course of presidential policy making, we should be cognizant of the possibility of improperly categorizing the data. Policy substance and political analysis are interlinked in a maximally informed investment strategy, and it is necessary to take these factors into account when analyzing advisory strategies. That said, this colloquy is only a quibble in a larger context of the policy-politics relationship, regardless of whether that relationship is symbiotic or antagonistic. Researchers can and should continue to employ operational definitions of neutral and political advice, but they must be aware of when those definitions may be in need of revision or qualification. That realization can be guided only by theorizing about the contextual and often conditional nature of presidential leadership.

One final methodological issue emerges from this analysis. When constructing operational definitions for research on policy competence, the Carter administration's experience suggests the importance of considering the president's theory of governing when determining what constitutes policy competence and responsiveness. The WHS may engage in responsive activity but couch its language in the parlance of policy substance. Researchers thus may erroneously classify information that is really responsive to presidential preferences as policy competence. To clarify the point, in Jimmy Carter's case, his theory of governing included a strong public goods component. Consequently, responsiveness was not always rendered in terms of what was good for *constituencies*, but, rather, what was good for *government* and the president's policy objectives. This often entailed substantive analysis by the White House. Researchers therefore need to be sensitive to the president's theory of governing when classifying information as substantive or responsive. I propose they do this by incorporating a conception of a higher form of responsiveness when analyzing presidential information patterns.

Still, the traditional framework involving responsiveness and policy competence was not particularly helpful in this study. Indeed, the notion of a higher form of policy competence was useful for pointing out the contributions of civil servants to the White House decision process, but it also served to muddy the analytical waters. In a sense, it emerged as the functional equivalent of a nonfalsifiable theory. I found it relatively easy to point out where civil servants fell short of this ideal but difficult to distinguish the higher form from that of bureaucratic parochial self-interest. If the higher form is of any analytic use, it is in the area of identifying the strategies of actors and not as benchmark for measuring the relative success or failure of advice offered by the various participants. If policy competence as an analytic tool is of to be of value, it cannot be directly applicable to explaining *all* cases. It may more accurately reflect reality (the goal of any research enterprise), but it is more useful as one among many variables, and not as the focus of an entire project.

EXTENDING THE ANALYSIS: WHERE TO NOW?

The best way to extend the analysis presented here and utilize the insights identified by the study is to expand the number of administrations studied. This book has examined one president, three categories, and six policies. Doing so has allowed me to systematically explore a set of questions relevant to my inquiry, and, to a lesser extent, consider competing or alternative hypotheses. I have also been able to give an account of the level of uncertainty derived from my analysis. In all cases, institutional aspects were found to vary systematically, while personal ones were not as amenable to systematic inquiry. This strengthened the amount of certainty I could derive from institutional and organizational explanations, although it proved less so for individual idiosyncrasies. Nevertheless, all my findings are suggestive of the need for more analyses that can further understand the longitudinal dimensions of advising, something that was not possible given the parameters of the cases studied here.

Welcomed studies would contain either a replication of my analysis, done using other presidents and presidencies, or go further in-depth into one of the three categories in order to ascertain the extent to which those findings would support or differ from my consideration of the Carter administration. Similar studies examining foreign policy rather than domestic policy would be equally useful. The juxtaposition of foreign and domestic politics would help to construct middle range generalizations of presidential use of information. Perhaps interesting differences as well as similarities could be identified. It would then be the task of the researcher to explain the reasons for any discrepancies or continuities uncovered. Finally, where this study has explored noncrisis domestic priorities, it would be valuable to examine domestic nonpriorities. Much of what emerges from a presidential administration includes policies that were not high on the president's priority list. A study comparing how information was collected, disseminated, controlled, and used in nonpriority situations with the findings presented here would be of great use to presidency scholars and aid in the pursuit of identifying continuity and variation in the Oval Office. In addition, different theoretical frameworks might be useful in providing alternative interpretations of what has been found both here and in the broader literature. For example, the new economics of organization, with its emphasis on agency theory, might contribute additional insights into the vagaries of presidential organization from other angles, and thus enhance our broader understanding of the dynamics of the office. The new institutionalist framework employed here has been useful for understanding institutional-personal trade-offs, suggesting the applicability of other questions of interest to presidency researchers.

FINAL THOUGHTS ABOUT ADVISING, RESEARCH, AND PRESIDENCY THEORY

Institutional analysis is still the best way for presidency scholars to learn about presidents. Scholars have long noted the need to seek generalization and understand continuity in the presidency. But that only tells part of the story. The presidency is sensitive to the idiosyncrasies of the individual occupying the office to perhaps a greater degree than any other single political institution. While the president is the leader of an expansive executive establishment, it is still an intensely political office. Thus, while generalization is certainly an important and coveted, if all too elusive, goal of presidential research,[19] presidency scholars should seek not only commonalties but a systematic understanding of the differences within and across administrations, and the consequences of those differences.[20] We know a lot about *presidents,* now it is time to understand the *presidency.* This study shows, for example, that individuals have a non-negligible effect on the character and content of policy. Formal structures and the political contexts within which presidents act are constraining influences, conditioning the incentives and ultimately influencing their policy preferences, but they are not determinative. Individuals have an impact on process—especially in the presidency, where intrainstitutional factors are not as set as in, say, Congress, but more so than in the Supreme Court. No one really disputes the importance of individuals, but the importance of individuals exists across as well as within administrations.

Efforts to understand the presidency need to understand intra-administration variation as well as longitudinal dynamics. This study has certainly not filled this order, but the theoretical framework employed and the empirical findings presented here suggest the appropriateness of such an approach. Nevertheless, it is probably not possible to provide fully reliable generalizations on all issues of interest to presidential scholars. This is not an attempt to duck the problem of generalization but a reflection on reality.

Middle-range generalization may take the form of *classifying* advisory networks, network breakdowns, successes, failures, and the like.[21] Efforts at generalization could then proceed in two broad sweeps. First, the differences among administrations could be identified. Second, the dynamics underlying these differences could be analyzed. Scholars would then further understand where and why presidential policy advice differs, how the confluence of individual and institutional factors contributes to policy success, and so on. While scholars who advocate taking the president out of presidency studies have valid concerns, they can be addressed by looking to differing variables and factors leading to success and failure, while supplementing the analysis with details necessary for understanding presidential variation.

For example, Terry Moe makes a strong, carefully reasoned argument that the scholarly community needs to limit the number of variables studied and then focus mostly, if not exclusively, on institutional dynamics.[22] I agree with that approach and have tried to craft this study in just that manner, exploring more the organizational and institutional properties of the presidency as they played out in the Carter administration. If we are to learn much in a systematic sense, it makes sense to limit what we are studying while remaining sensitive to the possible impact of other variables or circumstances. By focusing on fewer variables we gain seemingly greater understanding of the variation inherent in the office of the presidency. Using one presidency to test a theoretical framework developed independent of that case is certainly a step in the right direction. For example, I have limited the variables of interest so as to gain greater insight into how they varied from case to case and category to category. I have also looked at congressional impact on the administration's policy decisions, but without fully engaging in a study of congressional interactions with the White House. To do so would only have muddled what I intended to say about presidential advisory processes within the WHS (especially the DPS) and the EOP.

As a collective scholarly enterprise, some have argued that work in the presidency needs to be cumulative.[23] But cumulative knowledge can mean putting at least some emphasis on discovering what is different about presidents in similar and different situations, as much so as it is about studying institutional resources only. Indeed, one can follow on the other. This is not to suggest that we need to, or even can, study the presidency without giving systematic attention to the individuals who reside at 1600 Pennsylvania Avenue. Nor is it inconsistent with Moe's analysis, as some might be tempted to claim. Institutional characteristics temper what is possible for different individuals in otherwise similar circumstances.

Well-crafted studies of individual presidents in the context of institutional constraints can do much to further our progress and at a faster rate than has been the case in the past. That is why, for example, I have placed so much stock in the variant of the new institutionalism that I employed in this book. Likewise, primarily institutional studies can add much by taking into account how or why individuals might matter in what they bring to the table in terms of experience, political acumen, skill, ideology, and the like.[24]

The common core of presidency research is that studies need to begin with an explicit theoretical framework that then informs empirical findings. We need to construct testable theories and examine well-chosen cases that will further our goal of accumulating systematic knowledge of the office and its occupants. The two need not be mutually exclusive. Matthew Dickinson's well-crafted study of Franklin Roosevelt's advisory system, it seems to me, does just that.[25] Although he focuses mainly on Roosevelt (with reference to other presidents), he derives lessons that might be useful to the presidency.

Differences between presidents need to be placed in a broader historical and theoretical context. In this manner scholars could attain cumulative knowledge while simultaneously accounting for the importance of individuals. Of course, looking at only one president can only yield propositions that are suggestive for further work rather than prove definitive or general by themselves. But further research is always needed, and works such as Dickinson's help map out research strategies that enable us to pinpoint anomalous areas that, upon further study and refection, may not be so anomalous after all. It also allows us to confirm softer impressions and to disentangle the relationships of important actors within and outside the White House. Perhaps equally important, it allows us to come to terms with what we simply cannot know because the circumstances are so idiosyncratic or specialized that we cannot derive any lessons from them that are useful for the study of the presidency.

Individuals are inherently more difficult to pinpoint, and this makes things like temperament, personality, style, and worldview hard to include as variables. Differing individual styles within an institutional framework can lead to fundamentally different outcomes in policy decisions,[26] which is why I contend the new institutionalism should be the general direction of future research. This approach, with its organizational framework sensitive to individual vagaries, can help account for both, although the emphasis is on the constraining nature of institutional and organizational structures. In this book, Carter himself is often outside the realm of analysis, which focuses on the DPS. Nonetheless, his view of his office and his public-goods approach to politics had a profound impact on how the DPS went about its job of collecting, synthesizing, and disseminating information and advice. Many of the documents analyzed support this contention. Using elements of both research approaches will, in my opinion, lead us to more fruitful theorizing in a manner broadly consistent with Moe's suggestion, and in so doing gain considerable understanding of the issues and interaction of various forces in a well-specified arena.

In using the new institutionalism, the purpose of this study has been to further understand an institution and the interplay of political and substantive advice within that institution. Presidential advice, information, and the process of policy making are elements of any administration. It is my hope that this book has been able to contribute in a positive, albeit modest, way to the attempt to explain how the two modes of analysis can be integrated in a White House–centered operation, regardless of the policy-making location. While I have examined only one president, I have tried to show how the conclusions drawn from that analysis can be useful for clarifying our understanding of the office. More work needs to be done, and the judgments presented here will certainly be refined, reformulated, and, in some cases, refuted. Nevertheless, the process of further grappling with both the theoretical and empirical issues that this and other studies have raised can add insight and substance to our understanding of institutional dynamics writ large. The effort to do so can only enhance, clarify, or confirm much of what we know, think we know, or simply do not know about the American presidency.

Notes

PREFACE

1. See Matthew J. Dickinson, "Neustadt and New Institutionalists: New Insights on Presidential Power?" typescript, Center for American Political Studies, Occasional paper 95-4, Harvard University, 1995. See also Matthew Dickinson, *Bitter Harvest: FDR, Presidential Power, and the Growth of the Presidential Branch*.

2. Dickinson, "Neustadt and New Institutionalists," 10.

3. Richard E. Neustadt, *Presidential Power and the Modern Presidents: The Politics of Leadership From Roosevelt to Reagan*, 128–29.

4. Terry M. Moe, "The Politicized Presidency" in *The New Direction in American Politics*, ed. John Chubb and Paul Peterson.

CHAPTER 1. FOUNDATIONS OF PRESIDENTIAL ANALYSIS

1. Roger B. Porter, *Presidential Decision Making: The Economic Policy Board*, 1.

2. Alexander L. George, "The Case for Multiple Advocacy in Making Foreign Policy," *American Political Science Review* 66 (Sept., 1972): 751–85; and Alexander L. George, *Presidential Decisionmaking in Foreign Policy: The Effective Use of Information and Advice*.

3. This particular segment of the presidency literature is voluminous. What follows is only a brief beginning, but see, for example, Norman C. Thomas, "Presidential Advice and Information: Policy and Program Formulation" in *The Presidency in Contemporary Context*, ed. Norman C. Thomas; Charles E. Walcott and Karen M. Hult, *Governing the White House: From Hoover through LBJ*; James P. Pfiffner, ed., *The Managerial Presidency*, 2d ed.; John Hart, *The Presidential Branch: From Washington to Clinton*, 2d ed.; Matthew J. Dickinson, *Bitter Harvest: FDR, Presidential Power and the Growth of the Presidential Branch*; and John Burke, *The Institutional Presidency*.

4. See Charles O. Jones, *The Presidency in a Separated System*, chap. 3.

5. Karen Hult, "Advising the President," in *Researching the Presidency: Vital Questions, New Approaches*, ed. George C. Edwards III, John H. Kessel, and Bert A. Rockman.

6. This theoretical framework will be detailed in chap. 2.

7. Any work dealing with this trend must begin with Terry Moe's seminal essay, "The Politicized Presidency," in *New Direction in American Politics*, ed. Chubb and Peterson. Moe's perspective, especially that dealing with the politicization of the president's appointment power, is ably tested in Thomas Weko, *The Politicizing Presidency: The White House Personnel Office, 1948–1994*. For an early comment on the extent of the politicizing tendencies of the presidency, see Hugh Heclo, "OMB and the Presidency—The Problem of 'Neutral Competence'" *The Public Interest* 38 (winter, 1975): 89–98.

8. For a review of the tendency and, indeed, necessity for presidential scholars to rate

presidents, see Richard Rose, "Evaluating Presidents," in *Researching the Presidency*, ed. Edwards et al.

9. Terry Moe, "Presidents, Institutions, and Theory," in *Researching the Presidency*, ed. Edwards et al. Rational institutionalism has been the analytic focal point of a growing body of presidency literature. Terry Moe's work is arguably the driving force behind most, if not all, of this literature. For his work on the presidency, see esp. Moe, "Politicized Presidency"; Moe, "Presidents, Institutions, and Theory"; Moe, "The Presidency and the Bureaucracy: The Presidential Advantage" in *The Presidency and the Political System*, ed. Michael Nelson, 5th ed.; and Moe and Scott A. Wilson, "Presidents and the Politics of Structure" *Law and Contemporary Problems* 57 (spring, 1994): 1–44. For more general statements of the utility of the framework applied across a host of institutional settings, see Moe, "The New Economics of Organization," *American Journal of Political Science* 28 (Nov., 1984): 739–77; Moe, "The Politics of Structural Choice: Toward a Theory of Public Bureaucracy" in *Organization Theory: From Chester Barnard to the Present and Beyond*, ed. Oliver E. Williamson; and Moe and Gary J. Miller, "The Positive Theory of Hierarchies" in *Political Science: The Science of Politics*, ed. Herbert F. Weisberg.

10. Stephen Skowronek, *The Politics Presidents Make: Leadership from John Adams to George Bush*.

11. "Politics" is used in a number of ways throughout this book. It includes all of the factors just mentioned, as well as the more pejorative references to the Machiavellian manipulation of situations, people, or the factors that condition their interaction. I include more in-depth clarification of the term later in this chapter.

12. Although the consideration of the trade-offs, interaction, and substantive implications of policy and politically relevant information tends to be concentrated in studies of executive branch politics, their systematic contemplation has begun to be incorporated into a greater array of studies covering a variety of political settings and bearing a family resemblance to presidents and their staffs. One particularly useful example in the legislative arena is Richard Hall's discussion of "policy-relevant" information and "political intelligence," and how each is pursued and used by members of Congress, their "enterprise," and committee and subcommittee staffs. See Richard L. Hall, *Participation in Congress*, esp. 89–93.

13. See, among others, Peri Arnold, *Making the Managerial Presidency: Comprehensive Reorganization Planning, 1905–1996*, rev. 2d ed.; Burke, *Institutional Presidency*; Campbell, *Managing the Presidency*; Hart, *Presidential Branch*; Patrick J. Haney, *Organizing for Foreign Policy Crises: Presidents, Advisers, and the Management of Decision Making*; John Kessel, "The Structure of the Reagan White House" *American Journal of Political Science* 28 (May, 1984): 231–58; Richard Neustadt, "Presidency and Legislation: The Growth of Central Clearance" *American Political Science Review* 48 (Sept., 1954): 641–71; Walcott and Hult, *Governing the White House*; Dickinson, *Bitter Harvest*; and Pfiffner, ed., *The Managerial Presidency*.

14. Presidential staffing patterns have been the subject of a great deal of scholarly attention in recent years. Of the many excellent works in this area, see Shirley Anne Warshaw, "Staffing Patterns in the Modern White House," in *Presidential Policymaking: An End-of-Century Assessment*, ed. Steven A. Shull; Samuel Kernell, "The Evolution of the White House Staff," in *Can the Government Govern?*, ed. John Chubb and Paul Peterson; Dickinson, *Bitter Harvest*; and Hart, *Presidential Branch*.

15. Roger B. Porter, "Advising the President" *PS* 19 (fall, 1986): 868.

16. Richard Tanner Johnson, *Managing the White House: An Intimate Study of the Presidency*. Useful critiques can be found in Burke, *Institutional Presidency*, 55–59; and Porter, *Presidential Decision Making*.

17. Meena Bose makes essentially the same point in her discussion of the differing decision processes at work in the Eisenhower and Kennedy administrations. See her *Shaping and Signaling Presidential Policy: The National Security Decision Making of Eisenhower and Kennedy*, 99–101.

18. John Burke and Fred I. Greenstein, with Larry Berman and Richard Immerman, *How Presidents Test Reality: Decisions on Vietnam, 1954 and 1965*, 274–75.

19. The exploration and explanation of intra-administration variation within particular presidencies is not new to presidency studies. But the mark of a study can be at least partially measured by how well these studies enable us not only to understand the president under scrutiny, but also to understand the dynamics of the presidency generally. One example that considers one president is Erwin C. Hargrove, *Jimmy Carter as President: Leadership and the Politics of the Public Good.*

20. Many studies of Congress use these properties as the foundation of institutional analysis. An excellent recent example is Tim Groseclose and David C. King, "Committee Theories and Committee Institutions" (paper presented at the annual meeting of the American Political Science Association, Washington, D.C., 1997).

21. On the general nature of Congress as institution as well as various perspectives on the nature of equilibrium and strategy, see Kenneth A. Shepsle and Barry R. Weingast, eds., *Positive Theories of Congressional Institutions.* It is worth noting that both major strands of theory concerning the construction of a committee system, the distributive and the informational, share the view that the creation of congressional institutions reduce uncertainty by providing a means through which members can specialize, be it for reelection or collective good purposes. See, for example, David Mayhew, *Congress: The Electoral Connection*, and Keith Krehbiel, *Information and Legislative Organization.* For various perspectives on the dynamics of leadership in a political environment not terribly conducive to the assertion of strong leadership, see Barbara Sinclair, *Legislators, Leaders, and Lawmaking: The U.S. House of Representatives in the Postreform Era;* David Rohde, *Parties and Leaders in the Postreform House;* and Gary Cox and Matthew McCubbins, *Legislative Leviathan: Party Government in the House.* Finally, on the incremental nature of congressional change, see David C. King, *Turf Wars: How Congressional Committees Claim Jurisdiction.*

22. Jack Knight, *Institutions and Social Conflict*, 3.

23. For a description of each of these, as well as a slightly different discussion of organizational and institutional properties of the presidency, see Burke, *Institutional Presidency* 12–52.

24. I discuss various ways to discern the presidential institution when I consider the application of the new institutionalism to presidency research below.

25. On the variation in presidential use of the cabinet, the cabinet's status as a deliberative body, and cabinet-staff conflict, see James P. Pfiffner, *The Modern Presidency*, 111–22. Analyses of the dynamic properties of presidential reliance on the State Department versus the National Security Council can be found in Bert A. Rockman, "America's *Departments* of State: Irregular and Regular Syndromes of Policy Making" *American Political Science Review* 75 (Dec., 1981): 911–27; and Cecil V. Crabb and Kevin V. Mulcahy, *American National Security: A Presidential Perspective.*

26. Warshaw, *Domestic Presidency;* and Hart, *Presidential Branch.*

27. Lyn Ragsdale and John J. Theis III, "The Institutionalization of the American Presidency, 1924–1992," *American Journal of Political Science* 41 (Oct., 1997): 1280–1318.

28. Walcott and Hult, *Governing the White House*, 260–63.

29. There is an ever-expanding body of literature applied across several fields of political science that holds many of these characteristics of institutionalization in common. For analyses on the American political system, see, among others, Nelson W. Polsby, "The Institutionalization of the U.S. House of Representatives," *American Political Science Review* 62 (Mar., 1968): 144–68; Patrick J. Fett and Daniel E. Ponder, "The Deinstitutionalization of the U.S. Congress?" (paper presented at the annual meeting of the American Political Science Association, Chicago, 1995); Daniel E. Ponder and Russell D. Renka, "Reversing the Institutionalization of the U.S. Congress" (paper presented at the annual meeting of the Midwest Political Science Association, Chicago, 1998); Robert S. Gilmour, "The Institutionalized

Presidency: A Conceptual Clarification," in *The Presidency in Contemporary Context*, ed. Norman Thomas; Margaret Jane Wyszomirski, "The Discontinuous Institutional Presidency," in *Executive Leadership in Anglo-American Systems*, ed. Colin Campbell and Margaret Jane Wyszomirski; and Ragsdale and Theis, "Institutionalization of the American Presidency."

30. See, for example, Jack L. Walker, *Mobilizing Interest Groups in America: Patrons, Professions, and Social Movements*.

31. Nelson W. Polsby, *Consequences of Party Reform*; Mark A. Peterson, *Legislating Together: The White House and Capitol Hill from Eisenhower to Reagan*; George C. Edwards III, *At the Margins: Presidential Leadership of Congress*; Jon R. Bond and Richard Fleisher, *The President in the Legislative Arena*; Jones, *Presidency in a Separated System*.

32. Stephen J. Wayne, "Approaches," in *Studying the Presidency*, ed. George C. Edwards III and Stephen J. Wayne. Quote is at 17.

33. Many of these are detailed in John Hart, "Neglected Aspects of the Study of the Presidency," *Annual Review of Political Science* 1 (1998): 379–99.

34. Hult, "Advising the President," 112. See also Theodore C. Sorensen, *Decision Making in the White House*, 57–77.

35. See chap. 2 for a more complete treatment of this analytical lense.

36. This is the primary analytical framework employed in the book. I have covered it in only the briefest terms here. See chap. 2 for a far more detailed explanation of the properties of the staff shift framework.

37. Graham K. Wilson, "The Challenge to Neutral Competence: A Preface to a Panel," (paper presented at the annual meeting of the American Political Science Association, Washington, D.C., 1993), 8.

38. Policy competence, often referred to as "neutral" competence, has fallen out of favor in some circles for both political and conceptual reasons. As a matter of course, policy competence must be a major part of the explanation of this book. My study goes beyond an analytic focus on policy competence and responsiveness to include other important factors of presidential information. This includes a consideration of advisory strategies and an integrated look at interest group pressure, bureaucratic parochialism, failures of politicization, and the like. Useful studies exist of presidential and executive branch relations, interest group impacts on decision making, and presidential congressional relations. They are all valuable for their depth of coverage within their particular area of interest. This book integrates these components using document analysis and endeavors to provide as complete a picture as possible of Carter's attempts to garner, use, and disseminate advice and information.

39. Neustadt, *Presidential Powe*, esp. 44–63.

40. There is much controversy over the extent to which presidential popularity can be parlayed into enhanced bargaining successes with other institutions, especially Congress. Arguments positing little relationship between the two variables are found in Bond and Fleisher, *President in the Legislative Arena*, 181–83; and Edwards, *At the Margins*, 126–43. Cf. Peterson, *Legislating Together*, 199–201, for a slightly more optimistic view of presidential popularity and the propensity of presidents to take bolder action when they enjoy enhanced prestige.

41. See Dickinson, "Neustadt and New Institutionalists"; Dickinson, *Bitter Harvest*; and Hart, *Presidential Branch*.

42. The case analysis of the creation of the Department of Education in chap. 4 will help clarify this distinction.

43. Walcott and Hult, *Governing the White House*, 11.

44. Skowronek, *Politics Presidents Make*, 17.

45. On the problem of reification, see Andrew P. Vayda, Bonnie J. McCay, and Cristina Eghenter, "Concepts of Process in Social Science Explanations" *Philosophy of the Social Sciences* 21 (Sept., 1991): 318–31. For an extremely useful discussion of process and variance approaches as applied to the study of the presidency, see Karen M. Hult, Charles E. Walcott,

and Thomas Weko, "Qualitative Research and the Study of the U.S. Presidency" (paper presented at the annual meeting of the American Political Science Association, Washington, D.C., 1997).

46. Vayda et al, "Concepts of Process," 326.

47. See chap. 2 for elaboration.

48. Martha S. Feldman, *Order Without Design: Information Production and Policymaking*, 136. Cited in Edwin Hutchins, "Organizing Work by Adaptation," in *Organizational Learning*, ed. Michael D. Cohen and Lee S. Sproull, 50.

49. Joseph Califano, as Secretary of Health, Education, and Welfare, did hinder the process by various tactics and delaying mechanisms, as will be explained in the empirical chapters.

50. Dickinson, *Bitter Harvest*.

51. I am indebted to Matt Dickinson, whose thoughtful critique of my concept of policy success and failure forced me to clarify my thinking on this issue.

52. Quoted in John W. Kingdon, *Agendas, Alternatives, and Public Policies*, 2d ed., 132.

53. This definition has intellectual roots in Knight's treatment of coordination in social institutions. See Knight, *Institutions and Social Conflict*, esp. 7.

54. I spend a great deal of time detailing presidential incentives and the preferences that derive from them in chap. 2.

Chapter 2. Presidents, the Presidency, and Information

1. See, among others, Richard Waterman, *Presidential Influence and the Administrative State;* Moe, " Politicized Presidency"; and Weko, *Politicizing Presidency*. For a useful analysis of the institutionalization of domestic policy making in the presidency, see Shirley Anne Warshaw, *The Domestic Presidency: Policy Making in the White House*.

2. See Joel D. Aberbach and Bert A. Rockman, "Mandates or Mandarins? Control and Discretion in the Modern Administrative State," in *Managerial Presidency*, ed. Pfiffner, 2d ed.

3. This line of inquiry has taken hold mostly in the congressional literature, especially dealing with the nature of committee membership. The goal is to ascertain whether there is a legislator-bureaucrat connection in which bureaucrats reward districts represented by a member of Congress sitting on their oversight committee or subcommittee. See R. Douglas Arnold, *Congress and the Bureaucracy: A Theory of Influence*. For a different interpretation that sees the bureaucrat-legislator relationship in a different light, namely for the gains that can be made from decreasing information costs and utilizing greater expertise to execute programs, see D. Roderick Kiewiet and Matthew D. McCubbins, *The Logic of Delegation: Congressional Parties and the Appropriations Process*.

4. James W. Fesler, "Politics, Policy, and Bureaucracy at the Top," *Annals of the American Academy of Political and Social Science* 466 (Mar., 1983): 23–41; and Moe, "Politicized Presidency."

5. An excellent review of the president's use of the appointments powers for maximum control in the administrative presidency, see Waterman, *Presidential Influence*. The best treatment to date of the relationship between theoretical proposition and empirical reality in the politicization of the presidency is Weko, *Politicizing Presidency*.

6. I discuss the difference between presidential preferences and incentives later in this chapter.

7. See Woodrow Wilson, "The Study of Administration," in *Classics in Public Administration*, ed. Jay M. Shafritz and Albert C. Hyde, 2d ed.; and Max Weber, "Bureaucracy," in *Max Weber: Essays in Sociology*, ed. H. H. Gerth and C. Wright Mills.

8. For a systematic treatment of this view, see John Brandl, "How Organization Counts: Incentives and Inspiration" *Policy Analysis and Management* 8 (Aug., 1989): 489–93.

9. Patricia W. Ingraham and Carolyn R. Ban, "Models of Public Management: Are They Useful for Federal Managers in the 1980s?" *Public Administration Review* 46 (1986): 152–60.

10. Herbert Kaufman, "Emerging Conflicts in the Doctrines of Public Administration," *American Political Science Review* 50 (1956): 1057–73. Quotes are from pages 1060 and 1061, respectively.

11. Wilson, "Challenge to Neutral Competence," 8.

12. For an example of the second type and an effort to distinguish between the differing perceptions of roles inherent in each type of governmental actor set in comparative perspective, see Joel D. Aberbach, Robert D. Putnam, and Bert A. Rockman, *Bureaucrats and Politicians in Western Democracies.* For a similar attempt in the American context, see Cornell G. Hooton, *Executive Governance: Presidential Administrations and Policy Change in the Federal Bureaucracy.*

13. Fesler, "Politics, Policy, and Bureaucracy."

14. Colin Campbell, *Managing the Presidency: Carter, Reagan, and the Search for Executive Harmony,* 49.

15. See James P. Pfiffner, "OMB: Professionalism, Politicization, and the Presidency," in *Executive Leadership,* ed. Campbell and Wyszomirski.

16. After 1960, the effectiveness of the bureau declined as it became more politicized and its basic roles were superseded by presidential aids. Appointments began to take on a decidedly political flavor and the efficiency that was characteristic of a more neutrally competent organization declined. The current Office of Management and Budget (OMB) has evolved into more of a political as opposed to professional and policy resource that it was originally intended to be. For analyses of this phenomenon, see Heclo, "OMB and the Presidency"; and Larry Berman, *The Office of Management and Budget and the Presidency, 1921–1979.* An interesting insider account highlighting the sheer magnitude of power residing in the organization is found in David Stockman, *The Triumph of Politics: Why the Reagan Revolution Failed.*

17. Sidney M. Milkis, *The President and the Parties: The Transformation of the American Party System Since the New Deal;* and Polsby, *Consequences of Party Reform.*

18. Weko, *Politicizing Presidency.* His analysis broadly considers the rational choice approach to presidential policy making, of which agency theory is a major part.

19. Ibid., 153.

20. Ibid., 154.

21. For a somewhat different perspective, see Feldman, *Order Without Design.*

22. These examples emerged in the course of several conversations with Erwin Hargrove.

23. Andrew Rudalevige, "Testing the Politicized Presidency: The Origins of Presidential Legislation, 1946–95" (paper presented at the annual meeting of the Midwest Political Science Association, Chicago, 1997), see esp. tables 4, 5, and 6, as well as figs. 2 and 2a. See also his "The President's Program: The 'Politicized Presidency' and Policy Formulation" (paper presented at the annual meeting of the Midwest Political Science Association, Chicago, 1999).

24. See Thomas E. Cronin, *The State of the Presidency,* 161.

25. I explore the nature of this shift later in this chapter.

26. In an effort to be cumulative, my work dovetails with that of Matthew Dickinson and others who examine the nature of presidential activity in an uncertain environment. Dickinson, in particular, explores the idea of presidential staffing to reduce bargaining uncertainty, and my work uses his as a starting point. See Dickinson, *Bitter Harvest,* 8–9.

27. Paul J. Quirk, "What Do We Know and How Do We Know It?" in *Political Science: Looking to the Future,* vol. 4, *American Institutions,* ed. William Crotty. Quirk's admonition has been at least partially mitigated by Walcott and Hult, *Governing the White House.*

28. Hult, "Advising the President." This approach is also consistent with Charles O. Jones's ideas about presidential effectiveness. He writes: "The tests of presidential effectiveness—if not exactly strength or weakness—may be the extent to which communication is established between the White House and the departments and agencies, the clarity of policy messages that are communicated, and the degree of mutual support that results when mes-

sages are clear." Such a judgment is inherently difficult, but the effort is necessary in order to make sense of the degree to which staffing and advising functions of are faithful to and serve the president's stated goals and preferences. (Jones, *Presidency in a Separated System*, 60.)

29. Skowronek, *Politics Presidents Make*, 11–12. The reference is to President Polk, but Skowronek's use of the example is meant to illustrate the incentives characteristic of "every other president" (idem., *Politics Presidents Make*, 11).

30. This observation probably holds as well for second-term presidents who are often concerned with defining their legacy for the judgment of history.

31. This has been noted by several democratic theorists. But for a profound analysis of this view from both a negative and positive stance, see Robert A. Dahl, *Democracy and Its Critics*, 52–79.

32. See, for example, Milkis, *President and the Parties*, esp. 301–307.

33. For a brilliant analysis of the argument made in reference to voters in the electoral process, see Elisabeth R. Gerber and John E. Jackson, "Endogenous Preferences and the Study of Institutions," *American Political Science Review* 87 (Sept., 1993): 639–56.

34. I will on occasion refer to preferences in the way I referred to them first in the preceding explanation, i.e. as the president would "prefer" to accomplish a goal, though to do so would be inconsistent with structural incentives.

35. The economic approach stresses the importance of formal rules and structures as constraints on individual actions. Indeed, much of the formal analysis of Congress and legislative institutions uses this framework. See esp. Duncan Black, *The Theory of Committees and Elections;* William Riker, "Implications From the Disequilibrium of Majority Rule for the Study of Institutions," *American Political Science Review* 74 (1980): 432–37; and Kenneth Shepsle, "Institutional Arrangements and Equilibrium in Multidimensional Voting Models," *American Journal of Political Science* 23 (1979): 27–59.

The sociological approach argues that political institutions are relatively autonomous and adaptive entities, and the individuals within the organization have more or less discretion in performing their tasks. Their individual contexts and cumulative experiences order political life and, to an extent, do so in a relatively consistent manner over time and regardless of the individuals occupying them. On this approach, see James G. March and Johan P. Olsen, "The New Institutionalism: Organizational Factors in Political Life," *American Political Science Review* 78 (1984): 734–49; and idem., *Rediscovering Institutions: The Organizational Basis of Politics.* Placing the work of March and Olsen in the sociological camp is not entirely fair, given that their approach is not strictly sociological. However, their perspective does claim that institutions need not be "efficient" in the way that economic theorists seem to imply. A useful synopsis of various approaches subsumed under the rather broad rubric of the new institutionalism is Ellen M. Immergut, "The Theoretical Core of the New Institutionalism," *Politics and Society* 26 (1998): 5–34.

36. The roots of my thinking on this perspective, as well as a much more thorough explanation of its premises, are similar to what Searing calls the "motivational approach" to the new institutionalism, integrating sociological and economic perspectives on the interplay between individuals and institutions. See Donald D. Searing, "Roles, Rules, and Rationality in the New Institutionalism," *American Political Science Review* 85 (Dec., 1991): 1239–60.

37. For a critical perspective on the historical development of institutions, consult Karen Orren and Stephen Skowronek, "Beyond the Iconography of Order: Notes for a 'New Institutionalism'" in *Dynamics of American Politics: Approaches and Interpretations*, ed. Lawrence C. Dodd and Calvin Jillson.

38. The most thorough exposition of how the leadership ambitions of presidents are tempered by time and circumstance is found in Skowronek, *Politics Presidents Make.*

39. See also March and Olsen, "New Institutionalism," 742–46; and idem., *Rediscovering Institutions*, 10, 59, 74–76, 118, and 133–34.

40. Such a test is found in Weko, *Politicizing Presidency.*

41. Paul C. Light, *The President's Agenda: Domestic Policy Choice from Kennedy to Carter.*

42. Jones, *Presidency in a Separated System.*

43. Samuel Kernell, *Going Public: New Strategies of Presidential Leadership,* 3d ed., esp. 20–38.

44. As noted above, Dickinson's work is similarly concerned with presidential strategies to decrease a president's bargaining uncertainty. His work starts with Neustadt's bargaining paradigm and then examines the success of the Roosevelt administration's relatively small White House staff as compared with his successors in the modern era. See his *Bitter Harvest,* esp. 1–15, and chap. 8.

45. The centralized strategy is often closely aligned with the politicized strategy. However, I separate them for analytical convenience and, I hope, empirical accuracy.

46. Although the terms I use (e.g., policy director and policy facilitator) are similar to those used by George Edwards in his study of presidential-congressional relations, they imply different things. Edwards refers to the power of the presidency and the ability to influence policy making and congressional action, seeking to understand whether presidents can provide effective, purposive leadership. See his *At the Margins,* 4–6. My work refers explicitly to the responsibilities of the president's *staff* rather than to the president.

47. For reasons explained in the next chapter, this is not a major problem for my analysis because Pres. Jimmy Carter's approach to governance emphasized policy competence in his cabinet officials over responsiveness.

48. There are numerous fallacies of logic and inference in trying to link policy process with policy success. A good process may lead to poor policy, and a poor process may wind up yielding good policy. As I explain below, I define "success" or "good" in terms of presidential interests, and no further. For example, I classify the youth employment initiative (see chap. 3) as a success even though it did not make it through Congress, and the creation of a new Department of Education (also chap. 3) as a failure, even though it passed and remains in existence today. For other studies that warn against being too quick to link process and outcome, see Ryan Barrileaux, *The Post Modern Presidency: The Office after Ronald Reagan;* Burke and Greenstein et al., *How Presidents Test Reality;* and Joseph Pika, "White House Staffing: Salvation, Damnation, and Uncertainty" in *Executive Leadership,* ed. Campbell and Wyszomirski.

49. Ingraham and Ban, "Models of Public Management," 152.

50. See, for example, Bradley H. Patterson, *The Ring of Power.*

51. Moe, "Politicized Presidency," 239.

52. Nelson W. Polsby, "Presidential Cabinet Making: Lessons for the Political System," *Political Science Quarterly* 93 (spring, 1978): 15–25. Other works that cite the secular trend toward centralization include Margaret Wyszomirski, "The Deinstitutionalization of Presidential Staff Agencies," *Public Administration Review* 42 (1982): 448–58; Hugh Heclo, *A Government of Strangers: Executive Politics in Washington;* and Kernell, "Evolution of the White House Staff."

53. Wilson, "Challenge to Neutral Competence," 8.

54. For a similar argument, see Peri Arnold, "The Institutionalized Presidency and the American Regime," in *The Presidency Reconsidered,* ed. Richard W. Waterman, 220.

55. See also Jeffrey E. Cohen, *Presidential Responsiveness and Public Policy-Making: The Public and the Policies that Presidents Choose.*

56. Walcott and Hult, *Governing the White House.*

57. Walcott and Hult agree that the domestic policy apparatus is part of the deep structure of the White House. However, while they note that there has long been a domestic policy apparatus, they point to the creation of the Domestic Council in 1970 as the genesis of a "stable" entity. See Charles Walcott and Karen Hult, "The Domestic Policy Conundrum: White House Domestic Policy Organization" (paper presented at the annual meeting of the

American Political Science Association, Atlanta, 1989), cited in Hult, "Advising the President," 125. For a more comprehensive analysis, see their *Governing the White House.*

58. An analysis that argues the White House staff as a whole meets the criteria of an institution is convincingly made in Burke, *Institutional Presidency,* chap. 2.

59. Warshaw, *Domestic Presidency,* 93. More generally, see her chap. 4 for an interesting analysis of the process of developing the directions and functions of the Domestic Council and, later, the DPS.

60. Hart, *Presidential Branch,* 89.

61. Margaret Jane Wyszomirski, "The Roles of a Presidential Office for Domestic Policy: Three Models and Four Cases," in *The Presidency and Public Policy Making,* ed. George C. Edwards III, Steven A. Shull, and Norman C. Thomas, 130–50.

62. Among the many works in this area, see Thomas E. Cronin, "The Swelling of the Presidency," *Saturday Review* 1 (Feb., 1973): 30–36.

63. The classic presentation of this problem is Gary King, Robert O. Keohane, and Sidney Verba, *Designing Social Inquiry: Scientific Inference in Qualitative Research.* A particularly thoughtful and useful application of these and other methodological concerns of special relevance for presidency scholars is Karen M. Hult, Charles E. Walcott, and Thomas Weko, "Qualitative Research and the Study of the U.S. Presidency" (paper presented at the annual meeting of the American Political Science Association, Washington, D.C., 1997).

64. A study that focuses on the cabinet but also notes the usefulness of cabinet councils and task forces is James P. Pfiffner, "White House Staff versus the Cabinet" *Presidential Studies Quarterly* 4 (fall, 1986): 666–90.

65. See, for example, Thomas L. Gais, Mark A. Peterson, and Jack L. Walker, Jr., "Interest Groups, Iron Triangles, and Representative Institutions," in Walker, *Mobilizing Interest Groups.*

66. Useful analyses of presidential relations with the interest group community are found in Benjamin Ginsberg and Martin Shefter, "The Presidency, Interest Groups, and Social Forces: Creating a Republican Coalition," in *Presidency and the Political System,* ed. Nelson, 3d ed.; and Mark A. Peterson, "The Presidency and Organized Interests: White House Patterns of Interest Group Liaison," *American Political Science Review* 86 (Sept., 1992): 612–25.

67. See Paul J. Quirk, "In Defense of the Politics of Ideas," *Journal of Politics* 50 (Feb., 1988): 31–41; and Martha Derthick and idem., *The Politics of Deregulation.*

CHAPTER 3. ANALYTIC METHOD

1. See Brooks D. Simpson, "Historians and Political Scientists: Observations on Presidential Studies," *Congress and the Presidency* 20 (autumn, 1993): 87–91, for a provocative essay that calls for cross-fertilization of presidential scholarship in history and political science, each being informed and enriched by the other's work.

2. Within the voluminous literature of each, see Peterson, *Legislating Together;* Paul Brace and Barbara Hinckley, *Follow the Leader;* Cary Covington, "Congressional Support for the President: The View From the Johnson/Kennedy White House" *Journal of Politics* 48 (Aug., 1986): 717–28; Kernell, *Going Public;* and Jeffrey Tulis, *The Rhetorical Presidency.* See Lyn Ragsdale, "Studying the Presidency: Why Presidents Need Political Scientists" in *Presidency and the Political System,* ed. Nelson, 5th ed., 29–61, for an excellent effort to catalogue what presidential scholars employing diverse methodological and conceptual approaches have been able to generalize about the office.

3. It is, however, getting a bit easier to ignore these calls as presidency scholars have labored to improve the conceptualization, operationalization, and methods by which they approach whatever research task confronts them. This is increasingly the case regardless of whether one employs a qualitative or quantitative approach. For a review of the advances made by political scientists, see Hart, "Neglected Aspects," 379–99.

4. I have gained experience on both sides of the methodological "divide." Much of my recent work on the presidency utilizes quantitative techniques; for example, my "Presidential Leverage and the Presidential Agenda," uses Poisson regression analysis to uncover factors that impinge on presidents' activity, innovation, and administrative presidency decisions. On the other hand, my second book (in progress) deals with the phenomenon of organizational learning in the presidency. The first set of questions concerning the president's agenda are amenable and properly studied using the quantitative approach; the second on organizational learning, and questions I raise in this book, are not.

5. See Gary King, "The Methodology of Presidential Research," in *Researching the Presidency*, ed. Edwards et al. For a more general statement, see Gary King, Robert O. Keohane, and Sidney Verba, *Designing Social Inquiry: Scientific Inference in Qualitative Research*. Of course, not everyone agrees that the logics are one and the same. See the various perspectives presented in the symposium on *Designing Social Inquiry* in the June, 1995, issue of the *American Political Science Review*.

6. King, "Methodology of Presidential Research," 388, 402–409. For analyses focusing on only one president but taking lessons from the president in question and placing them in a larger analytical context, adding to our theoretical understanding of the presidency writ large, see, among others, Fred I. Greenstein, *The Hidden-Hand Presidency: Eisenhower as Leader;* Charles O. Jones, *The Trusteeship Presidency: Jimmy Carter and the United States Congress;* Hargrove, *Jimmy Carter as President;* and Dickinson, *Bitter Harvest*. See Quirk, "What Do We Know . . . ?," 37–66, for a call to focus on presidential decisions, rather than the individual president, as the unit of analysis. All of the books cited in this note, it seems to me, do just that.

7. King et al., *Designing Social Inquiry*, 109.

8. See Hargrove, *Jimmy Carter as President;* and Jack Knott and Aaron Wildavsky, "Jimmy Carter's Theory of Governing," *The Wilson Quarterly* (winter, 1977): 49–67.

9. A systematic consideration of personality impact on advice is outside the scope of this book. However, for a systematic exposition of the problems of disentangling the effects of personality on political performance, as well as useful suggestions and hypotheses concerning the conditions under which personality might prove crucial or even determinate in political activity, see Erwin C. Hargrove, "Presidential Personality and Leadership Style" in *Researching the Presidency*, ed. Edwards et al.

10. A similar argument can be found in Jeffrey K. Tulis, "The Interpretable Presidency," in *Presidency and the Political System*, ed. Nelson, 3d ed.

11. For one of many works that expand on this basic point, see James Johnson, "How Not to Criticize Rational Choice Theory: The Pathologies of 'Commonsense'," *Philosophy of the Social Sciences* 25 (1996): 77–91, esp. 85.

12. For perspectives that argue for the utility of using descriptive inference as a basis for systematically exploring political phenomena, see King et al., *Designing Social Inquiry*. See also Simpson, "Historians and Political Scientists." For a slightly different take emphasizing the explanatory enterprise of political science, see Lawrence C. Dodd, "Congress, the Presidency, and the American Experience: A Transformational Perspective," in *Divided Democracy: Cooperation and Conflict Between the President and Congress*, ed. James A. Thurber.

13. Quirk, "What Do We Know . . . ?"

14. There are notable exceptions that enter into both the quantitative and qualitative domains. Among quantitative efforts, see Covington, "Congressional Support." One of the best qualitative efforts remains Greenstein, *Hidden Hand Presidency*.

15. See his concise descriptive analysis of case studies and theory building in Cohen, *Presidential Responsiveness*, 186–88.

16. Hargrove, *Jimmy Carter as President*, 13, 16. Emphasis added. See also Jones, *Trusteeship Presidency*, 7–8; and Knott and Wildavsky, "Jimmy Carter's Theory of Governing."

17. Nelson W. Polsby, "Presidential Cabinet Making: Lessons for the Political System," *Political Science Quarterly* 93 (spring, 1978): 15–25. Quote is at 21.

18. This neutrality of cabinet officers may be part of a more general evolutionary dynamic in the modern presidency. Hart, for example, notes that cabinet member links with interest groups and political parties have declined. This pattern, he claims, predated Carter and took shape most notably in the Nixon administration. See Hart, *Presidential Branch*, esp. 137–40.

19. There were exceptions to this pattern. HEW's Joseph Califano, for example, was highly political in his approach to the job of secretary.

20. The case for understanding the problems presidents face in controlling and assimilating the various policy and political resources available to them has been elaborated in chap. 1. But also see Bruce Buchanan, "Constrained Diversity: The Organizational Demands of the Presidency," in *Managerial Presidency*, ed. Pfiffner; Richard Rose, "Organizing Issues In and Organizing Problems Out" in *Managerial Presidency*, ed. idem.; and Dickinson, *Bitter Harvest*, esp. 27–30.

21. See King et al., *Designing Social Inquiry*, esp. 28–29, 99–100, 109–12, and 223–24, for more on the necessity of multiplying the observable implications of a theoretical framework in order to better understand the dynamics under consideration.

22. This focus on policy is coming back into vogue in the presidential literature in spite of criticism to the effect that an analytical focus on policy lends insight into only that policy or president and has little to say in terms of theory. See Paul Light, "Presidential Policy Making," in *Researching the Presidency*, ed. Edwards et al., for a critique and rejection of that view. See also Steven A. Shull, ed., *Presidential Policymaking*.

23. More on this can be found in Cohen, *Presidential Responsiveness*, 186–87.

24. I will have more to say on this topic in the final chapter.

25. This is certainly not to argue that crisis decisions have little to tell us about presidents or the nature of decisions. Hargrove, for example, hypothesizes that personality is of critical importance in understanding how crisis decisions are made. See Hargrove, "Presidential Personality and Leadership Style." Haney has completed an interesting study, similar to my own except that it examines foreign policy crisis decisions, rather than domestic policy noncrisis proposals. Our work is similar in that we both note the importance of understanding the various and interactive roles of advice, advisers, and information in formulating choice. See his *Organizing for Foreign Policy Crises*. For an argument in favor of focusing on noncrisis decisions, see Hugh Heclo, *Studying the Presidency: A Report to the Ford Foundation*, 22–23.

26. See Jimmy Carter, *Keeping Faith: Memoirs of a President*. For empirical analysis which ranks all presidential priorities and contains all six policies above, see Patrick J. Fett, "Truth In Advertising: The Revelation of Presidential Legislative Priorities" *Western Political Quarterly* 45 (1992): 895–920. See esp. table 5, 905–906.

27. This is not to say memoirs or speeches are useless for this analysis. Indeed, I make extensive use of memoirs especially, mostly for the purpose of providing background to the policies under consideration. My point is simply that I use neither memoirs nor speeches as primary sources for the determination of success or failure.

28. This is an eminently testable hypothesis and one that should be explored. To do so here, though, would require a far different research design than the one employed and is thus outside the scope of this study. I hope to explore this particular hypothesis in more detail in future work.

29. Bert A. Rockman, *The Leadership Question: The Presidency and the American System*, 112.

30. See also Hargrove, *Jimmy Carter as President*.

31. For a similar, if now somewhat dated, treatment of these issues, one that compares across administrations, see James L. Sundquist, *Politics and Policy: The Eisenhower, Kennedy, and Johnson Years*.

CHAPTER 4. STAFF AS POLICY DIRECTOR

1. Neustadt, "Presidency and Legislation," 641–71.

2. Erwin C. Hargrove, *The Power of the Modern Presidency*, 30. Emphasis added.

3. See Moe, "Politicized Presidency"; and Richard Nathan, *The Administrative Presidency*.

4. The term is from Neustadt, *Presidential Power*.

5. This is consistent with the idea of an "expectations gap" between public expectations of the presidency and the institutional capacity of the presidency to fulfill those expectations. See, for example, Waterman, ed., *Presidency Reconsidered*.

6. This is not to argue that foreign policy directions are any easier to forge and maintain support for than domestic policy. The president usually has more latitude in making foreign policy decisions, though, at least as compared to domestic policy. Examples of presidents exercising considerable unilateral discretion in foreign policy making include Johnson and Nixon in the Vietnam War, Bush in the Gulf War, and Clinton in committing troops to Bosnia and launching the air campaign against Serbia. For the classic statement of multiple advocacy as a strategy for presidents in the foreign policy arena, see George, "The Case for Multiple Advocacy," 751–85. For an application to Cold War policy making, see Meena Bose, *Shaping and Signaling Presidential Policy*.

7. See, for example, Arthur M. Schlesinger, Jr., *The Imperial Presidency*.

8. Carter, *Keeping Faith*, 75.

This section relies heavily on Beryl A. Radin and Willis D. Hawley, *The Politics of Federal Reorganization: Creating the Department of Education*. Readers are referred to this book for a much more comprehensive description, which traces previous attempts at education reform and continues up through the implementation stage.

9. Radin and Hawley, *Politics of Federal Reorganization*, 37–38.

10. Ibid., 26.

11. Ibid.

12. Ibid., 40. See also David Stephens, "President Carter, the Congress, and the NEA: Creating the Department of Education," *Political Science Quarterly* 98 (1983), esp. 661–65.

13. Ibid. In addition, those who supported creating a Department of Education presented arguments to the effect that education was a neglected element of an already too large and unwieldy department.

14. Ibid., 26–27.

15. Ibid., 17.

16. Ibid., 25.

17. This dissension would become a major factor in the ultimate failure to secure a broad department.

18. These stories will be analyzed in the next chapter. On Carter's problems with Congress, see Jones, *Trusteeship Presidency*. On Carter's unwillingness to compromise on matters of principle that scuttled political possibilities for success, see Hargrove, *Jimmy Carter as President*. On the impact of these problems on the Department of Education, see Radin and Hawley, *Politics of Federal Reorganization*, 91.

19. Radin and Hawley, *Politics of Federal Reorganization*, 57.

20. For a much more thorough recapitulation of the dynamics of the early staffs, see ibid., 58.

21. Memorandum, "Arguments For a Department of Education," undated, Domestic Policy Staff Files (hereafter DPSF), Stuart Eizenstat Papers, Box 195, Jimmy Carter Library (hereafter JCL).

22. The five included the creation of a cabinet department which would encompass the education division and related HEW and outside programs; a Department of Labor and Education, adding the education division, head start, and school nutrition to Department of Labor programs; a Department of Health, Education, and Science, combining health research

and education programs of HEW, the science programs at the National Science Foundation and National Endowment for the Humanities; a Department of Science and Education, bringing these two together and providing a foundation for supporting education and basic research; and finally, a Department of Education and Human Development, pulling in some HEW programs from the Office of Aging and Childrens Bureau, some DOL programs, and ACTION, the national volunteer agency. See Radin and Hawley, *Politics of Federal Reorganization*, 62.

23. See Joseph A. Califano, Jr. *Governing America: An Insider's Report from the White House and the Cabinet*, 277.

24. The task force strategy will be analyzed in greater detail later in this chapter when I discuss the creation of the *plan* and not the *proposal*.

25. For a similar viewpoint, although one based more on the political gains that can be made from strategic activity with an eye toward congressional-executive relations, see John B. Gilmour, *Strategic Disagreement: Stalemate in American Politics*, esp. 3–15.

26. See Radin and Hawley, *Politics of Federal Reorganization*, 111, for a complete analysis.

27. For more on Kennedy's style in this regard, see sections on administration in Theodore Sorensen, *Kennedy: 25 Year Anniversary Edition;* and Arthur Schlesinger, Jr., *A Thousand Days: John F. Kennedy in the White House.*

28. Hargrove refers to this as "centralized collegiality." See Hargrove, *Jimmy Carter as President*, 30 and 32. See also Jones, *Presidency in a Separated System*, 90.

29. Cited in memorandum for Stuart Eizenstat from Beth Abramovitz, Nov. 1, 1977, DPSF, Stuart Eizenstat Papers, Box 195, JCL.

30. Califano, *Governing America*, 273.

31. Ibid., 276. Emphasis added.

32. Ibid.

33. Memorandum for President Carter from Joseph Califano, Nov. 26, 1977, DPSF, Stuart Eizenstat Papers, Box 195, JCL.

34. Ibid.

35. See "Califano Launches Drive to Keep the 'E' in HEW," in *National Journal* 10 (1978).

36. Memorandum for James McIntyre from Joseph Califano, Jan. 9, 1978, DPSF, Stuart Eizenstat Papers, Box 195, JCL.

37. This is the classic public administration problem that leads presidents to centralize policy making in the first place.

38. For analyses of these bureaucratic pathologies, see, among others, Anthony Downs, *Inside Bureaucracy;* Harold F. Gortner, Julianne Mahler, and Jeanne Bell Nicholson, *Organization Theory: A Public Perspective*, chaps. 5–8; David Mechanic, "Sources of Power of Lower Participants in Complex Organizations" in *Classics of Organization Theory*, ed. Jay M. Shafritz and J. Steven Ott, 3d ed.; and James Fesler and Donald F. Kettl, *The Politics of the Administrative Process*, chap. 3.

39. Even before this division of labor was agreed upon, there was confusion over which organization would be responsible for which tasks. As Willis Hawley put it: "Initially, Hamilton Jordan told me 'You take care of the proposal. Leave the politics to me.' And I actually believed him. This quickly changed." Interview with Willis Hawley, May 14, 1993, Vanderbilt University, Nashville, Tenn.

40. Memorandum for President Carter from Stuart Eizenstat, Dec. 2, 1977, DPSF, Stuart Eizenstat Papers, Box 195, JCL. First emphasis added. All subsequent emphases in original.

41. Radin and Hawley, *Politics of Federal Reorganization*, 79.

42. Ibid., 112.

43. Memorandum for Stuart Eizenstat from Bert Carp, Nov. 26, 1977, DPSF, Stuart Eizenstat Papers, Box 195, JCL. Emphasis in original.

44. As I argue later, having a "higher" form of policy competence makes it difficult from

an analytical standpoint to accurately assess the different types of information and/or modes of thought entering into the president's or the staff's decision calculus. But such a distinction, while perhaps hindering or defying systematic codification, can enhance descriptive accuracy.

45. Memorandum for Jack Watson from Jim Parham, Mar. 24, 1978, DPSF, Stuart Eizenstat Papers, Box 195, JCL. Emphasis added. A brief account of the concept of the "higher form" of neutral (or policy) competence can be found in Wilson, "Challenge to Neutral Competence."

46. Memorandum for Hamilton Jordan and Jim McIntyre, Jan. 9, 1978, DPSF, Stuart Eizenstat Papers, Box 195, JCL. Emphasis added.

47. For a full description and account of these problems, see Harrison H. Donnelly, "Separate Education Department Proposed," *Congressional Quarterly Weekly Report* (Apr. 22, 1978): 987–90. It is interesting to note, in a rational choice context, that the narrow department, which was the *least* preferred option of all actors, including the President (with the exception of the DPS) was the option accepted in the end.

48. Ibid.

49. Memorandum for President Carter from Jim McIntyre and Frank Moore, August 17, 1978. DPSF, Stuart Eizenstat Papers, Box 195, JCL. Emphasis in original.

50. Hargrove, *Jimmy Carter as President*, 64–65.

51. Memorandum for President Carter from OMB/PRP team, November 26, 1977, DPSF, Stuart Eizenstat Papers, Box 195, JCL.

52. For a sustained argument as to the veracity of this claim, see Cohen, *Presidential Responsiveness*.

53. Memorandum for President Carter from OMB/PRP Review Team, Nov. 26, 1977, DPSF, Stuart Eizenstat Papers, Box 195, JCL.

54. Memorandum for the President from Richard Pettigrew, Nov. 28, 1977, DPSF, Stuart Eizenstat Papers, Box 195, JCL.

55. Memorandum for President Carter from Raymond Marshall, Apr. 10, 1978, DPSF, Stuart Eizenstat Papers, Box 195, JCL.

56. Radin and Hawley, *Politics of Federal Reorganization*, 67.

57. Ibid.

58. Memorandum for Stuart Eizenstat from Beth Abramowitz, Nov. 22, 1978, DPSF, Stuart Eizenstat Papers, Box 195, JCL.

59. "Senate Committee Clears Education Department," *National Journal* 10 (July 22, 1978): 1185.

60. Jones, *Trusteeship Presidency*, 184–85.

61. Hargrove, *Jimmy Carter as President*, 60.

62. This predates the strengthening of the DPS. However, the example is illustrative of the power that it did have at the time and serves as an indication of the level of responsiveness it offered the President, which was only to increase after it was given more power.

63. Willis D. Hawley, interview with author, May 14, 1993.

64. The PRP was not incompetent by any stretch of the imagination. It was successful in some other areas of the president's reorganization efforts, but could not (for reasons I have already detailed) combine political and policy information in a coherent manner in the case of the Department of Education. Still, there were some problems of political naivete in other reorganization areas such as the proposed creation of a Department of Natural Resources.

65. Hawley interview.

66. Adapted from "The Carter Administration and Youth Employment," undated, Domestic Policy Staff Papers, Stuart Eizenstat Papers, Box 324, JCL.

67. Ibid.

68. The Ford administration couched its opposition to these programs on grounds of fiscal conservatism.

69. See James W. Singer, "Taking Aim at Youth Unemployment," *National Journal* 10 (Jan. 28, 1978): 143–44.

70. For an excellent analysis of this problem, see James W. Singer, "The Problem of Being Young, Black, and Unemployed," *National Journal* 10 (Sept. 16, 1978): 1456–60.

71. "Executive Summary of the Domestic Policy Review Memorandum on Youth Training, Employment, and Education Programs," undated, DPSF, Stuart Eizenstat Papers, Box 324, JCL.

72. Recall the PRP being told to ignore careerists in the Office of Education.

73. See memorandum for Walter Mondale from Stuart Eizenstat, Bill Spring, and Kitty Higgins, Jan. 31, 1979, DPSF, Stuart Eizenstat Papers, Box 324, JCL.

74. Memorandum for Stuart Eizenstat from Bill Spring and Kitty Higgins, Mar. 29, 1979, DPSF, Correspondence Papers, Box 114, JCL.

75. Memorandum for Stuart Eizenstat from Bill Spring and Kitty Higgins, Apr. 23, 1979, DPSF, Stuart Eizenstat Papers, Box 324, JCL.

76. Memorandum for Stuart Eizenstat from Bert Carp, Bill Spring, and Kitty Higgins, Oct. 13, 1979, DPSF, Stuart Eizenstat Papers, Box 325, JCL.

77. As will be discussed briefly, the initiative would fail—but only because of fiscal burdens, not because of any fundamental disagreement on ideology over what could have been a divisive issue, as are many proposals dealing with how to combat unemployment.

78. "Youth Budget Program is Big Budget Initiative," *National Journal* 12 (Jan. 19, 1980): 122–23.

79. Harrison Donnelly, "Budget Pressures Threaten Carter Youth Jobs Proposal," *Congressional Quarterly Weekly Report* 38 (Mar. 8, 1980): 679–81. Quote at 679.

80. Ibid., 681.

81. Harrison Donnelly, "Carter Youth Jobs Plan In Trouble as Education Programs Face Fund Cuts." *Congressional Quarterly Weekly Report* 38 (June 7, 1980): 1579–80.

82. These processes will be delved into a bit more deeply, though briefly, in the following sections.

83. Singer, "Taking Aim at Youth Employment," 143–44.

84. Memorandum for President Carter from Stuart Eizenstat, undated, DPSF, Stuart Eizenstat Papers, Box 324, JCL.

85. Donnelly, "Budget Pressures Threaten," 681.

86. Memorandum for Stuart Eizenstat from Bill Spring and Kitty Higgins, Apr. 23, 1980, DPSF, Stuart Eizenstat Papers, Box 324, JCL.

87. Support for this proposition will be presented in the following two chapters.

88. Memorandum for Vice President Mondale from Stuart Eizenstat, Bill Spring, and Kitty Higgins, Jan. 31, 1979, DPSF, Stuart Eizenstat Papers, Box 324, JCL. Emphasis added.

89. The distinction is not superficial. Paul Light notes that a complete analysis of the vice presidency must include not only the degree to which a vice president has access to and advises a president, but the degree to which the president is influenced by that advice. See Paul C. Light, *Vice Presidential Power: Advice and Influence in the White House.* A full exposition of Mondale's role is beyond the scope of this study, but it is noted that at least on the issue of youth employment, regarding both its political and substantive dimensions, Mondale had both access to and influence over Carter.

90. The OMB position was to maintain the status quo.

91. Memorandum for President Carter from Vice President Mondale, undated, DPSF, Stuart Eizenstat Papers, Box 324, JCL. Emphasis added.

92. These members included Senators Metzenbaum, Stafford, Randolph, Williams, Javits, Nelson, Eagleton, and Pell. Others included Schweicker, Cranston, Armstrong, and Representatives Ford and Miller. See memorandum for Stuart Eizenstat from Kitty Higgins, Mar. 19, 1980, DPSF, Stuart Eizenstat Papers, Box 324, JCL.

93. Memorandum for Stuart Eizenstat from Bill Spring and Kitty Higgins, Apr. 24, 1980, DPSF, Stuart Eizenstat Papers, Box 324, JCL.

94. See memorandum for President Carter from Stuart Eizenstat, Raymond Marshall, and Louis Martin, May 18, 1979, DPSF, Stuart Eizenstat Papers, Box 324, JCL. The president asked for this support in a speech delivered at Cheyney State University in May, 1979.

95. Memorandum for President Carter from Stuart Eizenstat, undated, DPSF, Stuart Eizenstat Papers, Box 324, JCL.

96. Memorandum for Secretaries of the Treasury, Defense, Interior, Agriculture, Commerce, Labor, HEW, HUD, Transportation, Energy, the Attorney General, Director of OMB, Chair of the CEA, Director of Community Services Administration, Director of ACTION, Chairperson of Equal Employment Opportunity Commission, and Administrator of the Veterans Administration, from Stuart Eizenstat, Apr. 18, 1979, DPSF, Stuart Eizenstat Papers, Box 325, JCL.

97. *Presidential Review Memorandum*, Dec. 18, 1979, Office of Staff Secretary Files, Box 160, JCL.

98. Ibid.

99. *Executive Summary of the Domestic Policy Review Memorandum (DPR) on Youth Training, Employment, and Education Programs*, undated, DPSF, Stuart Eizenstat Papers, Box 324, JCL.

100. *Presidential Review Memorandum*, Dec. 18, 1979.

101. Even though the youth employment initiative is seen as a model of centralized decision making in the White House, it is a "failure" in the sense that it was unable to be passed. Most members of Congress supported the principle of addressing the problems of unemployed youth. However, many were reluctant to vote for the creation of a new program when the budget process was dominated by congressional and administration attempts to cut back existing programs. The Congress voted to sustain existing levels but did not pass the new program. This was not so much a failure in the "political environment," as much as a failure to be able to back up the program's necessarily high costs with budgetary outlays. See James Singer, "A Tempting Target," *National Journal* 12 (Mar. 8, 1980): 406.

102. These are also found to be important to varying degrees in all three areas of policy making.

103. Gilmour, *Strategic Disagreement*.

Chapter 5. Staff as Facilitator

1. Aberbach and Rockman, "Mandates or Mandarins?"

2. To repeat, this does not argue that this is the only strategy in which policy and politics coincide. Rather, it is the strategy in which there is a more conscious effort to combine the two and not merely the by-product of executing either responsive or policy competence roles.

3. See, for example, Peterson, *Legislating Together*.

4. See Aberbach et al., *Bureaucrats and Politicians*.

5. For an analysis of the distinction between large/small issues and new/old issues, and the intensity of their impact on the political process, see Peterson, *Legislating Together*, 150–59.

6. This dynamic exists in the national security/foreign policy arena between the State Department and Department of Defense. Though each deals with policy beyond the shores of the United States, their perspectives differ greatly. The bureaucratic culture prevalent in the State Department is dominated by diplomats, diplomats-in-waiting, a long institutional history that lends a great deal of expertise to any particular problem coming before it. The Defense Department, on the other hand, is composed of strong technical expertise and scientific approaches to various problems. If responsibility for a certain policy initiative is delegated to the State Department (where it probably rightly belongs) and there is no coordinating role

for the White House, the types of advice, information, and perspective coming from each of these departments will likely conflict. Depending on the mechanism for translating perspective into policy, one viewpoint thus may be sacrificed at the expense of another. This state of affairs would risk forfeiting valid information from the Defense Department for the expediency of relying on institutional memory.

A similar dynamic exists in the foreign policy/national security arena between political and policy organizations. The State Department, as characterized above, competes with the National Security Council staff, usually characterized by short-term, political outlook with a propensity for infusing new ideas and perspectives for the president's ear. For an analysis of this dynamic, which has implications for the questions analyzed in this study, see Crabb and Mulcahy, *American National Security*.

7. It is fair to note that welfare reform became less of a failure as the policy moved through the process, as will be seen. This evolution raises some issues about the appropriateness of classifying welfare reform as a failure. Still, the fact that coordination took a long time to kick in and must bear at least some of the burden for the president's failure to achieve most of what he wanted lends credence to the idea that the welfare reform process was fatally flawed. Nonetheless, the evolutionary improvement of the process should alert the reader to the fact that good process can emerge. However, at least in the case of welfare reform, the improvement came too late to save the program for the president's political interests. I will have more to say on this in the case analysis.

8. Each story has been told in much greater detail than I am able to go into here. My use of secondary source material will be obvious in the text. Readers desiring a more comprehensive treatment of the cases should consult those sources.

9. This section relies heavily on Laurence E. Lynn, Jr., and David deF. Whitman, *The President as Policy Maker: Jimmy Carter and Welfare Reform*.

10. Lynn and Whitman, *President as Policy Maker*, chaps. 2 and 3. See also Edward D. Berkowitz, *America's Welfare State: From Roosevelt to Reagan*.

11. Lynn and Whitman, *President as Policy Maker*, 44.

12. Ibid, 37.

13. Califano, *Governing America*.

14. This is broadly consistent with Carter's public goods approach to governing. See Hargrove, *Jimmy Carter as President*.

15. Lynn and Whitman, *President as Policy Maker*.

16. Califano, *Governing America*, 325–26.

17. Memorandum from Joseph Califano to President Carter, Feb. 5, 1977, DPSF, Stuart Eizenstat Papers, Box 318, JCL.

18. Ibid.

19. Ibid.

20. Lynn and Whitman, *President as Policy Maker*, 58.

21. Memorandum from Jack Watson and Jim Parham to President Carter, Apr. 15, 1977, DPSF, Stuart Eizenstat Papers, Box 318, JCL. Emphasis in original.

22. Memorandum from Henry Aaron to Joseph Califano, Jan. 21, 1977. Quoted in Lynn and Whitman, *President as Policy Maker*, 59.

23. Memorandum from Jack Watson to President Carter, Apr. 26, 1977, DPSF, Stuart Eizenstat Papers, Box 318, JCL.

24. Lynn and Whitman, *President as Policy Maker*, 69.

25. Memorandum to President Carter from Joseph Califano, Apr. 11, 1977, DPSF, Stuart Eizenstat Papers, Box 318, JCL.

26. Memorandum to President Carter from Jack Watson, Apr. 15, 1977, DPSF, Stuart Eizenstat Papers, Box 318, JCL.

27. Hargrove, *Jimmy Carter as President*, 55.

28. See memorandum to the White House Staff from Arnold Packer, July 15, 1977, DPSF, Stuart Eizenstat Papers, Box 317, JCL.

29. Hargrove, *Jimmy Carter as President*, 57–58.

30. Memorandum for Henry Aaron from Arnold Packer, May 16, 1977, DPSF, Stuart Eizenstat Papers, Box 318, JCL. Emphasis in original.

31. Memorandum to the President from Stuart Eizenstat, Charles Schultze, and Bert Lance, May 20, 1977, DPSF, Stuart Eizenstat Papers, Box 318, JCL.

32. Wilson, "Challenge to Policy Competence."

33. Memorandum to President Carter from Joseph Califano, May 19, 1977, DPSF, Stuart Eizenstat Papers, Box 318, JCL.

34. Califano, *Governing America*, 325–26; Hargrove, *Jimmy Carter as President*, 55; Lynn and Whitman, *President as Policy Maker*, 52.

35. Memo to Stuart Eizenstat from Tom Joe, May 11, 1977, DPSF, Stuart Eizenstat Papers, Box 318, JCL. Emphasis added.

36. Quoted in Lynn and Whitman, *President as Policy Maker*, 192.

37. Ibid.

38. Memo to President Carter from Stuart Eizenstat, Bert Carp, Bill Spring, and Frank Raines, Apr. 26, 1977, DPSF, Stuart Eizenstat Papers, Box 318, JCL.

39. Memorandum to President Carter from Jack Watson and Jim Parham, May 23, 1977, DPSF, Stuart Eizenstat Papers, Box 318, JCL.

40. Memorandum to President Carter from Stuart Eizenstat, Bert Carp, Frank Raines, and Bill Spring, July 27, 1977, DPSF, Stuart Eizenstat Papers, Box 319, JCL. As good a job as they did in integrating policy and political advice, the staff did not seem to go far enough in incorporating some of Tom Joe's most devastating substantive critiques. See memo to Stuart Eizenstat from Tom Joe, July 27, 1977, DPSF, Stuart Eizenstat Papers, Box 318, JCL.

41. Memorandum for President Carter from Joe Califano, Ray Marshall, Charles Schultze, and Stuart Eizenstat, July 31, 1977, DPSF, Stuart Eizenstat Papers, Box 318, JCL. Emphasis in original.

42. This was especially the case with Carter's insistence on scrapping the whole system and rebuilding it with no increase in costs.

43. If there is such thing as a higher form of policy competence, perhaps this is an example of a higher form of responsiveness (i.e., combining substantively informed information with the traditional responsiveness function).

44. Kingdon, *Agendas, Alternatives, and Public Policies*, 222–25. He cites examples of non-random behavior such as who is invited to a meeting, what policies are advanced and with what timing, which solutions get joined to what problems, and so forth.

45. Carter, *Keeping Faith*, 91.

46. Hargrove, *Jimmy Carter as President*, 49.

47. David Howard Davis, "Pluralism and Energy: Carter's National Energy Plan," in *New Dimensions to Energy Policy*, ed. Robert Lawrence, 191–200.

48. Jones, *Trusteeship Presidency*, 137.

49. Hargrove, *Jimmy Carter as President*, 52; Barbara Kellerman, *The Political Presidency: Practice of Leadership from Kennedy Through Reagan*, 211.

50. Principles were developed in the process of Energy I, so I will not give them explicit attention here except where relevant to the story of proposal development.

51. Congressional Quarterly, "Case Study: Creation of an Energy Plan," *Congressional Quarterly Weekly Report*, Oct. 6, 1979, 2203.

52. Ibid.

53. A more complete explanation of organizational learning in the presidency, using energy legislation as a case study, is found in Daniel E. Ponder, "The Presidency as a Learning Organization," *Presidential Studies Quarterly* 29 (Mar., 1999): 100–14.

54. White Burkett Miller Center for Public Affairs, University of Virginia, *Project on the*

Carter Presidency, vol. 13, 77–78. Emphasis added. Quoted in Hargrove, *Jimmy Carter as President*, 53.

55. Memorandum for the President from Stuart Eizenstat, Apr. 21, 1979, Office of the Staff Secretary Files, Box 127, JCL. Emphasis added.

56. Ibid, 3.

57. Quoted in Larry Light, "White House Domestic Policy Staff Plays an Important Role in Formulating Legislation," *Congressional Quarterly Weekly Report* 37, Oct. 6, 1979, 2199.

58. See memorandum for Distribution from Gerald Rafshoon, June 1, 1978, DPSF, Stuart Eizenstat Papers, Box 198, JCL.

59. For an analysis of the "going public" strategy, see Kernell, *Going Public*. For an exploration of the various types of agendas, especially the decision agenda, see Kingdon, *Agendas, Alternatives, and Public Policies*.

60. See memorandum for President Carter from Stuart Eizenstat, undated, DPSF, Stuart Eizenstat Papers, Box 198, JCL.

61. Memorandum to Stuart Eizenstat from Ann Wexler, Apr. 19, 1979, Office of the Staff Secretary Files, Box 127, JCL. The memo also makes reference to other groups including energy workers, construction workers, churches, the scientific and academic communities, rural and farm groups, and state and local officials.

62. See memorandum for President Carter from Hamilton Jordan, Sept. 1, 1978, Office of the Chief of Staff Files, Hamilton Jordan Papers, Box 44, JCL.

63. See memorandum for President Carter from Stuart Eizenstat and James Schlesinger, Aug. 8, 1978, DPSF, Stuart Eizenstat Papers, Box 198, JCL.

64. The relationship between advisers and bureaucrats in these cases is akin to the monitoring strategy prevalent in the information economics literature, especially principal-agent models. The principal monitors the agent through a variety of mechanisms focused on various measures of employee productivity. While this analysis is not directly transferable to this particular study, there did exist a reciprocal monitoring strategy where each agent (WHS and civil servants) monitored the information, advice, and strategies of the other, pursuant to ideals for optimal policy design.

The introduction of principal-agent models and the more general application of information economics is relatively new to political science. However, much headway has been made toward understanding the dynamic relationships between various political actors, especially institutional relationships among the president, bureaucrats, and legislators. For excellent review articles, see Moe, "New Economics of Organization"; and Jonathan Bendor, "Review Article: Formal Models of Bureaucracy," *British Journal of Political Science* 18 (1988): 353–95. An explicitly theoretical application can be found in Thomas H. Hammond and Jack H. Knott, "Who Controls the Bureaucracy?: Presidential Power, Congressional Dominance, Legal Constraints, and Bureaucratic Autonomy in a Model of Multi-Institutional Policymaking," *Journal of Law, Economics, and Organization* 12 (1996): 121–68. For a critique of the underlying assumptions of the positive theory of bureaucratic control, see Jeff Worsham, Marc Allen Eisner, and Evan J. Rinquist, "Assessing the Assumptions: A Critical Analysis of Agency Theory," *Administration and Society* 28 (Feb., 1997): 419–40.

65. Lynn and Whitman, *President as Policy Maker*, 270.

66. Ibid, 263–64.

67. A general blueprint for this strategy is Richard E. Neustadt and Ernest R. May, *Thinking in Time: The Uses of History for Decision Makers*.

68. Quoted in Hargrove, *Jimmy Carter as President*, 53. Emphasis added.

69. These charges could also be leveled at Energy I.

70. The president's complaint was mainly that the plan was too complicated for people to understand. Carter argued that if he did not understand it, how would he be able to convince the public, much less Congress? (Carter, *Keeping Faith*, 96–97.)

71. See Rockman, *Leadership Question*, 115–24.

CHAPTER 6. STAFF AS MONITOR

1. See esp. Fesler, "Politics, Policy, and Bureaucracy," 23–41; Kaufman, "Emerging Conflicts," 1057–73; and Francis Rourke, "Politics and Professionalism in American Bureaucracy," *Public Administration Review* 52 (1992): 539–46.

2. The obvious corollary is the role played first by the BOB and later the OMB in acting as a central clearing house for budgetary and programmatic requests made by bureaucratic agencies and departments. Where once those requests went directly to Congress, they have for most of this century been submitted to OMB and cleared as being acceptable to the administration's larger program. An early assessment is Neustadt, "Presidency and Legislation," 641–71. See also Berman, *Office of Management and Budget*, esp. 40–41.

3. Another reason for using a "delegated strategy" is that it allows the White House to decrease its responsibility for controversial proposals and to deflect negative publicity from them to the departments and agencies in the executive branch. It also allows for increased use of symbolism, especially for "fulfilling" political promises, when the important thing for the president is to have done *something* so as to meet an obligation to address an issue. Doing this can satisfy that interest while leaving the president and the White House staff more or less free to pursue other priorities. These are theoretical possibilities, to be sure, and they no doubt occur in the White House from time to time. I must stress, however, that no evidence was found that this was the case in either of the issues examined in this chapter. That does not mean that the Carter White House did not pursue such a strategy on other issues, but such was not the case with the policies addressed here.

4. See Nelson W. Polsby, *Political Innovation in America: The Politics of Policy Initiation.*

5. No policy advanced by the president is made in a vacuum, especially those that are presidential priorities. Whether the category is decentralized, mixed, or centralized, both the agency and the president's staff have roles to play. On policy development, political context, and presidential priorities, see Peterson, *Legislating Together*, 216–67.

6. I provide detailed documentation of these claims below.

7. Elizabeth Bowerman, "Health Insurance—Carter For, Ford Against," *Congressional Quarterly Weekly Report* 34 (Oct. 9, 1976): 2917–19.

8. The top ten issues, in order of importance, were inflation, government spending (which would indicate a reluctance to incur the considerable cost of health insurance), unemployment, crime, tax reform, the energy situation, lack of trust in government, welfare, national health care, and defense spending. See George H. Gallup, *The Gallup Poll: Public Opinion 1972–1977*, 2:880.

9. George H. Gallup, *The Gallup Poll: Public Opinion 1978*, 89–90, 158–60, 202–203.

10. Bowerman, "Health Care," 2918.

11. John K. Inglehart, "The Health Policy Squeeze," *National Journal* 9 (Nov. 12, 1977): 1776.

12. See John K. Inglehart, "And Now, NHI," *National Journal* 10 (May 6, 1978): 725.

13. Elizabeth Wehr, "Dilemma Over National Health Insurance Delays Promised Carter Plan," *Congressional Quarterly Weekly Report* 36 (July 15, 1978): 1771.

14. Congressional Quarterly, "Carter Defends Policies in Speech to UAW," *Congressional Quarterly Weekly Report* 35 (May 21, 1977): 989–92.

15. Memorandum for Hamilton Jordan and Stuart Eizenstat from Peter Bourne, Aug. 1, 1977, DPSF, Stuart Eizenstat Papers, Box 240, JCL.

16. See "Health Plan Order" Directive to Joseph Califano from President Carter, July 29, 1978, DPSF, Stuart Eizenstat Papers, Box 240, JCL.

17. This position supports the broader conclusion presented at the end of this chapter that perhaps NHI would have been more successful from a presidential standpoint had it been created in a mixed environment.

18. These included John F. Filner, chairman and CEO of AETNA; Robert Kirkpatrick,

president and CEO of Connecticut General Life Insurance; and Morrison H. Beach, chairman and CEO of the Travellers Corporation. See memorandum to Fran Voorde from Stuart Eizenstat, Nov. 15, 1978, DPSF, Stuart Eizenstat Papers, Box 242, JCL.

19. Elizabeth Wehr, "Kennedy, Labor Launch Drive for National Health Insurance," *Congressional Quarterly Weekly Report* 36 (Oct. 14, 1978): 2956.

20. As to whether or not this is in fact the case (i.e., as a general strategy of agency fiscal protection) is not my purpose here. The classic statement of padding as a budgetary tactic is found in Aaron Wildavsky, *The New Politics of the Budgetary Process,* 2d ed., 90–94.

21. Memorandum for President Carter from Joe Califano, May 15, 1978, DPSF, Stuart Eizenstat Papers, Box 241, JCL.

22. Memorandum to Stuart Eizenstat form Joe Onek and Bob Havely, Sept. 8, 1977, DPSF, Stuart Eizenstat Papers, Box 240, JCL.

23. Memorandum to Stuart Eizenstat from Joe Onek and Bob Havely, Sept. 27, 1977, DPSF, Stuart Eizenstat Papers, Box 240, JCL.

24. Ibid.

25. Wehr, "Dilemma Over National Health Insurance," 1773.

26. Secretary's Advisory Committee on National Health Concerns to Hale Champion, Feb. 28, 1978, DPSF, Stuart Eizenstat Papers, Box 241, JCL.

27. Memorandum from Joe Onek to Stuart Eizenstat, June 12, 1978, DPSF, Stuart Eizenstat Papers, Box 242, JCL.

28. Elizabeth Wehr, "Carter Lists 'Principles' of National Health Plan," *Congressional Quarterly Weekly Report* 36 (Aug. 5, 1978): 2058–59.

29. Wehr, "Dilemma Over National Health Insurance," 1770.

30. Memorandum to President Carter from Joseph Califano, Nov. 3, 1978, DPSF, Stuart Eizenstat Papers, Box 240, JCL.

31. For a broader description, see ibid.

32. As will be shown below, HEW eventually shifted its style to a more cooperative posture. This was due primarily to increased pressure to do so by the White House accompanied by threats to remove HEW from its role as delegated agent.

33. This is also a problem in the purely centralized strategy. See chap. 4.

34. Memorandum for President Carter from Stuart Eizenstat, Jim McIntyre, and Peter Bourne, Jan. 12, 1978, DPSF, Stuart Eizenstat Papers, Box 241, JCL.

35. Memorandum to Stuart Eizenstat from Joe Onek and Bob Havely, Feb. 13, 1978, DPSF, Stuart Eizenstat Papers, Box 241, JCL.

36. See the memorandum to the secretaries of HEW, Treasury, Defense, Commerce, Labor, director of OMB, chairman of the CEA, and the administrator of the Veterans Administration from Stuart Eizenstat, Feb. 6, 1978, DPSF, Stuart Eizenstat Papers, Box 241, JCL.

37. Recall the President's Reorganization Project in the creation of the Department of Education, and the DPS as chair of the interagency coordinating committee in Energy II.

38. Memorandum to Stuart Eizenstat from Joe Onek, May 19, 1978, DPSF, Stuart Eizenstat Papers, Box 241, JCL.

39. Memorandum for Stuart Eizenstat from Joe Onek, May 25, 1978, DPSF, Stuart Eizenstat Papers, Box 241, JCL.

40. Memorandum for President Carter from Joseph Califano, June 26, 1978, DPSF, Stuart Eizenstat Papers, Box 242, JCL.

41. Wehr, "Dilemma Over National Health Insurance."

42. Memorandum to Vice President Mondale from Stuart Eizenstat, Aug. 22, 1978, DPSF, Stuart Eizenstat Papers, Box 242, JCL.

The strategy advocated by Richard Moe, referred to in the excerpt, involved formulating legislation that would cover only the first phase of NHI, and then push for broader political passage.

43. Ibid.

44. Fesler, "Politics, Policy, and Bureaucracy."

45. Memorandum for Hamilton Jordan from Stuart Eizenstat, July 5, 1977, DPSF, Stuart Eizenstat Papers, Box 240, JCL. Emphasis in the original.

46. Memorandum for President Carter from Joseph Califano, May 30, 1978, DPSF, Stuart Eizenstat Papers, Box 241, JCL.

Califano's advocacy of a delayed starting date was, interestingly, probably the most commensurate with what the political circumstances required.

47. Memorandum for President Carter from Charles Schultze and James McIntyre, May 31, 1978, DPSF, Stuart Eizenstat Papers, Box 241, JCL.

48. However, it has been documented elsewhere that the OMB by this time was becoming increasingly politicized, so much so that its neutral competence role was considered to be either disappearing or severely in decline. See Heclo, "OMB and the Presidency," 80–98.

49. See Wilson, "Challenge to Neutral Competence."

50. Memorandum for Stuart Eizenstat from Joe Onek, Nov. 27, 1978, DPSF, Stuart Eizenstat Papers, Box 241, JCL.

51. Memorandum for Stuart Eizenstat and Bert Carp from Jim Mongan, Mar. 4, 1980, DPSF, Stuart Eizenstat Papers, Box 241, JCL.

52. See Heclo, "OMB and the Presidency"; and Erwin C. Hargrove and Samuel A. Morley, eds., *The President and the Council of Economic Advisers: Interviews with CEA Chairmen*, 16, 19–20.

53. Memorandum for Stuart Eizenstat and Joe Onek from Peter Bourne, Nov. 9, 1977, DPSF, Stuart Eizenstat Papers, Box 240, JCL. Emphasis in original.

54. Memorandum for Stuart Eizenstat from Joe Onek, Dec. 20, 1977, DPSF, Stuart Eizenstat Papers, Box 240, JCL.

55. Memorandum for President Carter from Stuart Eizenstat, Feb. 8, 1978, DPSF, Stuart Eizenstat Papers, Box 241, JCL. Emphasis in original.

56. Memorandum for Stuart Eizenstat from Peter Bourne, Feb. 4, 1978, DPSF, Stuart Eizenstat Papers, Box 241, JCL.

57. The strategy focused on the need to "candidly establish labor's willingness to negotiate their withdrawal" from several positions. These included the maximum benefit package, the resistance to co-payments and deductibles, captive-only role for private insurers, and total health budgeting. If labor moved quickly, the administration would "reach with Fraser and Kirkland on working toward common ground on substance." If labor did not move as expected, the president would have three options, including, first, "[R]efuse to reach any decisions on the labor proposal until the NHI Principles PRM process has been completed," second, "[T]he President could make it clear that we have grave concerns with the labor package and will probably reject it," and, finally, "The President could simply reject the new proposal as unacceptable and say that the Administration will put forth its own proposal." (Memorandum for Stuart Eizenstat from Joe Onek, Mar. 9, 1978, DPSF, Stuart Eizenstat Papers, Box 241, JCL.)

58. Memorandum for President Carter from Joseph Califano and Stuart Eizenstat, July 22, 1978, DPSF, Stuart Eizenstat Papers, Box 241, JCL.

59. Memorandum for Stuart Eizenstat from Bert Carp, Joe Onek, David Calkins, and Bob Berenson, Nov. 11, 1978, DPSF, Stuart Eizenstat Papers, Box 241, JCL.

60. Memorandum for Stuart Eizenstat from Joe Onek and Bill Havely, Feb.10, 1978, DPSF, Stuart Eizenstat Papers, Box 241, JCL.

61. Ibid.

62. Further implications of this failure will be discussed at the conclusion of this chapter.

63. The citations are well known. See, for example, Wilson, "Study of Administration." Although his work would not be translated to English for more than six decades, the elements of bureaucracy are clearly stated in Weber, "Bureaucracy."

64. Ralph Hummel argues that this is not necessarily the fault of the men and women who

hold jobs in bureaucracy, but rather that the nature of bureaucracy creates an "inhuman be-ing" who is "headless and soulless," made that way by the nature of bureaucratic design which strives for just the efficiency and rationality called for by Weber and Wilson. See his *The Bu-reaucratic Experience*, 3d ed. A much more positive view is presented in Charles Goodsell's persuasive *The Case for Bureaucracy: A Public Administration Polemic*, 3d ed. Goodsell's chal-lenge to Hummel's characterization is made most directly in chap. 5.

65. See, for example, James Q. Wilson, *Bureaucracy: What Government Agencies Do and Why They Do It*, 236. B. Dan Wood and Richard W. Waterman, drawing on a variety of sources, offer a brief but lucid history of why this state of affairs arose and persisted through-out much of recent American history. See their *Bureaucratic Dynamics: The Role of Bureaucracy in a Democracy*, 2–5.

66. For an especially thorough analysis of these commissions and an explanation of the variation in the degree to which they achieved their goals in pursuit of administrative reform and reorganization, see Arnold, *Making the Managerial Presidency*.

67. See Erwin C. Hargrove, *Jimmy Carter as President*.

68. See Virginia Gray and Russell L. Hanson, eds., *Politics in the American States*, 7th ed.

69. Congressional Quarterly, *CQ Almanac 1978*, 824.

70. General Accounting Office, *Seminar on Civil Service Reform*, GA 1.13: GGD-8918.

71. Jones, *Trusteeship Presidency*, 160.

72. Felix A. and Lloyd G. Nigro, *Modern Public Administration*, 4th ed., 119.

73. For an analysis of the genesis of this state of affairs, see Schlesinger, *Imperial Presi-dency*, and Nathan, *Administrative Presidency*.

74. Nigro and Nigro, *Modern Public Administration*, 119.

75. Hargrove, *Jimmy Carter as President*.

76. Ibid., 162, 165.

77. For a treatment of political capital, see Light, *President's Agenda*, 25–33.

78. Polsby, *Political Innovation in America*, 8.

79. For a more complete explanation of incubative policies as compared to acute or crisis-induced innovations, see ibid., 146–74.

80. For an analysis of the implementation of the CSRA, which is outside the scope of this study, see James S. Bowman, "Restoring Confidence in Bureaucracy: Beyond Civil Service Reform," in *Bureaucratic and Governmental Reform*, ed. James Calista. Bowman pays special attention to the status of whistle-blower protection, the Office of the Special Counsel, and calls for a new brand of bureaucratic leadership focusing on ethical and moral concerns which, he argues, can only strengthen government and ultimately restore the public's con-fidence in its political institutions.

81. For a more complete description see Nigro and Nigro, *Modern Public Administration*, 118.

82. General Accounting Office, *Seminar*.

83. Congress was not traditionally disposed to acting with force on CSR. See Jones, *The Trusteeship Presidency*, 160–63.

84. Memorandum for Stuart Eizenstat from Steve Simmons, Nov. 2, 1977, DPSF, Stuart Eizenstat Papers, Box 169, JCL.

85. Nigro and Nigro, *Modern Public Administration*, 120.

86. Ibid; *CQ Almanac 1978*.

87. Nigro and Nigro, *Modern Public Administration*, 120–21.

88. "Civil Service Reform: Interest Group Support and Opposition," May 8, 1978, DPSF, Stuart Eizenstat Papers, Box 168, JCL. This source includes a complete listing of supporters as well as those who were only interested in veterans-preference issues.

89. Ibid.

90. Charles W. Jacobs, "Carrot and Sticking the Bureaucrats: Merit Pay in the Civil Ser-vice," Ph.D. diss., Harvard University, 1988, abstract.

91. Space precludes me from analyzing the nine separate components of CSR. However, as I suggest in the text, those components were not particularly controversial. Looking at veterans preference maintains comparative advantage given the controversial nature of other policies under examination in this book.

92. *CQ Almanac 1978*, 826.

93. Memorandum to Rick Hutcheson from Max Cleland, Jan. 20, 1978, DPSF, Stuart Eizenstat Papers, Box 169, JCL.

94. See memorandum for President Carter from Barbara Blum, Jan. 9, 1978, DPSF, Stuart Eizenstat Papers, Box 169, JCL.

For a similar analysis on subjects not related to CSR, see the memorandum from OMB to Rick Hutcheson of the DPS (Memorandum for Rick Hutcheson from Wayne Granquist and Harrison Wellford, Jan. 20, 1978, DPSF, Stuart Eizenstat Papers, Box 169, JCL).

95. Memorandum for President Carter from Hamilton Jordan, June 21, 1978, Office of the Chief of Staff, Hamilton Jordan Confidential File, Box 34, JCL.

96. Letter for Robert Nix from President Carter, June 20, 1978, DPSF, Stuart Eizenstat Papers, Box 168, JCL.

97. Kernell, *Going Public.* See also Tulis, *Rhetorical Presidency.*

98. *Public Papers of the President: Jimmy Carter*, 1351.

99. *CQ Almanac 1978*, 828.

100. Ibid., 826.

101. See Congress, Senate, *Civil Service Reform Act of 1978*, 95th Cong., 2d sess., Conference Report, Rpt. 95-1272.

102. Wilson, "Challenge to Neutral Competence."

103. An important exception to this logic may lie in the times when symbolic politics is the goal of an administration concerning a particular issue. For example, it may be more important for the administration to *appear* to be doing something about a problem, and not so much that solutions are implemented. In such a case, such a strong role for the White House agents may not be required, but some form of oversight, although minimal, might be desirable from the president's point of view.

104. See memorandum for President Carter from Stuart Eizenstat and James McIntyre, Feb. 24, 1978, DPSF, Stuart Eizenstat Papers, Box 168, JCL.

105. Memorandum for President Carter from Alan Campbell, Jan. 19, 1978, DPSF, Stuart Eizenstat Papers, Box 169, JCL. Emphasis added.

106. Memorandum for President Carter from Alan Campbell, undated, DPSF, Stuart Eizenstat Papers, Box 168, JCL. Emphasis added.

107. See memorandum for President Carter from Stuart Eizenstat, Sept. 22, 1978, DPSF, Stuart Eizenstat Papers, Box 168, JCL.

108. See memorandum to President Carter from Hamilton Jordan, June 21, 1978.

109. Alan Campbell, *Decision Memo: Civil Service Reform*, memorandum for the President, Jan. 18, 1978, DPSF, Stuart Eizenstat Papers, Box 168, JCL.

110. See memorandum for President Carter from Stuart Eizenstat and Rick Hutcheson, Sept. 21, 1978, DPSF, Stuart Eizenstat Papers, Box 169, JCL.

111. Ibid.

112. See Campbell, *Decision Memorandum.*

113. Memorandum for President Carter from Stuart Eizenstat, Si Lazarus, and Steve Simmons, Jan. 27, 1978, DPSF, Stuart Eizenstat Papers, Box 169, JCL.

114. For a more in-depth description of the events surrounding the controversy, see ibid.

115. Memorandum for President Carter from Stuart Eizenstat and Frank Moore, Jan. 27, 1978, DPSF, Stuart Eizenstat Papers, Box 169, JCL. Emphasis in original.

116. Ibid.

117. Moe, "Politicized Presidency."

CHAPTER 7. PRESIDENTS AND THE POLITICAL USE OF POLICY INFORMATION

1. The call for presidents to look more systematically at advising is found in Hult "Advising the President."

2. Empirical support for the proposition that not all priorities are fully centralized in the White House can be found in Rudalevige, "Testing the Politicized Presidency"; and idem., "The President's Program: The 'Politicized Presidency' and Policy Formulation" (paper presented at the annual meeting of the Midwest Political Science Association, Chicago, 1999). Rudalevige argues that there is perhaps less centralization of policy formulation than recent presidential literature has led us to expect.

3. The insight that successful political leaders are those that "control the political definition of their actions," is found in Skowronek, *Politics Presidents Make*, 17.

4. I will have more to say on this later in the chapter when I discuss prospects for theoretical development in presidency research.

5. See, for example, Aberbach and Rockman, "Mandates or Mandarins?"

6. In his extensive review of the literature on executive politics, Colin Campbell refers to these internal dynamics, such as the state-related imperatives an executive inherits and his "ever-expanding apparatus for controlling and guiding the entire state apparatus" as "gearbox issues." These gearbox issues, such as the relations between the president and his staff and then the character of this relationship with reference to executive branch administrators, have formed much of the context of the analysis presented in this book. See Campbell, "Political Executives and Their Officials," in *Political Science: The State of the Discipline II*, ed. Ada W. Finifter, esp. 390–92.

7. I develop this hypothesis and find support for it in Ponder, "Presidency as a Learning Organization," 100–14.

8. On the notion of a "term cycle," see Rockman, *Leadership Question*, 115–20. Light's development of a "cycle of increasing effectiveness" is found in Light, *President's Agenda*, esp. 37–38. Of course, the idea of a cycle of increasing effectiveness is coupled with and at least partly offset by a cycle of "decreasing influence" (idem., *President's Agenda*, 36–37).

9. Jones, *Presidency in a Separated System*.

10. This perception still looms yet today, although it is clearly outdated as evidenced by many of the works cited here. As one leading presidential scholar has observed, "Although these statements (about the stunted progress of presidential studies) may have been appropriate in the 1970s and early 1980s, they no longer seem as telling as they once were" (Lyn Ragsdale, "Review of Edwards et al, *Researching the Presidency: Vital Questions, New Approaches*," *American Political Science Review* 87 [Dec., 1993]: 1022).

11. But see Weko, *Politicizing Presidency;* Burke, *Institutional Presidency;* and Walcott and Hult, *Governing the White House* for important recent longitudinal studies that examine White House institutional development empirically.

12. The seminal work in this area remains March and Olsen, "New Institutionalism," 734–49. Refinements, extensions, and critiques can be found in, among others, March and Olsen, *Rediscovering Institutions;* Bert A. Rockman, "The New Institutionalism and Old Institutions" in *New Perspectives on American Politics*, ed. Lawrence C. Dodd and Calvin Jillson; and Orren and Skowronek, "Beyond the Iconography of Order."

13. For an analysis of the informal character of policy setting within a larger, more formalized structure, see Susan Webb Hammond, *Congressional Caucuses in National Policymaking*.

14. I discuss properties of organizations and institutions with special reference to the presidency in chaps. 1 and 2.

15. A similar argument is found in Burke and Fred I. Greenstein et al., *How Presidents Test Reality*, 274–75.

16. For one such recent analysis, see Colin Campbell, "Management in a Sandbox: Why the Clinton White House Failed to Cope with Gridlock," in *The Clinton Presidency: First Appraisals*, ed. Colin Campbell and Bert A. Rockman.

17. For an analysis of the importance of role in organization theory and how that might be parlayed into research on the presidency, see Martha S. Feldman, "Organization Theory and the Presidency" in *Researching the Presidency*, Edwards et al., esp. 272–74. For an application, see Ponder, "Presidency as a Learning Organization."

18. See Wilson, "Challenge to Neutral Competence."

19. This view is put forth most forcefully in King, " Methodology of Presidential Research."

20. The best attempt to understand presidential leadership in just this fashion is Skowronek, *Politics Presidents Make*.

21. For more on the concept of advisory networks, one that was not given extensive consideration here, see Hult, "Advising the President."

22. Moe, "Presidents, Institutions, and Theory."

23. Several scholars have made this claim and it is indeed one with which few are likely to quarrel. Matthew Dickinson, for example, is explicit in his intent to be cumulative in his book on FDR's advisory system (see *Bitter Harvest*, xiii).

24. Jeffrey Cohen's book is an excellent example of this type of work, combing institutional regularities in context of presidential responsiveness, with sensitivity for the different conceptions of the office held by the incumbents (see *Presidential Responsiveness*). Erwin Hargrove has made a career of developing longitudinal and context based theories of when and under what conditions individual skill makes a difference. His efforts are reflected in a number of areas, but see esp. his "Presidential Personality and Leadership Style." Many of his ideas are brought to fruition in *The President as Leader: Appealing to the Better Angels of Our Nature*.

25. Dickinson, *Bitter Harvest*.

26. An excellent example of just this dynamic is in Burke and Greenstein et al., *How Presidents Test Reality*.

Bibliography

Aberbach, Joel D., and Bert A. Rockman. "Mandates or Mandarins? Control and Discretion in the Modern Administrative State." In *The Managerial Presidency*, ed. James Pfiffner. 2d ed. College Station: Texas A&M University Press, 1998.

Aberbach, Joel D., Robert D. Putnam, and Bert A. Rockman. *Bureaucrats and Politicians in Western Democracies*. Cambridge, Mass.: Harvard University Press, 1981.

Arnold, Peri. "The Institutionalized Presidency and the American Regime." In *The Presidency Reconsidered*, ed. Richard W. Waterman. Itasca, Ill.: F. E. Peacock, 1993.

———. *Making the Managerial Presidency: Comprehensive Reorganization Planning 1905–1996*. Rev. 2d ed. Lawrence: University Press of Kansas, 1998.

Arnold, R. Douglas. *Congress and the Bureaucracy: A Theory of Influence*. New Haven, Conn.: Yale University Press, 1979.

Barrileaux, Ryan. *The Post Modern Presidency: The Office after Ronald Reagan*. New York: Praeger Press, 1988.

Bendor, Jonathan. "Review Article: Formal Models of Bureaucracy." *British Journal of Political Science* 18 (1988): 353–95.

Berkowitz, Edward D. *America's Welfare State: From Roosevelt to Reagan*. Baltimore: Johns Hopkins University Press, 1991.

Berman, Larry. *The Office of Management and Budget and the Presidency, 1921–1979*. Princeton, N.J.: Princeton University Press, 1979.

———. *Planning a Tragedy: The Americanization of the War in Vietnam*. New York: W. W. Norton, 1982.

Black, Duncan. *Theory of Committees and Elections*. Cambridge: Cambridge University Press, 1958.

Bond, Jon R., and Richard Fleisher. *The President in the Legislative Arena*. Chicago: University of Chicago Press, 1990.

Bose, Meena. *Shaping and Signaling Presidential Policy: The National Security Decision Making of Eisenhower and Kennedy*. College Station: Texas A&M University Press, 1998.

Bowerman, Elizabeth. "Health Insurance—Carter For, Ford Against." *Congressional Quarterly Weekly Report* 34 (October 9, 1976): 2917–19.

Bowman, James S. "Restoring Confidence in Bureaucracy: Beyond Civil Service Reform." In *Beyond Bureaucratic and Governmental Reform*, ed. James Calista. Greenwich, Conn.: JAI, 1986.

Brace, Paul, and Barbara Hinckley. *Follow the Leader*. New York: Basic Books, 1992.

Brandl, John. "How Organization Counts: Incentives and Inspiration" *Policy Analysis and Management* 8 (August, 1989): 489–93.

Buchanan, Bruce. "Constrained Diversity: The Organizational Demands of the Presidency." In *The Managerial Presidency*, ed. James P. Pfiffner. Pacific Grove, Calif.: Brooks/Cole, 1991.

Burke, John P. *The Institutional Presidency*. Baltimore: Johns Hopkins University Press, 1991.

Burke, John P., and Fred I. Greenstein, with Larry Berman and Richard Immerman. *How Presidents Test Reality: Decisions on Vietnam, 1954 and 1965*. New York: Russell Sage Foundation, 1989.

Califano, Joseph A., Jr. *Governing America: An Insider's Report from the White House and the Cabinet*. New York: Simon and Schuster, 1981.

"Califano Launches Drive to Keep 'E' in HEW." *National Journal* 10 (1978).

Calista, James, ed. *Beyond Bureaucratic and Governmental Reform*. Greenwich, Conn.: JAI, 1986.

Campbell, Colin. *Managing the Presidency: Carter, Reagan, and the Search for Executive Harmony*. Pittsburgh: University of Pittsburgh Press, 1986.

———. "Political Executives and Their Officials." In *Political Science: The State of the Discipline II*, ed. Ada W. Finifter. Washington, D.C.: American Political Science Association, 1993.

Campbell, Colin, and Margaret Jane Wyszomirski. *Executive Leadership in Anglo-American Systems*. Pittsburgh: University of Pittsburgh Press, 1991.

Carter, Jimmy. *Keeping Faith: Memoirs of a President*. New York: Bantam Books, 1982.

Chubb, John, and Paul Peterson, eds. *Can the Government Govern?* Washington, D.C.: Brookings Institution, 1989.

———, eds. *The New Direction in American Politics*. Washington, D.C.: Brookings Institution, 1986.

Clifford, Clark, with Richard Holbrooke. *Counsel to the President: A Memoir*. New York: Anchor Books, 1991.

Cohen, Jeffrey E. *Presidential Responsiveness and Public Policy-Making: The Public and the Policies that Presidents Choose*. Ann Arbor: University of Michigan Press, 1997.

Cohen, Michael, and Lee S. Sproull, eds. *Organizational Learning*. Thousand Oaks, Calif.: Sage, 1996.

Congressional Quarterly. "Carter Defends Policies in Speech to UAW." *Congressional Quarterly Weekly Report* 35 (May 21, 1977): 989–92.

———. "Carter Statements on Gas Deregulation." *Congressional Quarterly Weekly Report* 36 (1978): 713.

———. "Case Study: Creation of an Energy Plan." *Congressional Quarterly Weekly Report* 37 (October 6, 1979): 2203.

———. *CQ Almanac 1978*. Washington, D.C.: CQ, 1979.

Covington, Cary R. "Congressional Support for the President: The View from the Kennedy/Johnson White House." *Journal of Politics* 48 (August, 1986): 717–28.

Cox, Gary W., and Matthew D. McCubbins. *Legislative Leviathan: Party Government in the House*. Berkeley: University of California Press, 1993.

Crabb, Cecil V., and Kevin V. Mulcahy. *American National Security: A Presidential Perspective*. Belmont, Calif.: Brooks/Cole, 1991.

Cronin, Thomas E. *The State of the Presidency*. 2d ed. Boston: Little, Brown, 1980.

———. "The Swelling of the Presidency." *Saturday Review* 1 (February, 1973): 30–36.

Dahl, Robert A. *Democracy and Its Critics*. New Haven, Conn.: Yale University Press, 1989.

Davis, David Howard. "Pluralism and Energy: Carter's National Energy Plan." In *New Dimensions to Energy Policy*, ed. Robert Lawrence. Lexington, Mass.: Lexington Books, 1979.

Derthick, Martha, and Paul J. Quirk. *The Politics of Deregulation*. Washington, D.C.: Brookings Institution, 1985.

Dickinson, Matthew J. *Bitter Harvest: FDR, Presidential Power and the Growth of the Presidential Branch*. New York: Cambridge University Press, 1997.

———. "Neustadt and New Institutionalists: New Insights on Presidential Power?" Typescript, Center for American Political Studies, Occasional Paper 95-4, Harvard University, 1995.

Dodd, Lawrence C. "Congress, the Presidency, and the American Experience: A Transformational Perspective." In *Divided Democracy: Cooperation and Conflict between the President and Congress*, ed. James A. Thurber. Washington, D.C.: CQ, 1991.

Dodd, Lawrence C., and Calvin Jillson, eds. *The Dynamics of American Politics: Approaches and Interpretations*. Boulder, Colo.: Westview, 1993.

———, eds. *New Perspectives on American Politics*. Washington, D.C.: CQ, 1993.

Donnelly, Harrison H. "Budget Pressures Threaten Carter Youth Jobs Proposal." *Congressional Quarterly Weekly Report* 38 (March 8, 1980): 679–81.

———. "Carter Youth Jobs Plan in Trouble as Education Programs Face Funding Cuts." *Congressional Quarterly Weekly Report* 38 (June 7, 1980): 1579–80.

———. "Separate Education Department Proposed." *Congressional Quarterly Weekly Report* 36 (1978): 987–90.

Downs, Anthony. *Inside Bureaucracy*. Boston: Little, Brown, 1967.

Edwards, George C. III. *At the Margins: Presidential Leadership of Congress*. New Haven, Conn.: Yale University Press, 1989.

Edwards, George C. III, John Kessel, and Bert Rockman, eds. *Researching the Presidency: Vital Questions, New Approaches*. Pittsburgh: University of Pittsburgh Press, 1993.

Edwards, George C. III, and Stephen J. Wayne, eds. *Studying the Presidency*. Knoxville: University of Tennessee Press, 1983.

Edwards, George C. III, Steven A. Shull, and Norman C. Thomas, eds. *The Presidency and Public Policy Making*. Pittsburgh: University of Pittsburgh Press, 1985.

Ellis, Richard, and Aaron Wildavsky. *Dilemmas of Presidential Leadership*. New Brunswick, N.J.: Transaction Books, 1990.

Feldman, Martha S. *Order without Design: Information Production and Policymaking*. Stanford, Calif.: Stanford University Press, 1989.

Finifter, Ada W., ed. *Political Science: The State of the Discipline II*. Washington, D.C.: American Political Science Association., 1993.

Fesler, James W. "Politics, Policy, and Bureaucracy at the Top." *Annals of the American Academy of Political and Social Science* 466 (March, 1983): 23–41.

Fesler, James W., and Donald F. Kettl. *The Politics of the Administrative Process*. Chatham, N.J.: Chatham House, 1991.

Fett, Patrick J. "Truth in Advertising: The Revelation of Presidential Legislative Priorities." *Western Political Quarterly* 45 (1992): 895–920.

Fett, Patrick J., and Daniel E. Ponder. "The Deinstitutionalization of the U.S. Congress?" Paper presented at the annual meeting of the American Political Science Association, Chicago, 1995.

Gais, Thomas L., Mark A. Peterson, and Jack L. Walker, Jr. "Interest Groups, Iron Triangles, and Representative Institutions." In Jack L. Walker, Jr., *Mobilizing Interest Groups in America: Patrons, Professions, and Social Movements*. Ann Arbor: University of Michigan Press, 1991.

Gallup, George H. *The Gallup Poll: Public Opinion 1972–1977*. Vol. 2. Wilmington, Del.: Scholarly Resources, 1978.

———. *The Gallup Poll 1978*. Wilmington, Del.: Scholarly Resources, 1979

General Accounting Office. *Seminar on Civil Service Reform*. GA 1.13:GGD-8918. Washington, D.C.: General Accounting Office, 1988.

George, Alexander L. "The Case for Multiple Advocacy in Making Foreign Policy." *American Political Science Review* 68 (1972): 751–85.

———. *Presidential Decisionmaking in Foreign Policy: The Effective Use of Information and Advice*. Boulder, Colo.: Westview, 1980.

Gerber, Elisabeth R., and John E. Jackson. "Endogenous Preferences and the Study of Institutions." *American Political Science Review* 87 (September, 1993): 639–56.

Gerth, H. H., and C. Wright Mills, eds. *Max Weber: Essays in Sociology.* New York: Oxford
University Press, 1958.

Gilmour, John B. *Strategic Disagreement: Stalemate in American Politics.* Pittsburgh: University of Pittsburgh Press, 1995.

Gilmour, Robert. "The Institutionalized Presidency: A Conceptual Clarification." In *The
Presidency in Contemporary Context*, ed. Norman Thomas. New York: Dodd and Mead,
1975.

Ginsberg, Benjamin, and Martin Shefter. "The Presidency, Interest Groups, and Social
Forces: Creating a Republican Coalition." In *The Presidency and the Political System*, ed.
Michael Nelson. 3d ed. Washington, D.C.: CQ, 1990.

Goodsell, Charles T. *The Case for Bureaucracy: A Public Administration Polemic.* 3d ed. Chatham, N.J.: Chatham House, 1994.

Gortner, Harold F., Julianne Mahler, and Jeanne Bell Nicholson. *Organization Theory: A
Public Perspective.* Chicago: Dorsey, 1987.

Gray, Virginia, and Russell L. Hanson, eds. *Politics in the American States.* 7th ed. Washington, D.C.: CQ, 1999.

Greenstein, Fred I. *The Hidden Hand Presidency: Eisenhower as Leader.* New York: Basic Books,
1982.

Groseclose, Tim, and David C. King. "Committee Theories and Committee Institutions."
Paper presented at the annual meeting of the American Political Science Association,
Washington, D.C., 1997.

Hall, Richard L. *Participation in Congress.* New Haven, Conn.: Yale University Press, 1996.

Hammond, Susan Webb. *Congressional Caucuses in National Policy Making.* Baltimore: Johns
Hopkins University Press, 1998.

Hammond, Thomas H., and Jack H. Knott. "Who Controls the Bureaucracy?: Presidential
Power, Congressional Dominance, Legal Constraints, and Bureaucratic Autonomy in a
Model of Multi-Institutional Policymaking" *Journal of Law, Economics, and Organization*
12 (1996): 121–68.

Haney, Patrick J. *Organizing for Foreign Policy Crises: Presidents, Advisers, and the Management
of Decision Making.* Ann Arbor: University of Michigan Press, 1997.

Hargrove, Erwin C. *Jimmy Carter as President: Leadership and the Politics of the Public Good.* Baton Rouge: Louisiana State University Press, 1988.

———. *The Power of the Modern Presidency.* New York: Knopf, 1974.

———. *The President as Leader: Appealing to the Better Angels of Our Nature.* Lawrence: University Press of Kansas, 1998.

———. "Presidential Personality and Leadership Style." In *Researching the Presidency: Vital
Questions, New Approaches*, ed. George C. Edwards III, John H. Kessel, and Bert A. Rockman. Pittsburgh: University of Pittsburgh Press, 1993.

Hargrove, Erwin C., and Michael Nelson. *Presidents, Politics, and Policy.* New York: Knopf,
1984.

Hargrove, Erwin C., and Samuel A. Morley, eds. *The President and the Council of Economic Advisers: Interviews with CEA Chairmen.* Boulder, Colo.: Westview, 1984.

Hart, John. "Neglected Aspects of the Study of the Presidency." *Annual Review of Political Science* 1 (1998): 379–99.

———. *The Presidential Branch.* 2d ed. Chatham, N.J.: Chatham House, 1995.

Heclo, Hugh. *A Government of Strangers: Executive Politics in Washington.* Washington, D.C.:
Brookings Institution, 1977.

———. "The Office of Management and Budget and the Presidency: The Problem of Neutral Competence." *The Public Interest* 38 (1975): 80–98.

————. *Studying the Presidency: A Report to the Ford Foundation*. New York: Ford Foundation, 1977.

Hess, Steven. *Organizing the Presidency*. Washington, D.C.: Brookings Institution, 1988.

Hooton, Cornell G. *Executive Governance: Presidential Administrations and Policy Change in the Federal Bureaucracy*. Armonk, N.Y.: M. E. Sharpe, 1997.

Hult, Karen M. "Advising the President." In *Researching the Presidency: Vital Questions, New Approaches*, ed. George C. Edwards III, John H. Kessel, and Bert Rockman. Pittsburgh: University of Pittsburgh Press, 1993.

Hult, Karen M., Charles E. Walcott, and Thomas Weko. "Qualitative Research and the Study of the U.S. Presidency." Paper presented at the annual meeting of the American Political Science Association, Washington, D.C., 1997.

Hummel, Ralph P. *The Bureaucratic Experience*. 3d ed. New York: St. Martin's, 1987.

Hutchins, Edwin. "Organizing Work by Adaptation." In *Organizational Learning*, ed. Michael D. Cohen and Lee S. Sproull. Thousand Oaks, Calif.: Sage, 1996.

Immergut, Ellen M. "The Theoretical Core of the New Institutionalism." *Politics and Society* 26 (1998): 5–34.

Inglehart, John K. "The Health Policy Squeeze." *National Journal* 9 (November 12, 1977): 1776.

————. "And Now, NHI." *National Journal* 10 (May 6, 1978): 725.

Ingraham, Patricia W., and Carolyn R. Ban. "Models of Public Management: Are They Useful for Federal Managers in the 1980s?" *Public Administration Review* 46 (March/April, 1986): 152–60.

Johnson, James. "How Not to Criticize Rational Choice Theory: The Pathologies of 'Commonsense'" *Philosophy of the Social Sciences* 25 (1996): 77–91.

Johnson, Richard Tanner. *Managing the White House*. New York: Harper and Row, 1974.

Jones, Charles O. *The Presidency in a Separated System*. Washington, D.C.: Brookings, 1994.

————. *The Trusteeship Presidency: Jimmy Carter and the United States Congress*. Baton Rouge: Louisiana State University Press, 1988.

Kaufman, Herbert. "Emerging Conflicts in the Doctrines of Public Administration." *American Political Science Review* 50 (December, 1956): 1057–73.

Kellerman, Barbara. *The Political Presidency: Practice of Leadership from Kennedy Through Reagan*. New York: Oxford University Press, 1984.

Kernell, Samuel. "The Evolution of the White House Staff" in *Can the Government Govern?*, ed. John Chubb and Paul Peterson. Washington, D.C.: Brookings Institution, 1989.

————. *Going Public: New Strategies of Presidential Leadership*. 3d ed. Washington, D.C.: CQ, 1997.

Kessel, John. "The Structure of the Carter White House." *American Journal of Political Science* 27 (August, 1983): 431–63.

————. "The Structure of the Reagan White House." *American Journal of Political Science* 28 (May, 1984): 231–58.

Kiewiet, D. Roderick, and Mathew D. McCubbins. *The Logic of Delegation: Congressional Parties and the Appropriations Process*. Chicago: University of Chicago Press, 1991.

King, David C. *Turf Wars: How Congressional Committees Claim Jurisdiction*. Chicago: University of Chicago Press, 1997.

King, Gary. "The Methodology of Presidential Research." In *Researching the Presidency: Vital Questions, New Approaches*, ed. George C. Edwards III, John H. Kessel, and Bert Rockman. Pittsburgh: University of Pittsburgh Press, 1993.

King, Gary, Robert O. Keohane, and Sidney Verba. *Designing Social Inquiry: Scientific Inference in Qualitative Research*. Princeton, N.J.: Princeton University Press, 1994.

Kingdon, John W. *Agendas, Alternatives, and Public Policies*. 2d ed. New York: HarperCollins, 1995.

Knight, Jack. *Institutions and Social Conflict.* Cambridge: Cambridge University Press, 1992.

Knott, Jack, and Aaron Wildavsky. "Jimmy Carter's Theory of Governing." *The Wilson Quarterly* 1 (1977): 49–67.

Krehbiel, Keith. *Information and Legislative Organization.* Ann Arbor: University of Michigan Press, 1992.

Lawrence, Robert, ed. *New Dimensions to Energy Policy.* Lexington, Mass.: Lexington Books, 1979.

Light, Larry. "White House Domestic Policy Staff Plays an Important Role in Formulating Legislation." *Congressional Quarterly Weekly Report* 37 (October 6, 1979): 2199–2204.

Light, Paul C. "Presidential Policy Making." In *Researching the Presidency: Vital Questions, New Approaches,* ed., George C. Edwards III, John H. Kessel, and Bert Rockman. Pittsburgh: University of Pittsburgh Press, 1993.

———. *The President's Agenda: Domestic Policy Choice from Kennedy to Carter.* Baltimore: Johns Hopkins University Press, 1982.

———. *Vice Presidential Power: Advice and Influence in the White House.* Baltimore: Johns Hopkins University Press, 1984.

Lynn, Laurence E., Jr., and David deF. Whitman. *The President as Policy Maker: Jimmy Carter and Welfare Reform.* Philadelphia: Temple University Press, 1981.

March, James G., and Johan P. Olsen. "The New Institutionalism: Organizational Factors in Political Life." *American Political Science Review* 78 (1984): 734–49.

———. *Rediscovering Institutions: The Organizational Basis of Politics.* New York: Free Press, 1989.

Mayhew, David R. *Congress: The Electoral Connection.* New Haven, Conn.: Yale University Press, 1974.

Mechanic, David. "Sources of Power of Lower Participants in Complex Organizations." *Administrative Science Quarterly* 7 (1962): 349–64. Reprinted in Jay M. Shafritz and J. Steven Ott, eds. *Classics of Organization Theory.* 3d ed. Pacific Grove, Calif.: Brooks/Cole, 1992.

Milkis, Sidney M. *The President and the Parties: The Transformation of the American Party System Since the New Deal.* New York: Oxford University Press, 1993.

Moe, Terry M. "The New Economics of Organization." *American Journal of Political Science* 28 (November, 1984): 739–77.

———. "Political Institutions: The Neglected Side of the Story" *Journal of Law, Economics, and Organization* 6 (1990): 213–54

———. "The Politicized Presidency." In *The New Direction in American Politics,* ed. John Chubb and Paul Peterson. Washington, D.C.: Brookings Institution, 1985.

———. "The Politics of Structural Choice: Toward a Theory of Public Bureaucracy." Paper presented at the annual meeting of the American Political Science Association, Washington, D.C., 1988.

———. "The Politics of Structural Choice: Toward a Theory of Public Bureaucracy" in *Organization Theory: From Chester Barnard to the Present and Beyond,* ed. Oliver E. Williamson. New York: Oxford University Press, 1990.

———. "The Presidency and the Bureaucracy: The Presidential Advantage." In *The Presidency and the Political System,* ed. Michael Nelson. 5th ed. Washington, D.C.: CQ, 1998.

———. "Presidents, Institutions, and Theory." In *Researching the Presidency: Vital Questions, New Approaches,* ed. George C. Edwards III, John H. Kessel, and Bert Rockman. Pittsburgh: University of Pittsburgh Press, 1993.

Moe, Terry M., and Gary J. Miller. "The Positive Theory of Hierarchies." In *Political Science: The Science of Politics,* ed. Herbert F. Weisberg. New York: Agathon, 1986.

Moe, Terry M., and Scott A. Wilson, "Presidents and the Politics of Structure" *Law and Contemporary Problems* 57 (spring, 1994): 1–44.

Nathan, Richard. *The Administrative Presidency.* New York: John Wiley, 1983.

Nelson, Michael, ed. *The Presidency and the Political System*. 3d ed. Washington, D.C.: CQ Press, 1990.

———, ed. *The Presidency and the Political System*. 5th ed. Washington, D.C.: CQ, 1998.

Neustadt, Richard E. "Presidency and Legislation: The Growth of Central Clearance." *American Political Science Review* 48 (September, 1954): 641–71.

———. *Presidential Power: The Politics of Leadership from FDR to Carter*. New York: John Wiley and Sons, 1980.

———. *Presidential Power and the Modern Presidents*. New York: Free Press, 1990.

Neustadt, Richard E., and Ernest R. May. *Thinking in Time: The Uses of History for Decision Makers*. New York: Macmillan, 1986.

Nigro, Felix A., and Lloyd G. Nigro. *Modern Public Administration*. 4th ed. New York: Harper and Row, 1984.

Orren, Karen, and Stephen Skowronek. "Beyond the Iconography of Order: Notes for a New Institutionalism." In *The Dynamics of American Politics: Approaches and Interpretations*, ed. Lawrence C. Dodd and Calvin Jillson. Boulder, Colo.: Westview, 1993.

Patterson, Bradley H. *The Ring of Power*. New York: Basic Books, 1988.

Pelham, Ann. "Congress 'Ahead of the Game' on Energy." *Congressional Quarterly Weekly Report* 37 (1979): 1433–41.

Peterson, Mark A. *Legislating Together: The White House and Capitol Hill from Eisenhower to Reagan*. Cambridge: Harvard University Press, 1990.

———. "The Presidency and Organized Interests: White House Patterns of Interest Group Liaison" *American Political Science Review* 86 (September, 1992): 612–25.

Pfiffner, James P., ed. *The Managerial Presidency*. Pacific Grove, Calif.: Brooks/Cole, 1991. Revised and reprinted, College Station: Texas A&M University Press, 1999.

———. *The Modern Presidency*. New York: St. Martin's 1994.

———. "OMB: Professionalism, Politicization, and the Presidency." In *Executive Leadership in Anglo-American Systems*, ed. Colin Campbell and Margaret Jane Wyszomirski. Pittsburgh: University of Pittsburgh Press, 1991.

———. "White House Staff versus the Cabinet" *Presidential Studies Quarterly* 4 (fall, 1986): 666–90.

Pika, Joseph A. "White House Staffing: Salvation, Damnation, and Uncertainty." In *Executive Leadership in Anglo-American Systems*, ed. Colin Campbell and Margaret Jane Wyszomirski. Pittsburgh: University of Pittsburgh Press, 1991.

Polsby, Nelson W. *Consequences of Party Reform*. New York: Oxford University Press, 1983.

———. "The Institutionalization of the U.S. House of Representatives" *American Political Science Review* 62 (March, 1968): 144–68.

———. *Political Innovation in America: The Politics of Policy Initiation*. New Haven, Conn.: Yale University Press, 1984.

———. "Presidential Cabinet Making: Lessons for the Political System." *Political Science Quarterly* 93 (spring, 1978): 15–25.

Ponder, Daniel E. "The Presidency as a Learning Organization" *Presidential Studies Quarterly* 29 (March, 1999): 100–14.

———. "Presidential Leverage and the Presidential Agenda." Paper presented at the annual meeting of the American Political Science Association, Washington, D.C., 1997.

Ponder, Daniel E., and Russell D. Renka. "Reversing the Institutionalization of the U.S. Congress." Paper presented at the annual meeting of the Midwest Political Science Association, Chicago, 1998.

Porter, Roger. "Advising the President." *PS: Political Science and Politics* 19 (1986): 867–69.

———. *Presidential Decision Making: The Economic Policy Board*. Cambridge: Cambridge University Press, 1980.

Public Papers of the President: Jimmy Carter. Washington, D.C.: GPO, 1979.

Quirk, Paul J. "In Defense of the Politics of Ideas." *Journal of Politics* 50 (February, 1988): 31–41.

———. "What Do We Know and How Do We Know It? Research on the Presidency." In *Political Science: Looking to the Future.* Vol 4. *American Institutions,* ed. William Crotty. Evanston, Ill.: Northwestern University Press, 1991.

Radin, Beryl A., and Willis D. Hawley. *The Politics of Federal Reorganization: Creating the Department of Education.* New York: Pergamon, 1988.

Ragsdale, Lyn. "Review of George C. Edwards et al., *Researching the Presidency: Vital Questions, New Approaches.*" *American Political Science Review* 87 (1993): 1020–22.

———. "Studying the Presidency: Why Presidents Need Political Scientists." In *The Presidency and the Political System,* ed. Michael Nelson. 5th ed. Washington, D.C.: CQ, 1998.

Ragsdale, Lyn, and John J. Theis III. "The Institutionalization of the American Presidency, 1924–1992." *American Journal of Political Science* 41 (Oct., 1997): 1280–1318.

Riker, William. "Implications from the Disequilibrium of Majority Rule for the Study of Institutions." *American Political Science Review* 74 (1980): 432–37.

Rockman, Bert A. "America's *Departments* of State: Irregular and Regular Syndromes of Policy Making." *American Political Science Review* 75 (December, 1981): 911–27.

———. *The Leadership Question: The Presidency and the American System.* New York: Praeger, 1984.

———. "The New Institutionalism and Old Institutions." In *New Perspectives on American Politics,* ed. Lawrence C. Dodd and Calvin Jillson. Washington, D.C., CQ, 1993.

Rohde, David W. *Parties and Leaders in the Postreform House.* Chicago: University of Chicago Press, 1991.

Rose, Richard. "Evaluating Presidents." In *Researching the Presidency: Vital Questions, New Approaches,* ed George C. Edwards III, John H. Kessel, and Bert A. Rockman. Pittsburgh: University of Pittsburgh Press, 1993.

———. "Organizing Issues in and Organizing Problems Out." In *The Managerial Presidency,* ed. James P. Pfiffner. Pacific Grove, Calif.: Brooks/Cole, 1991.

Rourke, Francis E. "Politics and Professionalism in American Bureaucracy." *Public Administration Review* 52 (1992): 539–46.

Rudalevige, Andrew. "The President's Program: The 'Politicized Presidency' and Policy Formulation" Paper presented at the annual meeting of the Midwest Political Science Association, Chicago, 1999.

———. "Testing the Politicized Presidency: The Origins of Presidential Legislation, 1946–95." Paper presented at the annual meeting of the Midwest Political Science Association, Chicago, 1997.

Schlesinger, Arthur M., Jr. *The Imperial Presidency.* Boston: Houghton-Mifflin, 1973.

———. *A Thousand Days: John F. Kennedy in the White House.* Boston: Houghton-Mifflin, 1965.

Searing, Donald D. "Roles, Rules, and Rationality in the New Institutionalism." *American Political Science Review* 85 (December, 1991): 1239–60.

"Senate Committee Clears Education Department." *National Journal* 10 (1978): 1185.

Shafritz, Jay M., and J. Steven Ott, eds. *Classics of Organization Theory.* 3d ed. Pacific Grove, Calif.: Brooks/Cole, 1992.

Shepsle, Kenneth A. "Institutional Arrangements and Equilibrium in Multidimensional Voting Models." *American Journal of Political Science* 23 (1979): 27–59.

Shepsle, Kenneth A., and Barry R. Weingast, eds. *Positive Theories of Congressional Institutions.* Ann Arbor: University of Michigan Press, 1995.

Shull, Steven A., ed. *Presidential Policymaking: An End-of-Century Assessment.* Armonk, N.Y.: M. E. Sharpe, 1999.

Simpson, Brooks D. "Historians and Political Scientists: Observations on Presidential Studies." *Congress and the Presidency* 20 (autumn, 1993): 87–91.

Sinclair, Barbara. *Legislators, Leaders, and Lawmaking: The U.S. House of Representatives in the Postreform Era*. Baltimore: Johns Hopkins University Press, 1995.

Singer, James W. "The Problem with Being Young, Black, and Unemployed" *National Journal* 10 (September 16, 1978): 1456–60.

———. "Taking Aim at Youth Unemployment" *National Journal* 10 (January 28, 1978): 143–44.

———. "A Tempting Target," *National Journal* 12 (March 8, 1980): 406.

Skowronek, Stephen. *The Politics Presidents Make: Leadership from John Adams to George Bush*. Cambridge: Harvard University Press, 1993.

Sorensen, Theodore. *Decision Making in the White House*. New York: Columbia University Press, 1963.

———. *Kennedy: 25 Year Anniversary Edition*. New York: Harper and Row, 1988.

Stephens, David. "President Carter, the Congress and the NEA: Creating the Department of Education." *Political Science Quarterly* 98 (1983): 641–65.

Stockman, David. *The Triumph of Politics: Why the Reagan Revolution Failed*. New York: Harper and Row, 1986.

Sundquist, James L. *Politics and Policy: The Eisenhower, Kennedy, and Johnson Years*. Washington, D.C.: Brookings, 1969.

Thomas, Norman, ed. *The Presidency in Contemporary Context*. New York: Dodd, Mead, 1975.

Tulis, Jeffrey K. "The Interpretable Presidency" In *The Presidency and the Political System*, ed. Michael Nelson. 3d ed. Washington, D.C.: CQ, 1990.

———. *The Rhetorical Presidency*. Princeton, N.J.: Princeton University Press, 1987.

U.S. Congress. Senate. *Civil Service Reform Act of 1978*. 95th Cong., 2nd sess. Conference Report, Rpt. 95-1272.

Vayda, Andrew P., Bonnie J. McCay, and Christina Eghenter. "Concepts of Process in Social Science Explanations." *Philosophy of the Social Sciences* 21 (September, 1991): 318–31.

Walcott, Charles E., and Karen M. Hult. "The Domestic Policy Conundrum: White House Domestic Policy Organization." Paper presented at the annual meeting of the American Political Science Association, Atlanta, 1989.

———. *Governing the White House: From Hoover through LBJ*. Lawrence: University Press of Kansas, 1995.

Walker, Jack L., Jr. *Mobilizing Interest Groups in America: Patrons, Professions, and Social Movements*. Ann Arbor: University of Michigan Press, 1991.

Warshaw, Shirley Anne. *The Domestic Presidency: Policy Making in the White House*. Boston: Allyn and Bacon, 1997.

———. "Staffing Patterns in the Modern White House." In *Presidential Policymaking: An End-of-Century Assessment*, ed. Steven A. Shull. Armonk, N.Y.: M. E. Sharpe, 1999.

Waterman, Richard W. *Presidential Influence and the Administrative State*. Knoxville: University of Tennessee Press, 1989.

———, ed. *The Presidency Reconsidered*. Itasca, Ill.: F. E. Peacock, 1993.

Wayne, Stephen J. "Approaches." In *Studying the Presidency*, ed. George C. Edwards III and Stephen J. Wayne. Knoxville: University of Tennessee Press, 1983.

Weber, Max. "Bureaucracy." In *Max Weber: Essays in Sociology*, ed. H. H. Gerth and C. Wright Mills. New York: Oxford University Press, 1958.

Wehr, Elizabeth. "Carter Lists 'Principles' of National Health Plan." *Congressional Quarterly Weekly Report* 36 (August 5, 1978): 2058–59.

———. "Dilemma Over National Health Insurance Delays Promised Carter Plan." *Congressional Quarterly Weekly Report* 36 (July 15, 1978): 1770–73.

———. "Kennedy, Labor Launch Drive for National Health Insurance." *Congressional Quarterly Weekly Report* 36 (October 14, 1978): 2956.

Weko, Thomas J. *The Politicizing Presidency: The White House Personnel Office, 1948–1994*. Lawrence: University Press of Kansas, 1995.

Wildavsky, Aaron. *The New Politics of the Budgetary Process.* 2d ed. New York: HarperCollins, 1992.

———, ed. *Perspectives on the Presidency.* Boston: Little, Brown, 1975.

Wilson, Graham K. "The Challenge to Neutral Competence: A Preface to a Panel." Paper presented at the annual meeting of the American Political Science Association, Washington, D.C., 1993.

Wilson, James Q. *Bureaucracy: What Government Agencies Do and Why They Do It.* New York: Basic Books, 1989.

Wilson, Woodrow. "The Study of Administration." Reprinted in *Classics of Public Administration,* ed. Jay M. Shafritz and Albert C. Hyde. 2d ed. Chicago: Dorsey, 1987.

Wood, B. Dan, and Richard W. Waterman. *Bureaucratic Dynamics: The Role of Bureaucracy in a Democracy.* Boulder, Colo.: Westview, 1994.

Worsham, Jeff, Marc Allen Eisner, and Evan J. Rinquist, "Assessing the Assumptions: A Critical Analysis of Agency Theory" *Administration and Society* 28 (February, 1997): 419–40.

Wyszomirski, Margaret Jane. "The Deinstitutionalization of Presidential Staff Agencies" *Public Administration Review* 42 (1982): 448–58.

———. "The Discontinuous Institutional Presidency." In *Executive Leadership in Anglo-American Systems,* ed. Colin Campbell and Margaret Jane Wyszomirski. Pittsburgh: University of Pittsburgh Press, 1991.

———. "The Roles of a Presidential Office for Domestic Policy: Three Models and Four Cases." In *The Presidency and Public Policy Making,* ed. George C. Edwards III and Steven A. Shull. Pittsburgh: University of Pittsburgh Press, 1985.

"Youth Budget Program Is Big Budget Initiative." *National Journal* 12 (Jan. 19, 1980): 122–23.

Index

Joseph V. Hughes, Jr., and Holly O. Hughes Series in the Presidency and Leadership Studies

Bose, Meena. *Shaping and Signaling Presidential Policy: The National Security Decision Making of Eisenhower and Kennedy.* 1998.

Campbell, James E. *The American Campaign: U.S. Presidential Campaigns and the National Vote.* 2000.

Fisher, Louis. *The Politics of Shared Power: Congress and the Executive.* 4th ed. 1998.

Garrison, Jean A. *Games Advisors Play: Foreign Policy in the Nixon and Carter Administrations.* 1999.

Pfiffner, James P., ed. *The Managerial Presidency.* 2d ed. 1999.